THE
Debt-FREE &
Prosperous
Living™
HOME STUDY COURSE

by John M. Cummuta

Ninth Edition

Debt-FREE &
Prosperous
Living, INC.

Boscobel, WI

The Debt-FREE & Prosperous Living® Home Study Course ___
Ninth Edition

Twenty-Eighth Printing 2002

ISBN 1-883113-15-6

Published by Debt-FREE & Prosperous Living®, Inc.
310 Second Street
Boscobel, WI 53805
608/375-2900

Table of Contents

Part Two — The Specifics

Appendices

Part One – An Overview

A Whole New Outlook on Life

I'm going to help you go from debt to wealth, from owing nearly everyone to owning everything in your life...from being financially out of control to having a firm grip on your financial present and future. And none of what you'll read in this book is theory. I've done it, as have thousands of others who have read previous editions or attended one of our seminars.

I remember how I felt, when I first realized I could be debt-free, owning everything in my life, in just a handful of years.

But you have to understand, it wasn't just a light coming on over my head as I was comfortably cruising through life. I had just gone through a complete financial crash. My business' sole supplier went out of business...and overnight I was out of business too. My income went from really great to really zero in the course of a few weeks.

So I had to find an answer. I was being crushed by a debt load I could no longer support. And while it started as a desperate search for a way out from under that load, my journey eventually taught me a lot more than just a system to get myself out of debt. It showed me a whole new approach to life that revolutionized the way I looked at and used money. It opened to me a secure future I thought I'd never really achieve. And it was simple!

It was like moving from dark to light...from drowning to breathing freely...from stress to peace. And that's how you'll feel. It will take you from a life with no options to a life filled with endless options. It'll bring better sleep, better family relations, and more energy for life.

But before we start down that road, let's clarify our terms, so we don't get confused during the discussion.

First of all, there's only one real definition of "Financial

Independence" — that is, to be financially dependent on <u>no one</u>. And that's the goal of the Debt-FREE & Prosperous Living® system — to help you be completely independent of any job, any person and certainly independent of any need for government support, <u>ever</u>. It's what I call getting "un-vulnerable."

This program is built on the premise that the ideal situation would be for you to have NO debts and to have a substantial, ongoing monthly income at the same time — without having to work for it. In other words, I want to help you achieve, *in as short a time as possible*, a lifestyle where you own your home, your car(s), and all the other "stuff" in your life — and you have enough money in investments that you can live off the interest.

Can what you'll learn in this manual do that for you?

Yes! The Debt-FREE & Prosperous Living® system can save the average American family **over a hundred thousand dollars** in interest, and have them completely out of debt — including their home mortgage — in about seven years. Then it can help them build up more than **a million dollars** in simple, safe investments, by the time they would have paid off their mortgage the way the mortgage company has it set up. And our system shows them how to do all this *with the money they already bring home*!

That Kind of Success Requires a New Direction

To achieve this goal, you have to follow a new strategy. It's nearly impossible to reach this kind of freedom doing things the way you've always been taught — the way you've seen everyone else doing them. You first need to understand how you've been misled over the years, then you have to implement an efficient and sound strategy that will use your present income stream to get you to your financial freedom goal in the shortest possible time.

You'll notice, as we go through the following concepts, that many of them run counter to conventional wisdom. That's because conventional wisdom is frequently wrong. And it's wrong because it is "wisdom" being promoted by the businesses that profit greatly from our doing what's good for them — not for us. These businesses have us paying hundreds of thousands of dollars, over the years, for products and services we either don't really need, or that do not provide the happiness, bliss, and security we've been promised.

How We've Been Misled

If you're like most folks, this book may anger you. It'll be like a veil has been lifted from your eyes and you'll see how our economy is designed to make you work yourself to exhaustion — simply to accumulate wealth for the companies you do business with — not for you.

The most staggering example of this is a home mortgage. If you buy a home with a 30-year conventional or adjustable rate mortgage, you will pay for that loan about **three times**. Just multiply your monthly payment times 360 months and you'll see that the total you'll pay the mortgage company or bank is about three times the amount you borrowed from them.

That means that two-thirds of the total amount you'll pay your mortgage lender is interest. Interest is the profit the mortgage company makes for lending you the money to buy the house, and they obviously feel you should pay them nearly 200 percent interest!

Let's put some real numbers to this.

If you buy a $250,000 home, with a $200,000 mortgage, you'll end up paying about $600,000 over 30 years. **That's <u>four hundred thousand dollars</u> in interest to borrow two hundred thousand dollars!**

That means you'll have to work...week after week...year after year...to earn a **half million dollars or more**...so you can net four hundred thousand dollars after you pay income taxes — just so you can give it to the mortgage company as profit! Ask yourself — do they deserve a half million dollars of your hard-earned wealth more than you do? Are they doing you such a tremendous favor that you should wear yourself out, over three decades, to generate <u>nearly a half million dollars</u>...*that does not go to your wealth or to the value of your home*...but directly to their bottom line?

That's your money. You work for it. You pay taxes on it. <u>Yet they end up with it</u>. It's not fair, and I'm dedicated to helping you turn the tide of your wealth-building power to your benefit instead of theirs.

I'm going to help you craft a strategy for you and your family that will keep the maximum amount of the wealth you produce **in your hands**. Retaining and investing the money you waste on mortgage interest alone could change your life completely.

Just think about that four hundred thousand dollars. If you had it parked in mutual funds that averaged 10 percent return per year, you could enjoy a $40,000-a-year retirement income without ever touching the principal! And the exciting thing is we're not even talking about your having to earn any extra money to make this happen for you. This four hundred thousand (or whatever it works out to for you) <u>is money you're going to earn anyway</u>. We're just giving you control of who ends up with it: you or them.

By the way, if you have an accountant who tells you that you should never pay off your mortgage, "Because it's the last tax shelter for the average consumer," get a new accountant. Think about what they're saying. Let me translate it for you. They're really saying, "Keep on paying a dollar of interest to the mortgage company to get back 28 cents in tax deductions."

Let's assume you're in the 28 percent tax bracket. If you're in a different bracket, or the government has changed the numbers, just replace the appropriate amounts as you read this.

Each dollar of interest you pay the mortgage company is deductible from your taxable income, which saves you the 28 cents you would otherwise have paid to the government on that dollar. But, think about that. You're giving up a full dollar to save 28 cents. Whereas, if you pay off your mortgage, you will indeed have to pay 28 cents federal tax on each dollar not going to mortgage interest...but you're getting to keep the other 72 cents. Ask yourself, would you rather pay a dollar (mortgage interest) to save 28 cents, or pay 28 cents (tax) to keep the dollar? (See Appendix page A11.)

In the typical scenario, a full dollar is leaving your life on its way to the mortgage company, and Uncle Sam is giving you a 28 cent break on your taxes to ease the pain. But in the Debt-FREE & Prosperous Living® scenario, the only thing leaving your life is the 28 cents. You're 72 cents ahead on every dollar.

Our way is better, because 72 cents will always be more than 28 cents. **And you don't lose the tax deduction while you're paying off your debts...only when the mortgage is completely paid off.**

Let's Look at More Ways You're Being Taken Advantage Of

Car loans. Next to a home mortgage, the greatest draining away of your wealth is through auto loans. Lenders are willing to give you up to five, six and in some cases even more years to pay off a car these days, because the longer the amortization, the more the auto loan is like a mini home mortgage. The longer they can get you to stretch out the payments, the more total interest they'll get out of you for a given loan amount. If car finance companies thought they could get away with it, they'd offer you 30-year loans on cars. They'd love to get three times the price of the car back in monthly payments.

Insurance. It's been said that in no other expense area do people spend so much of their life's money with so little understanding of the value of what they're buying.

The first thing you need to do is recognize that insurance is a business, and both the insurance company and the agent are in that business to make as much money as they can. There's nothing wrong with that...as long as their profit motive doesn't color their recommendations for coverage and policy types.

The next thing you should recognize is that insurance companies don't lose money on insurance policies! Sure, a small number of them go out of business by making rotten outside investments, but they do not lose a penny on their insurance programs. That is a simple fact. When they sell you an insurance policy, they're gambling (with the odds in their favor) that bad things **will not** happen to you, and you (silly, if you think about it) are gambling that bad things will happen to you. Insurance companies never lose at this game.

Sure, there are a small number of people who file a big claim after paying only a few premiums. But, while it may appear the insurance company loses money in this situation, the fact is they have thousands of other people paying premiums, to whom nothing bad is happening. So they simply take the profit they're making on most people and easily cover the benefits they have to pay out to the few unfortunate ones. Insurers know, when they sell you a policy, that you are thousands of times more likely to be one of the fortunate ones who cost them nothing, and make them tons of profit!

They only bet on sure things. Which means that, if they're willing to sell you a policy, it's only because history and math have proven to them they're going to win. Another way to say it is — if they're willing to sell it to you, *you probably won't need it.*

Because you can't be certain you won't be one of the unfortunate few, there are some areas of your life you do want to cover with the correct types of insurance, but one thing you can be sure of is you almost certainly won't need all the coverages an agent would like to sell you.

I'll get into specific suggestions about how to properly buy insurance in a later section.

A Few More Misapplied Strategies

As I did the research for developing the Debt-FREE & Prosperous Living® system, I was amazed at how many of the financial "rules" we're taught (or just pick up) are wrong! And they're not just a little wrong. They can be deadly to our chances of ever achieving real financial independence in a desirable time frame.

The two untrue "truths" I found most difficult to break free from were the principles of "Saving money, a little at a time, as you go along through life" and "You need to develop a good credit rating...so use credit every chance you get."

Saving money as you go along. Every time you get conventional financial advice, it usually includes the instruction to build a little nest egg on the side while you work your way through life. Many authorities will counsel you to save 10 percent of your income as an investment for the future. They call it "Paying yourself first."

Now, in and of itself, this is not bad advice. It's just the way it's most often applied that causes people to move sluggishly toward their goals — instead of taking the shortest, fastest course. Efficiency comes from focusing on one task at a time. Saving a little on the side, while you simultaneously build up debt, or even work to pay off debt, is inefficient and slows you down.

Our Debt-FREE & Prosperous Living® strategy has proven to be the fastest, safest route to your financial goal: first you eliminate ALL debt — then you save. Another way to say that is, "go ahead and pay yourself first...and your first, best investment is paying off unpaid debt balances." We'll talk in detail about how to do this later.

You need a good credit rating. Believe it or not we're going to help you get to a point where your credit rating will be a non-issue to you. You won't need it to obtain credit, because you won't need any credit. You may want to check for damaging errors on your credit rating, because some employers and landlords use credit ratings as part of their hiring and leasing practices. But, when you finish the Debt-FREE & Prosperous Living® program, you'll never again need a credit rating to get credit.

Why Are We Obsessed with Using Credit?

Most Americans were never taught — by family or by the education system — how to manage their financial resources throughout the various stages of their lives. So they've become the unwitting students (and slaves) of Madison Avenue advertisers, the Hollywood culture builders, and the money-lending companies behind them.

Think about it. Where did you receive your personal financial training? Haven't you really been trained by TV and other advertising media on how you should live, what you should buy to show that you've arrived at a certain status level, and what kind of American Dream you should be chasing?

Are you not instructed by the media as to what kind of car you should be driving to look successful? Are you not shown what kind of house you should live in to be really happy, or what kind of clothes will make you socially acceptable? And doesn't everybody who's anybody go on a cruise every year?

All these images are continuously fired at you to make you want the things the people in the movies or commercials have…that make them happy, successful, etc. Then the advertisers come in, offering you just what you need to put yourself in that picture…and it comes with easy monthly payments, or it's available by using any major credit card.

See the process? They make you want things, by presenting them as being used or worn by people they make look desirable. Then they offer to sell you the clothes, car, golf clubs, whatever, on payments or with a credit card. They have an agenda.

I, on the other hand, am a teacher. I simply wish to show you a strategy that can get you to complete financial independence in the shortest period of time.

I want to help you reach a point where you're driving a late model, attractive car, and living in a comfortable home — but you have **no payments to make on anything**. Your only expenses will be food, heat, and minimal legal taxes. At that point you'll be insulated from layoffs, economic downturns, inflation and all the other woes that mentally and emotionally squeeze the average worker. You'll be beyond them, in a place few people reach — because they are continually misled to waste their wealth, or promise it away for decades to come.

A New Strategy

The new strategy I'm proposing is not based on assumptions or generalities, but on mathematics and probability. Sounds scientific, doesn't it? Well it's really pretty simple and straightforward, and it's based on the premise that you want to get debt-free and start building wealth in the shortest period of time — while protecting yourself from the bad things that have a reasonable probability of actually happening to you.

Let's start with the mathematics.

The key to achieving debt-freedom is the management of compound interest in your life. As you progress through these pages, you'll begin to see that compound interest is more powerful than you probably imagine — and right now it is likely stacked 100 percent *against* you. We'll be turning that around.

My Debt-FREE & Prosperous Living® system is based on a mathematical process that first shorts out compound interest working against you. It then shows you how to turn the "financial funnel" around so you can later maximize the power of compound interest working *for* you...funneling money *into* your life.

It really works, and faster than you likely think it could. This mathematical process has the average family completely out of debt, including their home mortgage, in about five to seven years...using nothing more than the money they already bring home. Imagine...no debts. No house payment, no car payments, no furniture payments, no credit card payments. Only eat, heat, and taxes.

Now let's look at the probability of bad things happening to you.

The key to protecting yourself from bad things that might happen to you involves Mathematical Probability. I'm talking about insurance here. You *probably* need to employ only those kinds of insurance that protect you from catastrophic occurrences, where the expense could wipe out you or your survivors. It is *probably* more cost-effective to assume the risk of insuring yourself from life's minor illnesses and accidents by max-imizing the deductibles on your policies. *Probability* shows us that this is most often cheaper than paying an insurance company higher premi-ums, month after month, to cover those minor costs for you.

The reason I've italicized the words *probably* and *probability* is because they represent how insurance companies look at the world. They only offer policies to people whom they believe will *probably* not have the problem being covered by the policy. And since insurance companies hire geniuses to determine these *probabilities,* I say we agree with the geniuses that these bad things won't happen to us.

We'll talk more specifically about this in a later section.

The real good news about insurance is that, after you're out of debt and have followed the Debt-FREE & Prosperous Living® system's invest-ment recommendations, you will soon have the resources to protect yourself from almost everything you are now buying insurance for — and you will need little or no insurance other than for personal liability.

Now let's begin examining the Debt-FREE & Prosperous Living® sys-tem in detail. The three major stages of our Debt-FREE & Prosperous Living® system are:

> **Stage 1: Operate 100% on cash — stop using <u>any</u> credit.**

> **Stage 2: Pay off ALL your debts, including any mortgages.**

> **Stage 3: Focus ALL available cash on wealth building.**

There's also a fourth stage that more and more North Americans are choosing. We call it *The New Paradigm.* It involves not only leaving the "fast lane," but taking the exit ramp. People following this strategy are choosing to leave fast-paced, high-pressure metropolitan lifestyles for more relaxed, less expensive, and safer small-town living. But this does-n't mean "living off the land," raising your own rabbits for food, and collecting aluminum cans for spending money.

I live in the country outside a small Wisconsin town, in a cedar home we built on 37 acres of woods and meadows. My airplane is parked in my hangar about 20 minutes from my driveway. This is not a bad way to live. None of our possessions are ostentatious, flashy, or new. But they meet our needs...**and they're paid for**. So...if this escape to a simpler, more affordable lifestyle fits you...

Stage 4: Move to a cheaper, safer, more enjoyable location.

By following the three or four stages of this strategy, you'll attain *real* independence in a relative handful of years — and you'll never need credit again. Most people following this strategy are completely debt-free, including their home mortgage, in five to seven years. And then they quickly build retirement wealth with all the monthly money they had previously been wasting on monthly debt payments.

Ask yourself: how much better off will I be, five to seven years from today, **if I continue on the course I'm on now?**

If you don't like the answer to that one, it's time to move to Stage 1.

STAGE 1

Operate on a 100% CASH Basis

Starting from Day 1 of your Debt-FREE & Prosperous Living® plan, operate 100 percent on cash.

I know it'll seem difficult at first to be focusing your resources on debt-elimination while simultaneously covering all your expenses with cash — but it can be done! And once your debts are paid off, you will **never** need credit again! Within months of paying off your debts you will become your own bank...your own credit card company. So you will never need to use the *other guys* again. All the money you had been sending to your creditors each month — plus what we call your Accelerator Margin™ — will be going into your savings after your debts are gone, so it won't take long for you to save up an amount higher than any credit card limit you might be offered. You won't need "Other People's Money," because you'll have plenty of your own.

But weaning yourself off credit will be as much psychological as mathematical. We've been taught in this economy to believe in credit. In fact, we have been indoctrinated that we cannot live without credit. Every step of the way we're told to get and keep a "good credit rating." Why? So we can get more credit, that's why.

I will address how to handle emergencies and unexpected expenses during these early stages, but first let's examine why the *cash based lifestyle* is really <u>better</u> than one built on credit.

Credit is Not Your Friend

Credit does nothing but diminish your lifestyle over time. It just makes everything cost more. Yes, you probably will need a loan to buy your first home. But even that could be accomplished without credit if you had sufficient patience. It might be hard to imagine right now, but you're going to prefer a life free of all loans, charge accounts, and credit cards.

Think about this for a moment: **When someone offers you credit – they're not giving you anything.** If they offer you a $5,000 Gold Visa card, they are not giving you $5,000. They are not adding a single dime into your life. They're simply moving up the date at which you can spend money that *you will have to earn* — and they're charging you a terrible price for letting you "use" $5,000 of their money.

So, the net effect is that — when someone offers you credit — they will actually reduce, not add to, the money you will have to spend over your lifetime.

Credit does only one thing: it raises the price of everything you buy with it. Credit takes more money away from you than the actual value (purchase price) of the thing you buy on credit. Usually a lot more than you think. And that extra money you're giving to the credit company is the same money you should be investing to produce your future retirement income.

People are literally giving away their future (retirement) wealth — to have a few extra things right now. But the true cost of using credit is much greater than they realize. So they drown in credit interest and wake up one day, old and wanting to stop working, only to realize they can't stop — because they still owe more and more interest on more and more debt. Debt they used to buy gadgets, trinkets, and other "had to have" junk they've long since stuffed into the attic, basement, closets, and garage.

How Bad It Really Is to Use Credit Cards

Suppose you carry four credit cards averaging 17 percent interest, and they have a combined outstanding balance of $5,200. If you pay only the minimum monthly payment of (usually two percent of the outstanding balance or $10 minimum payment). It would take you **40 years and 8 months** to pay them all off. And your payments would total **$16,990** over those four decades. That means — in addition to the original $5,200 you borrowed from the credit card companies — **you would have paid them $11,790 in interest!** Long after you would have thrown away the things you bought with the credit cards, you'd still be draining your wealth paying for them.

In this example, using a credit card would cause you to pay more than three times the value of whatever you bought! And you'd have to work many extra months to earn the $11,790 — just to help build the wealth of the credit card companies rather than your own wealth. Doesn't it make you mad when you see these numbers, and realize they're being used against *you* right now?

But it's worse than that, because research has shown that, when you use credit cards, you'll buy 112% more stuff, just because it's so easy to make the purchases. So not only does everything cost more, because of interest, but you buy twice as much stuff, making it a double whammy against your finances.

On the other hand, when you operate on cash the process becomes its own buying regulator. You'll think longer and harder about each purchase, so you'll be a lot less likely to buy things you don't need. And when you do buy something, it'll be only the size or amount necessary — because you'll be feeling the full payment at the time of purchase rather than in little bite-sized pieces over the next several decades of bill paying.

What's it Like to Operate on Cash?

You'll begin to see the benefits of operating 100 percent on cash long before you pay off your mortgage. Imagine that you're four or five months into the program and you've paid off a couple credit cards that each had a $50 monthly payment. You now have that $100 a month available to take care of life's little emergencies. But let's take it further down the timeline.

Imagine you've followed the Debt-FREE & Prosperous Living® system and paid off all your charge accounts, credit cards, and car loans — and you're now paying off your mortgage balance by adding in all the dollars that used to be wasted each month on those credit account payments. Then, one day the washing machine breaks.

Here's where most people would pull out a credit card to get it repaired, or they'd see an ad in the paper for a new one — with "low monthly payments" — and get themselves deeper in debt. But you just take the money you were going to add to your mortgage payment that month and use it to pay cash for the washing machine repair or replacement.

Using cash for this emergency would delay your debt-freedom date by *one month*, but it would not add a penny to your debt. Your washer would be repaired or replaced, and you'd be right back on your Debt-FREE & Prosperous Living® plan the next month.

OK, let's go a little further down the timeline.

Now imagine you've paid off your mortgage and you're putting all the money you used to be wasting on revolving credit debt and mortgage payments into your investments. Then suppose your car dies.

Here's where most people would crawl to the bank and beg for a car loan, but you just hold off on your investments for a month or two and buy a good used car for cash. Or, if necessary, you pull a little out of your liquid investment account and buy a better car — CASH.

Let's go for broke. Imagine you want to buy a new home.

Here's where most people grovel before a loan officer, beg for awhile, and show everything but their blood tests to prove they're worthy to pay hundreds of thousands of dollars in pure profit to the mortgage company for the privilege of using some of their money.

But you don't need a mortgage. You have a paid-off house and money in the bank. So you sell the house you now own, add in the difference from your investment account (if necessary), and buy your new home — CASH.

Then, the next month, you go right back to putting the full amount into your investments again.

Sounds liberating, doesn't it?

You'll Have to be Strong

Impulse buying is one of the most wealth-draining habits North Americans give in to. I call it "malling," because malls are where it most frequently takes place. You know, the "I've had a tough week so I deserve to buy myself something" syndrome. And, because it's so easy and painless to just flop down the old credit card to pay for it, impulse buying drives you deeper and deeper into debt.

You will find it's much harder to spend cash on something you don't really need than it was to just whip out the plastic to buy it. But if you really need...or even really want something...you can buy it with cash. Once you've paid off some bills and have a healthy Accelerator Margin™ each month, it can be redirected — at your discretion — to make important purchases. What freedom that will be, because you can fully enjoy the purchase without the nagging pressure and guilt of having to pay for it for months and years into the future.

I've mentioned the Accelerator Margin™ a couple times now, and you may be wondering about it. In just a bit I'll be explaining what it is, where it comes from, and how we use it in the Debt-FREE & Prosperous Living® system.

STAGE 2

Pay Off ALL Debt

In the next few pages I'll begin describing exactly how you'll pay off all your debts. The system is foolproof...except for one thing — **your commitment**. I cannot come over to your house and make you faithfully follow the steps of this plan. And while putting this system to work in your life won't be unbearably hard, it will be challenging. Only your commitment will keep you on the course. So, to seal that commitment I want you to give yourself some good reasons to follow through on your plan for Financial Freedom.

Before you go any further, turn to the *Financial Freedom Lifestyle To-Do List* on Appendix page A5 at the back of this book. On it I want you to list all the things you have always wanted to do, but never had the time to do. This is a list of the dream life you will live when this plan has worked its magic for you. Nothing is unimportant — put it all down.

Don't hurt yourself trying to think of things. Just relax and let the ideas flow. As I said earlier, this system has one goal: to give you back options in your life. Here's where you'll flesh out which of those options you'd choose. Whether it's traveling the world or learning how to paint portraits, there are no holds barred. It's your life...dream away.

Do it now. Then come back and continue reading.

Assuming you've finished your list, either cut it out of the book or photocopy it and hang it somewhere where you'll see it all the time — preferably where you sit to work on your bills. Anytime you feel your resolve for staying on the plan starting to flag, run to this list and read it again. And every time you do, just remember that — should you give up — **the huge ball of debt you are just barely carrying now will be more than you can bear in your older years**. In fact, it may crush you in the end, as it has others.

"OK," you might be saying, "I can see all the reasons *why* I want to pay off all my debts...but where am I going to find the money to do it?"

Finding the Money for Bill Payoff

Before you can actually begin paying off debts, I first need to help you put together what I call your "Accelerator Margin™." Your Accelerator Margin™ is the amount of money you'll add to the regular monthly payment of one bill after another — until they are all paid off.

As each debt is paid off, you'll add what used to be its monthly payment into your Accelerator Margin™, making it larger. This is like rolling a snowball down hill. It gets bigger and more powerful as each retired debt payment is added in. By the time you get to your home mortgage, your much larger Accelerator Margin™ should allow you to at least double your house payment until it's paid off.

If you're not yet making mortgage payments, you should use the Debt-FREE & Prosperous Living® system to pay off all revolving credit debt (bank cards, store charge cards, gas cards with any balance on them, car loans, and so on). Once your debts are gone, put all the money you've freed up into a money market account or Certificate of Deposit (CD) each month, to build up a down payment for your home.

As soon as you get into your new house, immediately start the process of paying off the mortgage using the Debt-FREE & Prosperous Living® system!

Notice that I said pay off all your debts first...*then* begin saving for your down payment. This is a critically important component of the system.

Don't Save Until ALL Debt Is Gone

Don't save any money until all debt is gone. This sounds like heresy to the "Put a little nest egg aside as you go through life" crowd, but it's what I recommend with this strategy. **You will achieve a lot more, a lot faster, by focusing your total available dollars on bill payoff.** If you spread your resources thin each month, trying to pay off bills while simultaneously trying to save some of your income, you'll see no significant results.

Here's why: let's say you currently need $4,000 net income each month to cover your debts and living expenses. Let's further say you can presently put together an Accelerator Margin™ of $400 — 10 percent of your monthly take-home income. (Don't worry about where this Accelerator Margin™ is going to come from. I'll explain that in a moment.) With those assumptions in place, we'll see how *conventional wisdom* would tell us to handle the situation.

Most financial planners would tell you to build up a six-month cash reserve before you start paying off debts. Based on the above scenario, you'd need to save six times $4,000 (your monthly requirement), or $24,000, to give you six months' worth of ready cash. If you divide the $400 you have available each month (your Accelerator Margin™) into the $24,000 cash reserve amount you plan to save up, you'll find that it will take you 60 months or **five full years just to build your cash reserve** — *before you can even start eliminating your debt.*

But, if you follow my Debt-FREE & Prosperous Living® system to the letter, you could be completely debt-free in those same five years <u>by paying off all debts first</u>!

What a Difference the System Makes

Let's examine the same scenario, but this time we'll follow the Debt-FREE & Prosperous Living® system to pay off all debt first.

We'll estimate that — after you've paid off your credit cards and revolving charge accounts, car payment, and mortgage — you could get by on just $2,000 a month, instead of the $4,000 a month you needed before your debts were eliminated. This reduction in monthly expenses means you'd only need $12,000 (instead of $24,000) in your six-month emergency fund.

That's great. But it gets even better. Because you eliminated $2,000 a month in monthly expenses, you now have that $2,000 to save each month. Plus you have the $400 original Accelerator Margin™ to save as well. This means you can put $2,400 a month into your emergency fund, so it would take only five months to fill it up to $12,000. **That's five months instead of the <u>five years</u> it would take if you didn't pay off your debts first!**

The bottom line is that the first way (the traditional way), you could save up your emergency fund in five years — <u>but still have most or all your debts</u>. The Debt-FREE & Prosperous Living® way it would take five months longer (5 years 5 months) — but **you'd have your emergency fund saved up <u>and</u> you'd own your home and everything else!** You would have no debts and money in the bank. That's financial freedom.

Now, maybe these numbers don't precisely match yours. But the point is the same. When you have little available to save each month...but you need a lot each month to get by...it'll take you forever to save up your six-month emergency fund. But when you have a lot available to save (because your income-sapping debts are gone), and you need relatively little to get by each month (because your income-sapping debts are gone), you can save up your emergency fund in a small fraction of the time it would have taken you had you not paid off your debts first. And you'll be **debt-free**!

Let me tell you how this first hit me.

We Were Stunned

When I first formulated this system, my wife and I sat down and ran our debts through the formula. We were stunned. Credit card bills, on which we had been paying the minimum payment or maybe a little more — month after month for years — were eliminated in just a few months! Car payments, gone in just a few more months! From that point we were able to more than *double* our mortgage payment, for a **total payoff time-line of only four years and seven months**. Just four years seven months from indebtedness to complete debt-freedom.

Imagine our excitement. We had 26 years left on our mortgage, and we had planned on just paying it out like everyone around us was paying their mortgages. Sure, we'd heard about mortgage reduction plans, but never really thought seriously about using one because we could never find the extra money to do it with, and those plans really didn't cut that much time off the mortgage

But with the Debt-FREE & Prosperous Living® strategy, we found the extra money to pay off our mortgage, by paying off all our charge accounts and car loans first. Then, using the same money we had been paying on credit cards and cars each month, **we accelerated the payoff of our home from twenty-six years down to four years**.

When I worked out the numbers, I was dumbfounded.

I considered the two scenarios before me. If we continued using our income the way we had been, the way everyone we knew was, we would've eventually paid off the house (in 26 years) and maybe put a few bucks in the bank during that time. But, it would have taken a quarter century to do it...while funneling hundreds of thousands of our hard-earned dollars to the mortgage company!

With the Debt-FREE & Prosperous Living® strategy, in 26 years we would own the same house, and by investing the nearly 22 years of additional payments that would have gone to the mortgage company and other creditors — we'd be millionaires! **And all this could be done with our same monthly income. It would not require any additional money to make it work!**

Let that sink in. <u>To apply the Debt-FREE & Prosperous Living® system to your life won't require an extra penny of income</u>. This system isn't magic, it's a *rerouting* and *refocusing* of your present income, to make it work more effectively for you rather than for your creditors. So you don't have to look for some get rich scheme. This program will make you rich with the money you're already earning.

For the strategy to be effective, however, you must concentrate your finances at one point of attack at a time. In the second stage of the Debt-FREE & Prosperous Living® strategy you'll be concentrating your money on paying off bills, so you don't want to weaken the mathematics by trying to save a portion of your income at the same time. Saving comes in stage three, after all your debts, including your home mortgage, are paid off. If you're concerned about possible emergency expenses, I'll address that a little further on.

But, if you need any further motivation to focus all your money in the payoff direction, let's consider the return on investment on both the bill-payoff and the savings sides of the equation.

If you're putting money into a savings or money market account at four, five, or six percent interest...or even government securities that generate seven or eight percent — while you are simultaneously paying 15 percent or more on credit interest — you're moving backwards at a rate of at least 7 to 11 percent a year. And when you compound that over several years, it becomes a staggering loss of your wealth.

NOTE: Investing your money into paying off a debt where interest is charged on the outstanding monthly balance gives you a return exactly equal to investing the same money into an interest-earning account with the same interest rate. For instance, that means that investing a thousand dollars towards paying off the balance of a debt on which 12% interest is charged, is the same as investing that thousand dollars into an investment that pays you 12% interest.

The main difference is that the return on investment for paying off a debt balance is GUARANTEED to stay at the interest rate being charged on that debt, whereas interest rates in most growth investments fluctuate. So, every dollar used to pay off the balance of, say, an 18.9 percent credit card is earning a GUARANTEED return of 18.9 percent! And that's an AFTER-TAX RETURN, so an equivalent investment would have to pay around 25% before taxes to yield the same after-tax benefit to you.

The Power of Compound Interest

When asked what was the most powerful invention he had ever seen, the great physicist, Albert Einstein responded, "Compound interest." Mayer Amschel Rothschild, the German merchant who founded the greatest banking dynasty in history, called compound interest, "The eighth wonder of the world."

But this power can be working *for you or against you*. Right now it is likely pumping your money the wrong way — and at a tremendous rate.

While savings account interest rates may be higher or lower at the time you read this, the interest rates you receive on money in a saving account, money market account, or Certificate of Deposit will generally be much lower than the interest rates you're paying on borrowed money and credit card purchases.

As an example, and without confusing the issue with the relatively inconsequential effects of taxes, it should be obvious that if you use a dollar to pay off a debt where you're being charged 15.7 percent interest, you are making a better return on your money than if you put it in an investment where you're earning a lower rate. In other words, you can make 15.7 percent (or whatever your credit cards charge) return on your money by using every available dime to pay off all your credit cards.

That means that every dollar you put into savings or investments, instead of bill payoff, is earning you less of a return than it could. In short, you do not want to invest in anything other than debt payoff until after you have NO debt remaining.

Even when it comes to your mortgage, where the interest rate appears to be lower than credit card levels, you're still getting an above-average return on your money by using it to pay off your mortgage. This is because paying off debt gives you a *guaranteed* return on investment, so you must only compare it with investments that would also *guarantee* their return. What investments guarantee their returns?

Growth/equity mutual funds <u>do not</u> guarantee their return. In fact, you can lose money in these funds. It's the same with bonds, real estate, precious metals, almost all types of securities.

The safest investments that do guarantee their return rates are U.S. Treasury instruments, such as bills, notes, and bonds. You'll find that long-term bonds generally offer the highest interest rate of the three, but this rate will always be slightly less than current mortgage interest rates. **So prepaying your mortgage will always give you a higher return on your money than the best comparable investment.**

And remember, there's more to this whole get-out-of-debt thing than just the dollars and cents of it. There's the security issue, and what that means to your stress level. The bottom-line goal of the Debt-FREE & Prosperous Living® strategy is to make you "un-vulnerable" to the negative consequences of debt. And nothing helps you feel more un-vulnerable than knowing that no one can foreclose on you and take your home away. No matter what life throws at you, you will always have a home to go to at the end of the day, and that's a good feeling.

When you own your home outright, you're insulated from the worst consequences of potential layoffs, mergers, inflation, and other bad things that can happen to your income stream. If all you need to bring home each month is enough money to eat, pay the light bill, and cover one twelfth of your property taxes, you're much less threatened by turns of events that emotionally paralyze other people. Just this reduction in stress could literally add years to your life...and they will be fun years.

And don't worry about the loss of your mortgage interest tax deduction or concern yourself with any other tax consequences. While you're paying off your mortgage, you're still getting your full tax deduction on the interest you pay. If you live in Canada, you know you have no mortgage interest deduction on your home, so that makes the elimination of your mortgage even more imperative.

By the way...did you catch it back where I said that your mortgage interest rate "appears" to be lower than credit card interest?

When I'm doing seminars I always have people asking why they should pay off their mortgage, when it has such a low interest rate, and they could make "so much more in the market." Then they start comparing mortgage rates among the class.

One person will say, "I've got a 7% mortgage."

Someone else will pipe in, "Yea...I got a 6.72% mortgage!"

I just smile and ask if anyone has brought along a payment coupon or statement from their mortgage. When I see a raised hand I simply ask, "How much of your current monthly payment is interest and how much goes against the principal balance?"

When I see their face go white I explain to the class that on a typical mortgage payment 92% to 98% of the payment is interest each month, and only 2% to 8% actually reduces the balance owed on the loan. So, while the mortgage company made you feel like you were getting a

6.72% or 7% mortgage, you're actually paying 92% to 98% each month. It would only be 6.72% or 7% if you paid the entire balance off in the first year. (See page F6 – A Horror Classic: "The Loan Principal That Wouldn't Go Away".)

See how insidious compound interest is when it's working against you?

By the way, I've heard some "wealth-building gurus" advocate mortgaging your home to the hilt, and investing the money to get rich! So you end up paying 92% to 95% interest on your mortgage, so you can make 10%, 20%, or 30% in the market. And, of course, there are no guarantees in the market, so you could <u>lose</u> 10%, 20%, or 30%. Nope! That makes no sense to me. The only kind of compound interest that can do you any good is compound interest working *for* you.

So let's get rid of all the compound interest draining your wealth away. The first step is to put together your Accelerator Margin™. This is the money you'll use to accelerate your debt payoff process.

Put Your Spending on a Diet

Consider all the ways you can trim your expenditures — to maximize the amount you can put into the payoff process.

I'll give you some specific suggestions a little later, but for now, begin thinking about ways you can reduce your insurance premiums, your car costs, possibly your house costs, your food and entertainment expenses, and even ways to save money when you're buying clothes and other personal and household needs.

You want to focus <u>all available money</u> into your bill payoff process. This does not mean you can't ever go to the movies or out to dinner. What it does mean is that you must understand the trade-offs. If you go out to dinner, that might add a month onto the payoff time for a certain bill — thereby delaying, to some extent, the day when you'll be completely debt-free. If it's worth it to you to make that trade, go ahead.

On the other hand, beware of the initial urge to shut off all forms of fun completely. You'll get frustrated and quit your plan entirely. Be willing to indulge yourself now and again — just know what you're trading and make sure it's worth it to you.

By the way, at Debt-FREE & Prosperous Living®, Inc., we publish a companion newsletter to this book. It too is called Debt-FREE & Prosperous Living®, and it provides subscribers with ongoing education, information, and emotional support. The way we see it, this book provides the overall strategy, and the monthly newsletter provides the ongoing tactics and motivation to most successfully implement the Debt-FREE & Prosperous Living® system in your life.

If you didn't receive information about subscribing to the Debt-FREE & Prosperous Living® newsletter when you got this book, just go to our website: *www.getdebtfree.com*, and click on the "Tools To Do It Yourself" button to find out more about our newsletter and other products we have available.

A Note About Bankruptcy

Bankruptcy is sometimes the only option for people whose circumstances have changed to the point where it's no longer *possible* to make their income meet their outgoing obligations. It is *not*, however, a proper debt-elimination tool for someone who *can* pay their bills. The problem is that bankruptcy lawyers have encouraged a lot of people who could pay their debts to just dump them through the bankruptcy laws — leaving their creditors holding the bag.

While it's arguable the credit companies deserve to lose some money, considering how they push credit on all of us, the ethics of someone who is mathematically capable of making their monthly payments using bankruptcy as a method for achieving debt-freedom troubles me. The bankruptcy laws were established to protect people who — through no fault of their own — got into an impossible financial situation. Bankruptcy was never meant as a way of getting rid of annoying bills, as a convenience for undisciplined consumers.

I went through a bankruptcy once, because I had lost my income through no fault of my own. But, I chose a Chapter 13 bankruptcy, so I could eventually pay everyone back — which I did. I didn't want to cheat my creditors. I just wanted to stop them from adding unending interest to the balances, and have them reduce their payment requests to levels that fit my new, lower income. The court made them do those two things, and I paid them all off in less than three years.

I'm not trying to pass judgment on people who declare bankruptcy, and if you've done that, I understand the pressures that make a person choose that course. What I am saying is that — if you can currently make your monthly payments, even if it's tight — the Debt-FREE & Prosperous Living® system **can** help you pay off all your debts in a handful of years. Plus, as soon as the first debt gets paid off, you have more free money each month, and that amount grows as each subsequent debt is eliminated. So the tightness or pressure you feel right now begins being relieved quickly and goes away fast.

For what it's worth, following the Debt-FREE & Prosperous Living® system will also preserve and enhance your credit rating, especially compared to the negative effects a bankruptcy or even Consumer Credit Counseling leaves behind.

STAGE 3

Then, Focus ALL Available Resources on Building Wealth

Once you've paid off all your debts, including credit accounts, car loans, and home mortgage(s), you then want to take the same total amount you were paying on your debts each month — including your now very large Accelerator Margin™ — and focus that into wealth-building investments.

> **NOTE: I frequently advise people who've fought and won a long, valiant debt-elimination battle, to take one or even two months' Accelerator Margin™ and reward themselves with a vacation or some other indulgence. It gives you something to look forward to as you slug your way through the debt-elimination process, and it gives you a preview of the lifestyle you'll be able to live when you build up sufficient investments.**

For starters, your wealth-building strategy should consider both possibilities and probabilities. We'll start with possibilities.

It is possible that something unforeseen might come up, like a breakdown in your car or a major appliance, so the first order of business after the debts are gone is to put that six months worth of required income into a liquid (easily convertible to cash) account, such as a money market account, CD, or an assets management account. This way you can easily withdraw any amount you might need to meet an emergency. Shop around, because there are significant differences between interest rates paid by various financial institutions.

Many discount investment brokerage companies offer competitive money market accounts along with debit cards, check writing, and other useful financial services. Get a copy of *Money, Worth*, or any other investment magazine, or watch CNBC, CNNfn, or any other financial news network to see ads for these brokerage companies. Get their information and decide which one's best for you. If you'd like some help making these choices or setting up these accounts, seek out a good financial advisor.

Make sure that, whichever type of account you choose for your emergency cash fund, it is both interest-bearing and liquid. You'll notice, however, that I included Certificates of Deposit as an option. One consideration with CDs is that you'll pay a penalty if you withdraw any of the money prior to the certificate's maturity date. But that penalty is usually just two or three months' interest. While that can be considerable, CDs usually pay significantly higher interest rates than passbooks or money market accounts. If you're pretty sure you'll rarely need to make withdrawals, a CD or several staggered CDs may be a better choice for your emergency fund.

Now Invest for Wealth-Building

Once you have your emergency fund built up, you can begin concentrating ALL your investment money each month into less liquid but higher-growth investments. I recommend you invest through Mutual Funds. These can be stock funds, bond funds, or other types of investments that are managed by professionals with proven track records. I *do not* recommend you do your own investing in individual stocks. I have never met any nonprofessional investor who — over time — came out ahead of the average mutual fund manager.

Of course, if you find the research and drama of selecting your own individual security investments rewarding, by all means...do it. But, do it with a portion of your investment portfolio you could stand to lose...because you might. Picking and timing stocks is not for the faint of heart. On the other hand, most folks find that mutual funds can build their wealth without changing the color or density of their hair.

I'll get into more detail about mutual funds later in this book, but let me state right here that mutual funds are an investing mechanism — not a specific investment. There are mutual funds through which you can invest in every type of security you could buy individually on your own. There are *stock* mutual funds, *bond* mutual funds, *money market* mutual funds, *gold and precious metals* mutual funds, *foreign securities* mutual funds, *utilities* mutual funds, and the list goes on. So — when I say "mutual fund" — I'm not necessarily saying "stock market."

Mutual funds respond to market influences just like their underlying securities. For example, there are good and bad times for investing in stocks, just as there are for bonds or any other kind of security, so when those times come you should treat mutual fund investing in those types of securities the same way you'd treat individual securities of that type. When the Federal Reserve begins raising interest rates, for example, you may consider selling some *stock* mutual fund shares and investing in *money market* mutual funds. You'd still be investing through mutual funds, just not stock funds.

Some stock mutual funds have produced annual growth rates exceeding 100 percent — for a given period of time. Of course, they occasionally have off years where they end up with negative growth (like we saw in the Tech Wreck of 2000). But over time, stock mutual funds generally provide you with the most wealth-building power for your hard-earned money — while freeing you from having to personally research each individual company you might consider investing in.

The time-proven fact is that, over decades, you can't beat the money-growing power of the U.S. stock market — and the simplest way for most people to invest in the market is through mutual funds.

NOTE: Throughout the investment stage of your Debt-FREE & Prosperous Living® plan you will, of course, maintain the necessary insurance to cover you from catastrophic occurrences, such as a totaled car or open-heart surgery. After you've built up an estate that can take care of your heirs in your absence, you may not need to carry much of the insurance you did during your wealth-building years.

What About Taxes on My Investments?

While taxes should never be your primary reason for selecting or not selecting a given investment, you should at least consider the effects of taxes on the growth of your investments. Many experts try to make this sound like an incredibly complex issue, but there are essentially three tax statuses for investments: tax-free (also called tax-exempt), tax-deferred and non-tax-deferred.

Tax-free investments are usually debt obligations of a governmental body. The most popular are tax-free municipal bonds. They are free from federal income taxes, and in some states, municipal bonds issued <u>in that state</u> are free from state income taxes as well (called double tax-free). These investments yield lower returns than taxable investments, but you must consider the value of not having to pay the taxes on your growth. (See Appendix page A4.)

Tax-deferred means letting the interest and capital gains accumulate in your account without your having to pay *current* taxes on them. But you do have to pay taxes on the money as you take it out of a tax-deferred account. The taxes are not eliminated, they're just deferred until later. And if you take the money out of a tax-deferred account before you reach the qualified age required for that type of account, you'll pay penalties in addition to income and capital gains taxes.

The most common mechanisms in the U.S. for tax-deferred investing are the Individual Retirement Account (IRA), the SEP-IRA (for self-employed), the Keogh (for self-employed) and the 401(k) and 403(b) plans offered by many employers. The Canadian equivalent of the IRA is the Registered Retirement Savings Plan (RRSP).

A tax-deferred plan should definitely be a part of your investment strategy, because the increased value of having the full interest amount, in addition to the principal, compound each month is incredible (see the IRA growth table on Appendix page A12).

It can make a difference of hundreds of thousands of dollars in your future wealth to have this month's interest earn interest itself next month — without being taxed in the process.

When you reach retirement age, you can begin withdrawing money from your tax-deferred account, and only pay income taxes on the money you take out, <u>as you take it out</u>.

> **NOTE: There is a variation of the basic IRA in the U.S. It's called the Roth IRA. The significant difference in this type of IRA is that, instead of getting a front-end tax deferral on the money you put into the IRA, you make Roth IRA contributions with after-tax dollars...but pay no tax on withdrawals. Consult your tax advisor to see if this option will benefit you.**

One of the key benefits of these types of investment shelters is that, when you normally begin withdrawing the money at retirement, you'll need less to live on each month, so you'll take it out in lower amounts than your current income. This will put you in a lower income tax bracket, so the taxes on the dollars you're taking out will therefore be lower than they would be if you paid them now, when you're in your higher income (tax bracket) years. But you can be sure *you will pay taxes on the money one way or another — at one time or another.*

Investments that are neither tax-free nor tax-deferred are subject to current income and capital gains taxes each year.

Since tax shelters such as IRAs and 401(k)s have maximum contribution limits, you'll eventually have more money to invest each month than you can put into these shelters. You'll then be choosing between tax-free investments such as municipal bond funds and taxable investments such as growth mutual funds. What you're after in these comparisons is maximum "after-tax" growth of your wealth, so when you compare tax-free and taxable investments, be sure to compare the *after-tax* gain on the taxable investment with the yield of the tax-favored investment. Many times the taxable investment will out-produce the tax-free investment, even after you pay the taxes. (See Appendix page A4.)

You are Now Becoming Wealthy

Like I said earlier, when my wife, Lois, and I worked out our debt-elimination and wealth-building plan we were first angered by how much of our wealth the mortgage company and other creditors had been siphoning off. But then when we realized that **the same money we were already spending every month could pay off the same house we were already paying for — plus earn us millions in interest, in the same amount of time we would have been paying on the mortgage**, we felt like a thousand-pound weight had been removed from our shoulders.

You see, the reason I had begun researching these systems and methods in the first place was that I'd come to believe that if I did not find some "magic bullet" to quickly make me hundreds of thousands of dollars, *I would probably have to keep working until the day I died*. I saw no day in my future where there would be no bills and money in the bank.

What scared me was that I was already making good money — but no matter how much I earned, we still seemed to be constantly running in place. It was like being on a treadmill. I was huffing and puffing, but no scenery was going by. We had a nicer TV and newer cars, but we still weren't gaining any ground towards financial independence. We were still just living from month to month.

In fact, we were actually worse off than when I had made less money, because now we had larger payments and bigger balances on everything. And we were paying a higher percentage in taxes. This meant I was trapped — I had to continue bringing in big bucks just to pay the bills...just to keep what we had...and little or nothing was building for the future.

This was real pressure, because I knew that I had to maintain this high income level at all costs, or we would be in serious trouble. I was definitely not feeling financially independent. In fact, I was feeling even more dependent than when I had a smaller income. I was feeling vulnerable to the economy, to my employer, to anything that could upset my income stream.

Then, when I developed the Debt-FREE & Prosperous Living® system and discovered that there really was a way to achieve financial independence — a way that did not require a bunch of extra money, but was simply a method of redirecting the money we were already bringing in

— I got excited. It was a system that could not only get us out of debt, but could make us rich — *using the income we were already bringing home.* For the first time I felt like we really had a chance to live out the kind of future we had hardly dared dream about before.

And then I realized that a side benefit of the strategy was that **I would never need credit again.**

Sound Like a Dream?

It's not a dream.

Never needing credit is just the way people who are not up to their necks in debt can live. In fact, people using cash can live a better lifestyle than people operating on credit. I'll prove it to you.

Did you ever hear the saying, "Money talks"?

It really does...when it's real money. It is not nearly so loud when you have to ask for financing. But if you have the dough, you can often strike bargains that are never available to the credit purchaser.

Just as an example: I bought a Pontiac Grand Prix a few years ago from a dealer — and I got it for *half price*! I know that I only paid half price, because I verified it with *Consumer Reports* auto pricing service.

I got the car, which was used but in nearly new condition, for half price, because I stood in the dealership with my checkbook. I tapped the checkbook on the salesman's desk and said, "I'm going to write a check to buy a car *today.* Now I can write the check here...or I can walk across the street and write a check at the dealer over there. You decide."

Well...they decided all right. They decided not to let real money get out the door, and I drove away in a wonderful car with all the trimmings — for half price! Someone interested in that same car — but asking for bank financing — would have had no bargaining leverage, so they would have paid nearly the asking price. Then they would have been taken to the cleaners with the finance charges, ending up paying thousands more than I did for the same car.

CASH IS KING!

Even when it comes to buying homes...or maybe I should say especially when it comes to buying homes.

In today's economy, more and more people are losing their homes. It's not your fault, but it could be your good fortune...if you have cash. You can visit the sheriff's tax sales in your county or parish and often buy homes for pennies on the dollar. Some of these houses are incredible values, and when you've bought one, you **own** it. You continue to operate on cash, with no mortgage payments.

But, if you're still not convinced that using cash can give you a better lifestyle than using credit, let's do a little simple math. Suppose you and I make the exact same income, but you buy most of the stuff in your life on credit while I pay cash. It's true that, in the very beginning, you'll be able to get a few things before I do, but this is only a brief illusion of a better lifestyle.

Let's say we both walk into an electronics store and we both buy the same TV. You use a credit card, I write a check. You're going to pay more for that TV than I do, because you'll pay the price *plus* interest. I'll only pay the price. Now let's go to a car dealer. We'll say we both like a $20,000 car. I'll get it for $20,000, while you'll end up paying $25,000 or more for it when you add in the interest on your payments.

See what's happening? You're paying more than I am for everything. And if we both have the same income...I'm going to be able to buy **more** of everything, over time, than you will. So...even if we use the materialistic yardstick of "things" as a measure of quality of lifestyle, I'll end up living a better lifestyle than you because I used cash instead of credit. And while you sweat bullets to pay your bills each month...I'll have no bills other than food, utilities, and property taxes.

Cash wins!

Using Credit Actually Lowers Your Standard of Living

When you're in debt, you're forced to live like you make less income than you actually do — because when you made those credit purchases in the past, you committed a portion of the income you are making today to those creditors.

So, if 92 percent of your after-tax income goes to credit debt payments, including your house (the national average), those purchases from the past are forcing you to live on only 8 percent of your present after-tax income. Someone who is completely debt-free, and making exactly the same income as you, has that 92 percent to spend or invest. They get to live on 100 percent of their after-tax income, because they operate on **cash.**

However, before you can get to the cash stage, you have to move through the debt elimination stage. And there are some significant obstacles to watch out for. The same obstacles that helped get you into the dilemma you're in today.

The Monthly Payment Trap

Our North American economic system has trained us to think only in terms of monthly payments. When we go to buy a TV, or a car, or even a home, we think in terms of how big a monthly payment we can afford — not how much the purchase is really costing us. This thinking pattern gets us in deep, deep trouble.

We don't ask ourselves even the most basic consumer questions. Is it good for us? Are we being ripped off? Is it absurd to pay 21 percent interest on a TV, or to pay nearly three times for our home over the course of a 30-year mortgage? We just say, "I want it. I want it now. It fits in my monthly income."

And you know why we never think beyond the monthly payment?

Because, "Everyone's buying with monthly payments, so it must be the right thing to do. Dad bought his cars and the house I grew up in this way, so it must be right. Shucks, everyone pays 30 years for a house. How else could anyone afford one...huh?"

I had a friend once tell me that — if they had offered him 10-year financing on a recently purchased new car, he probably would've taken it, because it would've given him lower *monthly payments*.

We go into the marketplace to buy something and the only two numbers we consider are our monthly income and the total of our monthly expenses. This tells us how much income is available monthly for new or additional monthly payments. Or we look at a specific credit card to see how much room there is before we go over our credit limit. Whatever room there is between our current balance and our credit limit is seen as spendable credit! It's almost as if it's our patriotic duty to keep our monthly payments equal to our income.

That's Absolutely the Wrong Way to Look at It

Merchants and the money-lending companies behind them have us trained to look at the wrong part of the equation. Read my lips: **it does matter how much the total cost is!** It matters to your future wealth, and it matters more than you probably imagine.

I was recently looking at a full-color insert a Chicago-area furniture store had stuffed in that city's Sunday paper. For each suite of furniture there were big red numbers giving a monthly payment...with a little asterisk after each payment amount. After some searching, I found...in tiny black numbers...the full price. At the bottom of the front page, in big yellow letters in a bright red box, it said, "NO MONEY DOWN."

This ad typifies how merchants use our *monthly payment* and *"gotta' have it now"* weaknesses against us.

First of all, the meaning of the little asterisk after each bright red monthly payment amount was found in a little patch of ridiculously small print at the bottom of the last page of this mini catalog. There I found that the "Low Monthly Payments" were based on an Annual Percentage Rate interest of 31.5 percent! Then, to add insult to injury, the "Low Monthly Payments" also required 10 percent down!

But didn't they say "NO MONEY DOWN" on the front page? Yep. They just sort of lied...that's all. On the same page where, in bright letters, they said "NO MONEY DOWN," they also showed me "low monthly payments" that required a down payment! Of course, I wasn't supposed to really find this out until I was in the showroom, where the salesperson would have me in a headlock...while my wife is saying, "Oh, honey, wouldn't this look great in our bedroom?"

And, if I ever got around to reading the fine print on the sales contract, that is where I'd probably discover the 31.5 percent interest rate. But, by then, both my wife and I would be envisioning the wonderful (junk) furniture in our home, and we'd be too psyched up to be stopped by the interest rate on the "low monthly payments."

Let's examine one example from their catalog, a bedroom set that has a "Low Monthly Payment" of "ONLY $54.51 per month." Right next to that it says, "SALE...$949" in itsy-bitsy letters. Well, thanks to their 31.5 percent interest rate, I would end up paying $1,722.22 for that $949 bedroom set — over 23 months. That is an extra $773.22 in interest — just for using their "Easy Monthly Payments"!

The problem is the average consumer never figures this out. They just pay the payments...and the $773.22 interest...and then wonder why they never have any money to spend (or invest) each month.

Think about this: *every penny of interest you pay is money you have to earn...money that should be contributing to your wealth...but instead you are donating it to the wealth of your creditors.* Do you really think they deserve it more than you and your family do?

The bottom-line truth is that you're only going to be able to generate a certain amount of wealth in your life, and you can't afford to waste any of that wealth making your lenders rich. You need to keep as much of it as possible for yourself!

It still amazes me when I think back, about how I would routinely sign mortgage papers, reading the financing disclosure pages that told me how much interest I would be paying over the life of the loan — and I never seemed to wonder how I would replace the hundreds of thousands of dollars I was promising to the mortgage company.

I had promised to give my mortgage company more than $200,000 on the house we lived in when our finances collapsed. You know...$200,000 is not that easy to come by. And I'm sure I could find better uses for it than the mortgage company could. How about you?

Credit stinks! There's no other way to look at it. You can live a better, less stressful, more fulfilled life using cash. And obviously, when I say "cash," I'm including checks, debit cards, cyber cash, or any other medium that transfers your currency to make the purchase. It's not borrowed money.

Stop thinking "Monthly Payment," and start thinking about the total cost of things you buy. When you do, you won't be so quick to take the credit option. And if that's not clear enough, let me state for the record that — with the possible exception of getting your first home — **you do not ever want to use credit for anything**.

Part Two – The Specifics

Step One Towards Debt Elimination

Now we're going to start putting the philosophy we've been discussing to work. The first step in applying the Debt-FREE & Prosperous Living® system to your finances is to find your initial Accelerator Margin™. This is the money that will prime your debt payoff pump. Right now it's buried in your current monthly spending, so we'll be discussing many savings opportunities later in this manual. We also teach ways to build your Accelerator Margin™ in our monthly Debt-FREE & Prosperous Living® newsletter.

The Accelerator Margin™ does not have to be a lot of money. It's like the snowball you begin rolling downhill. By the time you get to the bottom, it has become a boulder-sized ball you can make a snowman with. But it all started with a little snowball.

The amount you're shooting for in putting together your Accelerator Margin™ is at least 10 percent of your monthly, net household income. If your only debt is your mortgage, shoot for 25 to 30 percent of your monthly income for your Accelerator Margin™.

In other words, if you bring home $3,000 a month, you are trying to put together a $300 monthly Accelerator Margin™. If you think you can't afford that, keep reading and we'll show you how it can be done. On the other hand, if you can afford more, do it. This is not a game you want to stretch out. The goal is to pay off all debts in the shortest period of time. That is the fastest track to true financial independence. (Use Appendix pages A7-A9 to help develop your Accelerator Margin™.)

Let's first look at places where extra money might be hidden in wasted purchases or monthly expenditures. As we mentioned before, you can blow a lot of money just in the way you buy your car(s), your home, and your insurance. So we'll concentrate on these, because they offer the highest monthly potential for finding hidden Accelerator Margin™ money.

Obviously, you don't buy a car every day, but you probably will buy one at some point over the next few years, and what I'm sharing with you is a "Lifetime Strategy." <u>Debt-FREE & Prosperous Living® is a lifestyle</u>, not just a mathematical tool for paying off debts. I am therefore including some tips on how *not* to buy a car, so when you do...you won't simply hand over thousands of dollars that should be building your economic freedom. Most car dealers are plenty rich enough without you tossing your hard-earned money on their pile.

Here we go:

1. Don't ever buy a brand-new car. Buy nothing newer than two years old. The reason: a new car loses nearly half its value in the first two to three years. Yet you can buy two-year-old cars that are in "Like New" condition, with plenty of life left in them. Plus, the first owner will get any bugs worked out under the warranty. Let the poor soul who bought it new take the 50 percent bath on the car's depreciation — not you. Buying a brand-new car is simply throwing thousands of dollars down the chute. If you're hooked on new car smell, they sell spray cans of it at auto-parts stores.

2. Don't ever take more than 36 months financing on a car. I offer this tip with some reservation. My firm belief is that you should *never* buy a car with borrowed money. But if you are absolutely stuck, and must take a loan out — do not let it be for more than 36 months. People who take longer loans always owe more than the car is worth, until the last few months. Later in the book I'll show you how to pay off your car loans — and then my advice is to *never finance another one as long as you live.*

3. Don't ever take "Credit Life Insurance" on a car loan or a mortgage. This is incredible, if you really think it through. The car dealer or mortgage company is asking you to pay for an insurance policy on which *the bank* is the beneficiary, and on which the dealer or mortgage company makes a commission when they sell it to you. Worse yet, they frequently fold the insurance into the financing, so you're paying interest on the insurance! You can better protect your heirs with a term life insurance policy that will produce enough money to pay off the car(s) and the house. Check all your loan papers to see if you already have credit life. If you do, first make sure you have sufficient life insurance to pay off these loans, then cancel the credit life coverages. When you do, watch how your monthly payments drop.

> **NOTE: Whenever I recommend that you cancel any insurance, for which I also indicate a more cost-effective replacement (as I did in #3 above), ALWAYS GET THE REPLACEMENT POLICY IN FORCE BEFORE YOU CANCEL THE COVERAGE YOU WILL BE DROPPING.**

4. Never take extended warranties. Like most other forms of insurance, warranty policies are never likely to be needed by the person paying for them. With most products, if they're going to break down, they'll do it within the initial (free) manufacturer's period. If it was likely that your car, stereo, washer, microwave, or TV would have the troubles covered by an extended warranty, *they would not sell the warranty to you*. And if a salesperson tries to make it sound like an extended warranty is "free," ask him or her specifically if there is any charge to you for that coverage — either up front or in your payments. Cancel all extended warranties and get refunds for the unused time on them. I used to buy extended warranties on everything I purchased, until one day I realized that...I have never made a claim on one in my entire life. With savings I have since realized, I could afford to fix any of the once-covered products that might break.

5. Life insurance. The purpose of life insurance is **not** to make your survivors rich, should you die. It is to assure them a continuance of your income stream, should you stop producing it yourself. For most people the best value is to buy term life insurance, with a sufficient death benefit amount that, if it were invested in a good *income* mutual fund, the total return would equal your present monthly income. The next step is to put together a trust (your banker or lawyer can help) that will be the beneficiary of your life insurance. The trust should then be set up to invest the money from your insurance policy and pay your survivors the interest income as a continuation of your income stream.

Once you have a sufficient amount invested in your retirement portfolio – such that it's monthly interest income could supply enough for your survivors to live on in reasonable comfort – you really won't need life insurance any more. That's why I suggest term insurance...because you only need it for a certain term, until your investments build up.

However, each person's circumstances are different, and there are situations where term might not be the optimum answer. So I suggest you find an insurance agent or financial planner you trust, and ask them to evaluate your individual insurance needs. This evaluation should be repeated every three to five years, because circumstances and laws change.

Just make sure you have your advisor explain to you – in terms you can understand – why the course he or she is recommending is superior, in their professional opinion, to buying term insurance combined with separate investments.

6. Automobile insurance. If you naively accept all the coverages and deductible levels your insurance agent offers in their "standard package," you'll likely end up paying hundreds of dollars a year more than you need to.

For example, the "Medical" coverage on your car insurance policy may be redundant. You likely already have a medical (health insurance) policy that covers you and your family both in and out of the car — 24 hours a day. Non-dependents that might be hurt in your vehicle would likely be taken care of by the liability portion of your policy, so if you have a solid health insurance package, the "Medical" coverages on your car insurance may well be unnecessary. You can only get treated for your bodily injuries once, yet if you have health insurance and "Medical" coverage on your car insurance — you will be insured twice, to cover one set of expenses.

Your agent may also recommend "Road Service" and "Rental Car" coverages, but you'll likely never even remember you have them should you ever get into the highly unlikely situations in which these coverages actually apply. Most people forget they have Road Service coverage on their car insurance or — more likely — they never need it. The Rental Car coverage is of almost no value because it pays so little (at the time of this writing, State Farm pays $10 a day).

As for deductibles, we'll discuss them in detail later, but just raising your auto insurance deductible to $1,000 could cut your premiums by 40 percent.

7. Personal liability insurance. You are probably carrying two or more separate liability coverages: one on each auto, another on each recreational vehicle (motorcycle, boat, jet-ski, etc.), and another on your homeowner's policy. The purpose of liability insurance is that — should you or your property injure someone to the point where they could sue you — the insurance would pay them, so you don't end up with a court ordering you to sell your home and other assets to satisfy the judgment against you. **Generally speaking, you probably only need liability coverage equal to about twice your net worth.** And <u>you want the highest deductibles available, so as to keep the premiums to a minimum</u>. Do not waste premium money betting that you will have an accident or liability claim. Bet that you won't — the insurance company is betting you won't...and they're rarely wrong.

If you have your auto and homeowner's insurance through the same company, look into dropping your auto and home liability coverages to the minimums allowed and getting a $1 million "Umbrella" liability policy that will cover you under all circumstances.

I made all of the above suggested changes in my auto and homeowner's insurance coverages during lunch one day, and I'm saving $261 a year — while maintaining more than adequate protection.

8. Medical insurance is the same. If you pay for part or all of your medical (health) insurance coverage yourself, take the highest possible deductible you can stand. Unless you or a family member is particularly prone to illness, all you really need medical insurance for is to protect you from the huge bills that can come from a major illness. Bills that could drain your savings and investments. If you insist on having a coverage level that will pay for every sniffle, *you will likely pay through the nose in the form of higher monthly premiums!* In most cases, the increased premiums you'll pay over a year for a lower deductible or for more coverage will cost you more than carrying a higher deductible and covering your incidental medical expenses yourself.

> **NOTE: Insurance laws vary in each state, so before making these changes discuss them with a trusted insurance advisor.**

These have been just a few suggested changes where I know you are probably paying more each month than you have to. And every dollar you are wasting on these excess expenditures is a dollar that is not currently free to be added to your Accelerator Margin™.

Once you see how much just a few extra Accelerator Margin™ dollars can speed up your debt elimination, you'll become as ruthless as I am in finding every possible penny. Besides, it's *your* money. Why should you give one penny more than you must to anyone other than those with whom you choose to share it?

Look at every expense area you have. Are you really using all the premium (extra charge) cable TV channels you're paying for each month? Could you brown-bag it to lunch more often than you do? Do you pay someone to cut the grass or shovel the snow, when you could do it yourself? Are you paying $25 to have Jiffy Lube® change your oil, when you could do it for less than half that price. Are you paying a premium to eat frozen/precooked meals when you could cook more nutritious meals from scratch — for a fraction of the cost? Are you paying full price for all your groceries when your weekly newspaper and the World Wide Web are stuffed with discount coupons?

I'm not talking about living like a Tibetan monk. I'm just suggesting there is money flowing out of your hands each month that could get you out of debt faster. Is it worth it to search out this money? **Well, if you found just $100 a month and applied it to a $100,000, nine percent, 30-year-fixed mortgage, <u>you'd save $75,394 in interest</u>.**

CIA is Stealing Your Money

Here's a tool to help you find unnecessary expenditures: I call it CIA. No, that doesn't stand for Central Intelligence Agency. It represents

Convenience, Indulgence, and *Appearance.*

We waste money on Conveniences, like eating the expensive frozen prepared meals instead of making less expensive meals ourselves. When we pay others to do tasks we could easily do much more cheaply ourselves. When we take the kids to McDonald's after the Little League game instead of making a snack at home. When we waste five dollars a day ($100 a month) on eating lunch outside of work, rather than taking a few minutes to make a lunch to bring to work in the morning.

We waste money on Indulgences when we go to the mall after a hard day or week, because we "deserve" some kind of treat. That treat generally uses up money we really don't need to spend — and it's frequently charged on a credit card, which makes the cost even higher and the indulgence more damaging. We indulge ourselves with expensive credit-card dinners (again usually prompted by a hard week). We waste money on indulgences when we buy expensive toys, usually on credit, to help us make up for the "tough" life we live. These indulgences drain more from the average North American's financial resources than he or she might imagine. Most people are stunned when they research and compile indulgence expenditures.

We waste money on Appearances when we try to keep up with the Joneses. Let me tell you something — the Joneses are going bankrupt. Everything they have is in hock, and if they lost their income, they'd probably be homeless in a month or two. They are living an illusion, and you will be too if you try to compete with them. Forget trying to impress people with your possessions. Wait until you retire early — then they'll really be impressed!

Examine your life ruthlessly to see where you're wasting money on CIA, and eliminate those wastes. You'll probably be able to find the majority of your Accelerator Margin™ from this examination alone. And when you see how powerful your Accelerator Margin™ is in eliminating debt, you'll scour your finances for every available penny. See Appendix pages A7-A9 for help in putting together your Accelerator Margin™.

Let's Estimate When You'll Be Completely Debt-FREE

To get a rough idea of how long it will take you to get completely out of debt — **including your mortgage** — we'll use the Debt-Elimination Time Calculator form on Appendix page A14.

First total up all your debt balances. This number, including your mortgage balance, will be an impressive amount. But you'll be encouraged when you see what happens as we short-circuit the devastating impact of compound interest working against you — by paying these bills off by the shortest mathematical route.

Next, determine your Accelerator Margin™. You should look for every possible source of money to include in your Accelerator Margin™, because paying off debt balances is the best possible investment of your money. It gives you the highest return on investment.

For this reason, I recommend you include any amount you normally put into savings each month, because you're going to stop saving for right now. I even recommend you consider temporarily suspending any savings that are coming out of your paycheck at work and add that monthly amount to your Accelerator Margin™. You want to get as much monthly income working on the pay-down as possible. Your money will do you a lot more good paying off 20 percent debt than it will earning two to five percent in a savings account.

> **NOTE: Many people ask me about 401(k) or 403(b) plans they have at work. These are great retirement investment plans, because you're immediately earning around 50 percent on your money just from your employer's contribution. Plus the growth of the total investment accumulates tax-deferred until you begin taking distributions in retirement. What I recommend is that you continue investing in your 401(k) or 403(b), but not a penny more than your employer will match. Put all the rest into your Accelerator Margin™ until your debts are completely paid off — then raise your 401(k) contribution to the maximum percentage of**

your pay that is allowed.

Now locate your approximate total debt amount in the Total Debt Amount column, along the left edge of the Debt-Elimination Time Calculator chart. Then run your finger across to the right until you reach your approximate total monthly amount available for paying on all your bills — including your mortgage. This income amount should include both your Accelerator Margin™ and the normal minimum monthly payments on all your bills, but not the money that will go towards non-debt, monthly expenses like food, utilities, gasoline, and insurance.

When you've located this monthly amount, follow that column up to the line at the top of the table and you'll see the approximate number of years it will take you to get **completely out of debt**.

This chart will show you why you want to put the most you can into your monthly payoff Accelerator Margin™. The lower the monthly amount you can muster against your total debt load, the longer it will take you to pay it off. And the longer the payoff takes, the greater the portion of your money that will be going towards interest rather than principal.

Most people can pay off all their debts, including their mortgage, in around five to seven years, and the more you can put into the process the shorter that time frame. Let's see an example of how it might work:

If your debt, including your mortgage, totaled $100,000 — and the total monthly income (including all Accelerator Margin™ amounts) you had available for paying on your debt was $2,500 — you would first locate $100,000 in the left-most column, then look across to the right and find "2,489." This is the amount closest to the $2,500 you have available each month. Then run your finger up to the top of that column and your answer is four years! All your debts — **including your home mortgage** — would be paid off in just four years.

Be honest with yourself — what plan do you currently have, or have you ever heard about, that could get you totally debt-free in that short a time?

To get a handle on how brief that time is, simply think back four years. Doesn't it seem like just yesterday? Well that's how quickly you'll be looking back and remembering how hard it was carrying your heavy load of debt around.

Another feeling you'll have at that time is complete freedom and "un-vulnerability." That's not to say you'll quit your job or radically change your life when you're debt-free. You might...you might not. The point is, for the first time in your life, you will be in a position to *make that choice.*

No boss will be able to hold your job over your head, because you can survive without it. You could easily live on unemployment or savings until you found other work, or you could even work at McDonald's, if you had to, and still be OK. Or maybe you'd just choose to move to a less-expensive area and start a home-based business. The important thing is that the pressure would be off, and you'd have options.

Think about how many people (maybe yourself included) spend every day sweating out the economy, or their company's stability. According to a recent NBC television report, America has lost 25 percent of its jobs in just the last 10 years, and is still losing 2,200 jobs every day!

People are nervous, uneasy, stressed.

Layoffs start coming around and people panic because they know they cannot survive without their whole paycheck every month. But when you have no debts, all you need to worry about is eating, heating, and paying taxes. That takes a lot less money each month than you're spending now, so even a small savings account could sustain you for a relatively long period of time. No need to panic.

Once you begin building your investments — which starts happening the months after your mortgage is gone — you'll quickly build up a more-than-sufficient emergency reserve. After just a few months, you'll have as much in the bank as any credit card would ever offer you as a credit line — so you can be your own credit card or bank from that moment on. By the end of the first year, you'll have more in your savings and investments than you probably dare to dream right now.

As I mentioned earlier, when Lois and I first worked out our plan, we were stunned. If we had continued paying our bills and mortgage according to the way good little consumers are supposed to — 26 years down the road we would've owned our home and maybe (I'm being optimistic) had $100,000 put away.

Taking the same money, but using our Debt-FREE & Prosperous Living® debt-elimination and wealth-building strategy — 26 years down the road we would own the same house, plus have $3.8 million in investments! All this with the same money we were already bringing home! Think about that — you pay it out one way and you end up with the house and a little money (maybe). Pay the same money out the Debt-FREE & Prosperous Living® way and you end up with the same house...and <u>you're a millionaire</u>.

Which way would you choose?

That's what I thought.

Now Let's See Exactly How Long It Will Take

Before I tell you how to pay off all your debts, let's make sure you cannot make any more debts or increase the ones we're trying to pay off.

Cut up and throw away all your credit cards, with the possible exception of travel and entertainment cards that can't carry a balance (like American Express) and gasoline cards for road emergencies when you don't have cash with you. But never, never, never carry a rolling balance on these gas cards.

There is no justification for keeping the credit cards — none. If you find yourself trying to make excuses, think of how an alcoholic would sound explaining why he or she should be able to keep a fully stocked bar...while they are simultaneously trying to give up liquor!

What About Emergencies?

You may also hear yourself asking, *"What if an emergency comes up?"* I understand that concern, but we have to make sure it's not just an excuse to keep a credit card that will eventually be abused. Here's my answer to the question: If you have a savings account holding a couple thousand dollars or more, you have no reason to keep any credit cards. But, if you really don't have any money available for a true emergency, keep one credit card *that charges no annual fee*. You're going to pay this card off in its normal priority, which I'll explain a little further down, but you're not going to use it except in a real emergency.

In fact, I'll help you avoid using it. What I want you to do is rinse out a metal can, like a soup or vegetable can, fill in with water, drop the credit card in it, and pop it in the freezer. The reason we're putting the card in the metal can is so it can't be defrosted in the microwave. If you get tempted to use the card, you'll have to wait for it to thaw out the natural way. That may be enough time for you to cool down while the can warms up. This card is for emergencies only.

Once your debts are gone and you've saved up your emergency fund, destroy the credit card.

Another excuse you may hear yourself using is, *"I just use my credit cards during the month, then pay them off as soon as the bills come in."* The truth is that using a credit card — even with the intention of paying the whole thing off when it comes in — causes people to spend more than twice as much as they would if they were writing a check or laying down cash, because plopping down the plastic is too painless and too convenient for impulse buying. Impulse buying destroys your financial health.

The plain truth is that credit cards are nothing but consumer cocaine. They're pushed like cocaine, with credit card companies literally bombarding consumers with credit card offers. And they're used like cocaine, with consumers buying things just to give themselves a pick-me-up or quick rush of pleasure...but the consequences (like cocaine) are long term pain and suffering.

What if Your Job Requires You to Use a Credit Card?

Sometimes a person's work or lifestyle requires them to carry plastic. A salesperson, for instance, needs a charge card to rent a car, get a hotel room, and buy a client lunch. There are a couple options here other than holding onto a credit card.

My first choice is an American Express card, because it's not a "credit card." You're supposed to pay the full balance off every month, so it will not allow you to go into debt and start paying interest on a balance. I also need to make it clear I'm talking about the basic, green American Express card here. Gold and Platinum American Express cardholders are frequently offered lines of credit. Don't go there.

And American Express also offers the Optima™ card. Do not take this card, because it's a credit card. It allows you to carry a balance, and it charges interest. Don't let this wolf in sheep's clothing into your wallet.

If you feel you need something like a Visa card or MasterCard, then get an "Off-line Debit Card" from your bank.

The card I'm talking about looks and works like a regular Visa or MasterCard credit card, but instead of building up debt (on which interest is charged), the money is taken directly from your checking account. In other words, using the debit card is just like writing a check, but with the convenience of a credit card. The important point about debit cards is that, since they operate like a check, you have to have the money in your account. This will give you the same emotional spending discipline as writing a check, rather than the lack of discipline fostered by true credit cards.

You may find some car rental agencies and an occasional hotel balk at accepting a debit card, but they'll gladly accept American Express.

Now Let's Get Down to Paying Off Your Debts

DEFINITION: For the purposes of this system, a debt is an owed amount <u>that can be completely paid off</u>. Monthly, ongoing costs such as food, taxes, or utilities are EXPENSES, and although you want to minimize them, they are not to be included in this debt-elimination program because they can never be totally paid off.

The first thing you want to do is get all your debts together. Now write down each account's total balance and its corresponding required minimum monthly payment on the *Calculating Your Debt Payoff Priority* form on Appendix page A15 in the back of this manual.

NOTE: When I say "minimum monthly payment," I mean the minimum payment allowed by that creditor. If you're in the habit of adding a little to certain debt payments, like your mortgage, <u>STOP doing that</u>. Just pay the minimum payment allowed for each debt each month, and put all other available dollars into your Accelerator Margin™.

When you have them all written down, divide the *Total Balance* amounts by their respective *Monthly Payments* and put the answers in column 4.

For example: Let's say you have a Visa card with a $500 balance and a minimum monthly payment of $25. You would divide $500 by $25 and get an answer of 20. The answer does not mean anything in and of itself, but it is the first step in determining the proper order in which to pay off all your bills.

Do this for each bill, and record the answer to each division in the appropriate column 4 box on the *Calculating Your Debt Payoff Priority* form.

Next, starting with the <u>lowest</u> division answer, number the bills from "1" to whatever number of bills you have to pay off. Put these numbers in the *Priority* column. For example, if you had two bills (say the Visa above and a department store charge) — and the Visa division gave you the answer of 20, while the department store came out at 17 — the department store account would be *Priority* number "1" and the Visa account number "2."

These numbers indicate the order in which you should pay off your debts. You would pay off the department store first and the Visa account second.

You do not care which account has the highest interest rate, because this system accelerates bill payoff so that you will not be paying enough months of interest for it to make a significant difference. You are going to beat your creditors at their interest game and turn off the flow of money they have been siphoning out of your financial life.

Now Watch the Power of Mathematics Working for You

OK, it is time to start rolling the bill-payoff snowball downhill. During this process you will be focusing all your Accelerator Margin™ on <u>one debt at a time</u>, paying minimum allowed payments on all other debts. This is the fastest route to debt-elimination. Spreading money out over several debts at a time only makes it take longer, costing you money and enthusiasm.

On Appendix page A15, enter the full Accelerator Margin™ you've accumulated in box A at the top of the form, then add it to the regular payment for the first debt to be paid off. With this total amount (the regular monthly payment plus the Accelerator Margin™) being paid on the first debt each month, calculate how many months it will take until the debt is completely paid off.

For example, if you put together a $200 Accelerator Margin™ and added it to the Visa account payment we talked about above, you would be paying $225 a month, and you'd completely pay the bill off in 2.2 months! However, since we don't pay our bills in tenths of a month, it will take you 3 months to completely pay off the Visa account, and you'll have $125 of your Accelerator Margin™ left over in the third month. This $125 will be added to the payment of the second priority debt in the same (third) month. So its balance will already be $125 lower when you start working on it in earnest in month four.

You would put the $225 in column 6 across from the first debt, and enter 3 months in column 7. Then you would subtract the $125 remaining Accelerator Margin™ from debt #2's balance and show the new, lower balance in its place.

Then, in month four, you take all of what you had been paying on the Visa account — the $200 Accelerator Margin™ plus the $25 normal Visa payment, plus debt number two's payment — and enter the total amount in the *Margin Roll-up* (column 6) box next to the second debt to be paid off. If that debt had a monthly payment of, say $50, you would be paying a total of $275 each month on that debt. It too, would likely be gone in a few months, and you would then be adding the full $275 (your new, higher Accelerator Margin™) to the payment of the third debt to be paid off — and so on down through all your debts.

By the time you get to larger debts, like your car payment, your Accelerator Margin™ will have grown to an impressive amount. Both you, and whoever gave you your car loan, will be amazed at how quickly you'll pay it off.

When you've knocked off all the regular revolving credit accounts, including any car payments, you'll be ready for the big one — your mortgage payment. In most cases people following the Debt-FREE & Prosperous Living® system have completely eliminated all their debts, except their mortgage, in one to two years. They then frequently have an Accelerator Margin™ equal to their mortgage payment, sometimes as much as twice their mortgage payment. This means they can at least double their mortgage payment every month.

Don't be demoralized if it takes you a little longer to get through the debts that precede your mortgage. Some people take longer than two years to get to the mortgage but still end up debt-free in a total of between five and six years.

NOTE: Contact your mortgage holder directly and ask for SPECIFIC instructions on how to make additional principal prepayments along with your regular monthly payment. Ask them to mail written guidelines to you if they have them. In most cases, the Additional Principal Prepayment forms on Appendix page A13 will work.

When you add your now-large Accelerator Margin™ to your mortgage, you'll begin knocking off principal at an incredible rate. Your equity in your home will skyrocket — for two reasons:

1. 100 percent of your Accelerator Margin™ is reducing your principal balance (adding to your equity — the portion of the house you <u>own</u>).

2. The portion of your regular monthly payment that is interest will be falling dramatically, because it is calculated each month on the "remaining unpaid balance." Since your Accelerator Margin™ is pounding down this unpaid balance, the interest calculation will be performed each month on a smaller and smaller balance amount. So more and more of your regular monthly payment amount will also be applied to the unpaid principal balance, further accelerating the payoff process.

IMPORTANT: As soon as you reduce the principal balance to less than 80 percent of the home's appraised value — check with the lender to be sure they are no longer charging you for Mortgage Protection Insurance. This will eliminate the MPI monthly premium, meaning that even more of your total payment will be going to principal reduction.

Now let's get back to the *Calculating Debt Payoff Priority* form on Appendix page A15. Totaling the figures in column 7 will tell you the total number of months your debt-elimination plan will take. Divide this number by 12 and you'll know how many years it'll take until you're completely debt-free.

You should track your progress every month against this *Calculating Debt Payoff Priority* schedule. This will help you avoid frittering away money on nonessentials, while you think you're paying off your debts. If you know when a debt is supposed to be paid off — and it's not — you know you've been undisciplined in following your plan (or you had an emergency that required the Accelerator Margin™ that month). And you know exactly how far off schedule you are. Remember, our goal is not to fool ourselves into thinking we're addressing the problem — it is to get the job done!

Assuming you'll follow your debt payoff plan, you will soon be in a position to say, "Good-bye forever" to credit, credit ratings, and all the headaches and humiliation that go with credit.

By the way, don't let yourself slip into the negative emotional trap that "this is some kind of super-restrictive *budget.*" This is not a budget — it's a *spending plan* or a resource allocation plan that simply guides you in how to best use your financial resources. It's not a restrictive approach to using money, but rather it's an aggressive approach to building a future of your own design. Most importantly, it's making you "un-vulnerable," and eventually...financially independent.

You're not giving things up. In fact, you are gaining a few important things, like control and ownership of your own life — and freedom of choice about what you do with the rest of that life — not to mention what to do with the hundreds of thousands of dollars of interest you otherwise would have paid to creditors.

What About Emergencies Now?

If the TV breaks down, you don't worry, because **you're debt-free!** You just take a small part of what you're now investing each month and get the TV fixed. If it can't be repaired, take a little more money and get a new one.

Need a new car? Hold off on your investing schedule for a couple months and buy one <u>cash</u>.

Need a new home? Sell the one you own, add a little from your savings and investments if necessary, and buy a new one <u>cash</u>!

You'll never need credit again, so you won't be sweating out your credit rating.

> **NOTE: Your credit rating can unfortunately be used for other things these days, such as a qualification factor for getting a job or a promotion, for renting a place to live, even for opening a bank account in some areas. So don't irresponsibly damage your credit rating if you can avoid it, just because you think it now has no purpose. I disagree with the ways people are using our credit records, but I can't change the rules by myself. We must therefore deal with reality as it exists. We can, however, voice our opinions to our Congressperson and Senators about how our credit records should and should not be used.**

Introducing The "Lucky Family"

Appendix pages A1 through A4 illustrate a case study we completed on what we call the "Average American Family" or the "Lucky Family". We've compiled numbers from credible sources such as RAM research, the National Association of Realtors, as well as others and created the Lucky Family for the purpose of demonstrating the power of the Debt-FREE & Prosperous Living® system.

Appendix pages A1 through A4 illustrate a case study we completed on what we call the "Average American Family" or the "Lucky Family". We've compiled numbers from credible sources such as RAM research, the National Association of Realtors, as well as others and created the Lucky Family for the purpose of demonstrating the power of the Debt-FREE & Prosperous Living® system.

Reviewing the case study in the first few pages of Appendix A demonstrates why the Debt-FREE & Prosperous Living® system is the most effective way to create real financial freedom. Here's an overview of what you'll find on those pages:

• The Lucky Family will be completely debt free, including their home mortgage, in less than seven years.

• They will save over $105,000 in interest payments in that time-frame.

• And by the time they would have paid off their home the traditional way (thirty year mortgage), they will accumulate over $1.2 million dollars in wealth.

These calculations, which would take a math professor to compute, are easily performed with our proprietary DebtFree™ for Windows™ software. You can find out more about this powerful debt elimination tool on our web site: *www.getdebtfree.com* by clicking on the "Tools To Do It Yourself" button.

OK...Let's Start Building Your Wealth

When you're out of debt, you can take the whole Accelerator Margin™ amount you were paying on your mortgage and concentrate it ALL on wealth production. This monthly amount should now include what was your mortgage payment, plus the payment amounts from all the other debts you paid off before the mortgage, plus your original Accelerator Margin™ — combined.

If you don't yet have a six-month income cushion in a liquid investment account such as a money market account, build that up first. Since your monthly income requirements are now much lower (no more debt), you should be able to put six months' worth away in just a few months. Then it'll be time to start focusing on investment vehicles that will give you the best possible return — with the relative safety of having your money in the hands of experienced investment managers.

I'm talking about mutual funds.

Once you start investing, your mailbox will suddenly be stuffed with packages from investment advisors who will try to sell you on their special "Insider," "Contrarian," or "Scientific" investing systems — all of which will supposedly make you "rich...rich...rich" beyond your wildest dreams. These systems "can't lose," so their proponents say. Why, you could "double your money overnight." They may even tell you that mutual funds are for babies...folks who don't have nerve enough to do "real" individual-security investing.

Well, they're wrong on all counts. Most super-duper, can't-lose deals are either total fabrications, or they're only good for the insiders. And unless you're a broker for the company making the stock offering, or an owner of the company whose stock is being offered — you are *not* one of the insiders. You're just one of the suckers who's going to help make them "rich...rich...rich."

The other point is that mutual funds are real investments. When you buy shares in a mutual fund, you are, in essence, buying shares in a company whose business is investing — they use your money to buy stocks, bonds, precious metals, money market instruments or whatever asset or security the fund is designed to invest in. As the values of the securities your mutual fund manager has purchased for the fund go up, or as those securities pay dividends, your wealth increases.

It is just like owning stock in IBM. If the demand for IBM stock goes up, the value of your shares increases. When you buy shares in a mutual fund, and the securities the fund manager purchases with your money go up in value (on average), the value of your mutual fund shares increases. Or, if the fund intends to keep share values constant, you'll be given more shares to compensate for the growth of the internal securities.

The main reason I recommend mutual funds is that they give you every benefit you should be looking for in your investing strategy. One of the main concepts behind our Debt-FREE & Prosperous Living® investing philosophy is "simplicity with safety." Mutual fund investing is simple and quite a bit safer than investing in individual securities.

Suppose your brother-in-law or some newsletter financial guru shows you how he or she made a fortune by putting all their eggs in Afghan silkworm farms. It may have worked out that way...under those specific circumstances...for that individual. But a turn in the silk market could've wiped him or her out overnight. Mutual funds, on the other hand, may not always offer you the big gains individual securities might...for a moment in time — but they will offer you solid return potential, while giving you considerable protection against crashing and burning.

This protection comes from their inherent *diversification*. I'll explain diversification, as well as other mutual fund characteristics in the next section. So let's find out what mutual funds are and how they work.

What Exactly Are Mutual Funds?

Mutual funds began in Europe early in the nineteenth century, with the first U.S. mutual fund forming in 1924. They're just what they sound like: a fund created by people "mutually" pooling their money for the purpose of investing it. The people who have pooled their money (bought shares) in the fund are actually the "owners" of a company (the mutual fund), and their company goes out and invests in other companies, in government debt instruments, in money markets, in precious metals, and the like.

The owners of this investing company (the shareholders in the mutual fund) then participate in the profits or losses from these investments, proportionately to their number of shares in the fund. Mutual fund shareholders include individuals like you and me, as well as institutions, such as banks, insurance companies, and pension funds.

One of the great benefits of putting your money into a mutual fund is that the fund's investments are being coordinated by an experienced fund manager, who generally has years of documented success in the market. He or she also has a staff of specialists who continually monitor and analyze all the information that can impact the performance of your fund's investments.

This level of experience and breadth of resources are far beyond what you or I could likely hope to have if we were investing on our own. And the large pool of investment funds at the manger's disposal allows him or her to *diversify* or spread the fund's risk out over a number of individual securities.

Each mutual fund invests in a *diversity* of stocks, or bonds, or whatever type of security it's designed to invest in. The fund is therefore insulated from being devastated by a drop in a single security.

For example, if a fund invests equally in 100 different stocks, five of those stocks could lose all their value, yet your net asset value in the fund would be reduced by only five percent, because those five stocks only represent five percent of the fund's holdings. Whereas, if you had invested the same amount of money you put into the mutual fund into any one of the five companies that failed — you could have lost <u>one hundred percent</u> of your money.

Of course it's highly unlikely that five companies held by any mutual fund would go out of business. Any fund manager who selected stocks that poorly would be out of a job in a month. What's more likely is that some stocks in the fund may go own, but other stocks held by the fund might just as likely hold their value or go up. So it's possible that the overall gains in the stocks that go up could offset or exceed the losses from those that go down.

It's highly unlikely you or I could afford to spread our risk as broadly as a mutual fund automatically does for us. Most mutual funds are invested in at least 100 securities. For you to accomplish the same amount of diversification would take a considerable amount of money. Even if the average price per share across the 100 companies is just $25, it would cost you $25,000 just to buy 10 shares of each stock. And that's before considering brokerage commissions. Whereas, you could invest in a mutual fund for as little as $1,000, and get the same 100-stock diversification protection as would have cost you $25,000 when buying individual stocks.

To assure this important diversification for mutual fund investors, government regulations forbid a mutual fund from investing more than five percent of its assets in a single company. And the fund cannot own more than 10 percent of any company's total capitalization. The benefit for you and me is that single stocks within a fund may rise and fall, but no one company's securities can represent a large enough percentage of our mutual fund to sink it. This helps keep our money at minimum risk.

Even with diversification your investment in a mutual fund can go down. If you're invested, say, in a "high-tech" mutual fund — a fund which invests in leading-edge technology companies — and that entire sector of the market turns downward for a period, the value of your mutual fund holdings will go down. But not nearly as much as you likely would have lost had you invested the same money in an individual technology company. So the diversification benefit of mutual funds helps even in the down times.

Of course, you'd only really experience the "loss" if you sold your mutual fund shares at the lower value. In most cases, unless circumstances forced you to sell, you'd just hang onto the shares waiting for the next market upturn. When you invest for the long-term, as you should, the one thing you never want to do is knee-jerk react to short-term (less than five years) marketing conditions.

Mutual Funds Live in Families

Most mutual funds are a part of what's called a family of funds. A mutual fund family is simply a group of separate mutual funds marketed by the same overall management company.

You'll want to simplify managing your investments and moving money between funds (when the economy dictates) by looking for fund families that offer funds in the Stock, Bond, Precious Metals, and Money Market categories. That way it'll be simpler to move your money from one kind of fund to another when necessary, without a lot of fees, and with a single phone call. When you move money from one fund to another, within the same family of funds, the movement will be less complicated and cheaper.

Another advantage of investing in mutual funds, versus trying to do your own individual-security investing, is what we could call economies of scale. Since the fund manager is running a big company, he or she saves money on all the clerical, analytical, and other specialty help needed to be successful. And having all these economists, consultants, and other specialists gives the fund manager access to more powerful and timely information than you or I would likely have available to us.

Yet another advantage of mutual fund investing is that the fund does all the paperwork for you. You'll get regular statements, either monthly or quarterly, showing your investments and redemptions (buying and selling shares), and any income you've received during that time. You'll be able to compare these summaries with the individual confirmations you received each time you made a transaction.

At tax time you'll be issued a Form 1099, which shows your taxable growth, from income and capital gains, over the previous calendar year. Be aware that a copy of each Form 1099 is also sent to the IRS, so don't think you can "forget" to include any gains from your investments on your tax return.

Another benefit of mutual funds, that fits in precisely with our Debt-FREE & Prosperous Living® philosophy, is that — because the fund manager is minding the store for you — you can generally relax while your assets are growing in value...paying you income...or both. That makes mutual funds the perfect investment for retirement. You can travel, play golf, or whatever else floats your bass boat, while your experienced fund manager and his or her staff of specialists are hard at work making you richer.

No having to become a financial genius. No trying to time the market and throw the dice. Mutual funds are comparatively safe, they're simple, and they let you sleep. The three S's: Safe, Simple, Sleep. Those are key ingredients to the type of lifestyle I want to live — and the kind I believe you want to live too.

Types of Mutual Funds

There are essentially two types of mutual funds: Open-End funds and Closed-End funds. Most mutual funds you'll hear about are open-end funds.

Open-end funds can issue and sell new shares to the public as long as there are people willing to buy them. In other words, the pool of investors can grow indefinitely for an open-end fund. There are both pros and cons to this ability of the fund to grow.

The main advantage is that a large fund has the resources to increase diversity and, therefore, protect its shareholders from being adversely affected by a drop in any single stock or even a single industry. But that same "larger pie" situation precludes a larger fund from benefiting in a dramatic way from a gain in any individual security or selection of securities within the fund.

For example, if a large fund has five percent of its holdings in the healthcare sector, while a smaller fund has 25 percent of its investments in healthcare companies, a big gain in the healthcare stocks would have a much greater positive effect on the smaller fund than the larger one.

Conversely, should healthcare take a beating, shareholders in the smaller fund would feel the impact more keenly than those in the larger fund.

When an open-end fund sells shares, it's issuing new shares. This is called a primary distribution, and because these are new shares, the Securities and Exchange Commission (SEC) requires the fund to offer all potential investors a prospectus. This is a document detailing data about the fund's financial soundness, as well as its purpose and strategy. I'll take you on a tour of a prospectus a little further down.

When you buy shares in an open-end fund, you're buying new shares directly from the fund. When you sell shares, you are selling them back to the fund, not to other investors. When you invest, you are increasing the fund's asset pool, and when you sell back shares, the money comes out of the asset pool to pay you back. You'll generally have your money within a couple days of selling your shares.

Closed-end funds, on the other hand, issue a specific, limited number of shares. These shares are then traded like stocks, on exchanges, and their value — from day to day — is determined by marketplace supply and demand.

With open-end funds, the value of your shares is determined by the collective value of the underlying investments being made by the fund manager. But the market value of a closed-end fund share is primarily based on the demand (or lack thereof) for the shares in the fund itself.

This can work in your favor if the fund is doing well and demand is high. However, you could also find yourself in a situation where — even though the securities held within the fund are doing well — the demand for shares in the fund is weak, causing the market value of your shares to drop.

The value of a mutual fund share — whether the fund is open-end or closed-end — is its Net Asset Value, or just NAV. The NAV is simply the total assets of the mutual fund divided by the total number of shares outstanding. If the fund has assets of $100 million, and there are a million shares distributed, each share has a NAV of $100.

When demand for shares in a closed-end fund is not strong, shares will trade at a discount off the NAV. If demand is high, shares in the fund will trade at a premium above the NAV. Trading closed-end fund shares takes more skill and knowledge than does open-end fund trading. If a closed-end fund is trading at a premium, you must know whether market circumstances justify the higher price. If shares are trading at a discount, you must know if it's enough of a bargain.

Loads, No-Loads...What Are They?

"Loads," in mutual fund terms, are Sales Fees or Commissions you're required to pay to buy and/or sell shares in a given mutual fund.

Load funds add these commissions or sales charges onto your purchase or, more correctly, they take it out of the money you're investing — unless you specifically add additional money to cover the load. These charges can be substantial, running up to 8.5 percent. That would be $850 on a $10,000 investment!

But the effect of the load can be worse than just $850, because — when you invest the $10,000 — whoever sold you the shares would take out their $850 first, and actually only invest $9,150 for you in the fund. That means not only would you lose the $850, but you'd also lose all the dividends and capital gains you might have realized on the shares the $850 could have bought you. Over the course of 10 years, in a fund netting 12 percent growth, that would cost you $2,805 in future assets, because they took the $850 load out of your $10,000 investment.

History has not shown that loaded funds perform any better than no-load funds, so there does not seem to be any redeeming value for the penalty of having to pay the sales commissions. If an advisor recommends a loaded fund to you, have him or her show you — using numbers you can understand — why the fund will likely outperform similar no-load funds sufficiently to *more than* make up for the load. Paying the load is, in a sense, paying for the advisor's advice. You, as the consumer, must decide whether their advice is worth the cost. If it is, then go with their recommendations.

Most through-the-mail marketed funds are *no-load*.

When I talk about loads, in most cases I'm talking about front loads, which mean commissions are deducted from your investment before it gets invested. There are also funds that charge their load on the back end, when you sell the shares. These redemption fees, as they are often called, can run up to 6 percent. Most commonly they're reduced by 1 percent each year you hold the shares — so after six years you could sell them without having to pay any load.

But keep in mind that back-end loads or redemption fees are being charged on your money <u>after it grows</u>. That means that, while a 6 percent backend load might seem lower than a 7.25 or 8.5 percent front load, it is most often being calculated on a larger asset, and therefore can be quite a chunk of change...your change.

Some funds calling themselves "no-load" charge backend redemption fees, so read the prospectus.

Some mutual funds will also charge you up to 1.25 percent for what are called 12b-1 fees. These are nothing more than the fund's way of charging you to help pay their marketing costs. A true no-load will either not have this charge at all or it will be less than .25 percent. But be careful. Some funds claiming to be no-loads do charge marketing fees greater than .25 percent, and because these fees are not legally considered commissions (loads), they get away with using the "no-load" label. **Read the Prospectus!**

A true no-load fund is one on which you pay NO sales fees, redemption fees, exit fees, or marketing fees.

Low-load funds are marketed just like no-loads, except that they charge a one to two percent fee to cover the costs of advertising, handling your telephone questions, printing and mailing of sales materials, and so on. Some of these funds can be good performers, so do not completely discount them. When you feel more comfortable in evaluating the true value of one fund versus another, you can determine for yourself whether a given fund's potential might be worth one to two percent for their overhead costs.

I prefer no-load funds myself, but, as we all know, in life...nothing is perfect. There are a couple of potential disadvantages to no-load funds.

The first is that no-loads do not have a lot of money for advertising (because they're not getting it from you and me through fees), so you'll need to find them rather than waiting for them to find you. There are a host of magazines and online investment information sites where you can find information about top-performing no-load funds, so use this research time as an educational opportunity. The more you dig, the more you'll understand about how mutual funds work, and how to compare them.

The second potential disadvantage of smaller, no-load funds is that, because they can't afford to do big-time advertising, they may remain small, and therefore never gain the economies of scale enjoyed by the larger funds. They may also have a hard time attracting the more successful money managers away from larger funds. This possible downside is something you just need to be aware of as you watch your investments from year to year. If one of your funds seems to be going nowhere, it may be time to look for a faster-growing fund.

How to Read a Mutual Fund Prospectus

The prospectus is structured according to government specifications, so you can imagine what delightful reading it is. But it does contain information you need to understand in order to make an enlightened investment decision.

You should never invest in a mutual fund based solely on the company's advertising. The prospectus is the only place where the fund's feet are held to the fire to tell the truth about specific aspects of the fund, using specific language. So understanding this fine-print document is imperative for every responsible investor.

Let's look at what's in a typical prospectus.

THE FRONT PAGE

Some funds are strategically positioned to undertake higher risks for greater potential gains, while others are not quite so venturesome, and will therefore generate somewhat lesser gains (as well as lesser potential losses). The front page of a fund's prospectus will tell you the fund's investment objective, such as Aggressive Growth, Growth, or Income. Usually the higher the "growth" potential, the higher the risk. Now let's go inside.

1. KEY FEATURES OF THE FUNDS

This is a quick encapsulation of the fund's objectives, automatic investment features, liquidity, costs, management, shareholder services, and reporting.

2. SUMMARY OF EXPENSES

This is where you'll be told about Loads. Loads are sales commissions you pay, either upon purchasing shares in the fund, upon redeeming shares, or in some cases…both. This section will also tell you about 12b-1 fees. These are charges the fund withdraws from your account to help them cover their marketing expenses. They should never be above one percent, and on money funds or index funds, they should be below a half percent. Total operating expenses of a money fund should be under one percent, and should not exceed two percent regardless of the fund type.

3. CONDENSED FINANCIAL INFORMATION

This is a table of data and ratios that detail fund performance over a period of previous years. You should always be aware that past performance is no guarantee of future performance. But — I'll add — it sure beats throwing a dart from across the room.

4. INVESTMENT OBJECTIVES AND POLICIES

Here's where you find out what the fund does with shareholders' money. It tells you how they plan to invest, and what they expect to accomplish. For example, if a fund invests in stocks, its objective will be "capital appreciation." This section also tells you how the fund manager expects to handle volatile market situations. If the policy is to stay "fully invested at all times," you can expect significant ups and downs in the fund's performance. But, if the fund moves substantial portions of its assets into Treasury instruments or cash when the going gets rough in the stock market, the ride will be smoother...and the potential gains somewhat lower. You know — the risk-reward connection.

5. SECURITIES AND INVESTMENT TECHNIQUES

This section explains which types of securities the fund can hold, and what percentage of each type. It also describes the fund's authority to borrow money.

6. MANAGEMENT OF THE FUNDS

The record of the fund manager is an important factor in choosing a mutual fund. Funds advertise their best performance numbers, over their most productive recent years. However, many times the fund manager whose leadership produced that performance has moved along to another position. Look for management stability (more than three years) — and that the current manager is the one who generated the performance they're bragging about.

You'll also find information here about the fees and expenses the manager charges the fund.

7. DISTRIBUTIONS AND TAXES

This section will tell you how the fund will determine how much money it has made or lost, how frequently they'll make that calculation, and how frequently they'll pay out or reinvest your share of that money. This is also where you'll find the fund's intentions as to taxable distributions of income or gains to fund shareholders. You'll also be told about your potential federal, state, and local tax liabilities from the fund's proceeds.

8. SHARE PRICE CALCULATION

Just like it sounds, this section describes how the fund determines a share's Net Asset Value (NAV). See Closed-End funds on page 66 for a definition of NAV.

9. HOW THE FUND SHOWS PERFORMANCE

This section explains how the fund's marketing people come up with the performance figures shown in their ads and other promotional materials.

10. TAX-ADVANTAGED RETIREMENT PLANS

Most mutual fund families offer a service whereby you can invest money into their various funds through the tax-advantaged structure of an IRA, Keogh, or other corporate retirement plan. In other words, the money you put into your IRA could be invested in the mutual funds you designate — and the growth would then compound tax-deferred. This section of the prospectus explains how that can be done.

11. GENERAL INFORMATION

This is information about the fund company and about other funds they offer.

12. HOW TO PURCHASE SHARES

Here's where you'll find out whether you're required to have a brokerage account with the fund family to purchase shares in their funds. This section also describes any minimum initial purchase amount requirements, as well as ongoing purchase minimums.

13. HOW TO EXCHANGE BETWEEN FUNDS

Commonly called "switching," this section tells how you can move your invested money between funds within the company's family of funds.

14. HOW TO REDEEM SHARES
This section tells how to sell your shares back to the fund, and how the redemption price is calculated.

While formats may vary somewhat, these data should be available in every mutual fund's prospectus. Read it, understand it, then invest with confidence.

Mutual Fund Categories

There are five basic categories of mutual funds: stock funds, stock and bond funds, bond funds, money-market funds, and specialty funds.

Stock funds are mutual funds that buy stock in other companies. Stock is equity in the company, which means you are a part owner of the businesses in which your mutual fund invests.

Normally stock funds are designed for Growth; some are designed for Aggressive Growth. The more aggressive the fund's investment philosophy, the riskier the investments it will make, because it will usually be buying stock in newer, smaller companies. Companies that may have a tremendous upside potential, but may also fail to achieve that potential. Growth and Aggressive Growth funds should constitute a portion of every investor's portfolio, but the percentage of one's assets invested in aggressive stock funds should be reduced with the investor's age and decreasing capital-risk tolerance.

Young investors who are looking for large capital appreciation over the long-term, and who have time to recover from possible losses from riskier funds, should keep 50 to 80 percent of their assets in Growth and Aggressive Growth funds. But as the investor ages (approaches and reaches retirement), assets should be shifted more towards income-producing funds, with a small portion (minimum 10 to 20 percent) remaining in growth funds to keep the portfolio ahead of inflation. (See Appendix page A17.)

International stock funds buy only foreign (non-U.S.A.) stocks. *Global* stock funds buy stocks from all around the world, including the U.S. These types of funds usually invest conservatively, in major, proven corporations.

Stock and bond funds, sometimes called balanced funds or growth and income funds, split their holdings between stocks and bonds. Bonds differ from stocks in that, while stocks are actual ownership in a company, bonds are essentially loans to the company. Stock is equity in the company; bonds are debt instruments where the holder of the bond does not own any equity in the company, but the company (or government body) owes the bond-holder the money...and pays interest on that debt throughout the "maturity" period.

Balanced funds can be good for your retirement years because they offer the security and income production of bonds while still providing some growth through their stock component.

Bond funds have historically been good, solid income generators. However, interest rates have tremendous influence over the market value of bonds.

> **A rule of thumb: for every point short-term interest rates rise, long-term government bonds lose 10 percent to 12 percent in capital value. The reverse is also true: for every point short-term interest rates decline, long-term government bonds gain 10 to 12 percent in capital value. Of course, you would only realize that loss or gain if your bond mutual fund sold the bonds they hold while their value was different from when you purchased your fund shares. The prospectus will tell you how the mutual fund would react to such market conditions. Read it.**

Another factor with government bonds is that they're backed by the full faith and credit of the U.S. government, but what they forget to remind you is that the federal government is backed by you. While the creditworthiness of the U.S. government is as good as it gets on planet earth, we all still have to keep our heads in the game and elect fiscally responsible political leaders to keep things on track.

Then there are non-government bonds offered by corporations. Some are solid, some are shaky.

Many bond mutual funds available today own more speculative, riskier bonds — what some people call *junk bonds*. The polite term is *High-Yield* bonds. These are simply bonds from less proven companies, which are willing to pay higher interest rates to attract money. The High-Yield bond fund investor is lending money to companies that have not yet proven their ability to hang together through tough times. There is at least some risk that some of the companies in the fund may not be able to cover their interest obligations or even pay back the principal when those tough times come. The word is "risk." If you can tolerate it, there are some good High-Yield mutual funds out there. If you can't...leave them alone.

One noteworthy shortcoming of bonds is that, with the exception of junk bonds, most pay interest rates that – after taxes – don't work out to be much above inflation. That means, to optimize bonds' performance in your portfolio, you need to time your entry into bond funds to when the Prime Rate is beginning to fall, so you can benefit from both their income generation *and* their capital value appreciation.

There are many types of bond funds, such as municipal bond funds, high-grade corporate bond funds, high-grade tax-exempt bond funds, high-yield corporate bond funds, and so on. While defining each of these fund types is beyond the scope of this book, you can find many good books on mutual funds at both your local library and bookstore.

Each fund type has its own pros and cons, and each fits a different investment circumstance. For instance, if you are in a high tax bracket, you may find that tax-free municipal bonds give you solid returns without adding to your tax woes.

Money market funds invest primarily in short-term IOU's from banks and America's strongest, most stable corporations. Some invest in short-term notes from the federal, state, and local governments.

Many of these funds let you write checks directly out of your account, but these checks can often be limited to amounts over $500, and there are usually restrictions on how many checks you can write in a month.

Money market mutual funds usually pay higher interest rates than the so-called money market accounts offered by banks and Savings & Loans. Most brokerage accounts let you select a money market fund in which they will park any money you don't have currently invested in other funds or securities. These are often called "sweep" funds. So, as you pull money out of one investment, the brokerage company puts it into your "sweep" money market fund. There it stays until you give them another order to buy other mutual fund shares or securities with it.

Specialty funds include such things as sector funds and funds that invest in hard assets like gold and other precious metals.

Sector funds are mutual funds that invest all or most of their asset pool in companies in a single industry or segment of an industry. There are sector funds for high technology, transportation, healthcare, utilities, and so on.

The idea behind sector funds is that, while the stock market overall may be down or listless, a specific industry may be hot. In the late 1990s the technology sector was hot. So, if you had gotten into a technology mutual fund as the sector started its climb, you would've enjoyed incredible growth, sometimes exceeding 100 percent per year.

The obvious downside is that, if you poorly time your move into a sector fund, you can lose money just as quickly, as many tech investors discovered in 2000. Most often — by the time the average citizen is hearing about how hot a sector is — it's already cooling down and the smart money is on the way out.

Gold and precious metals funds are volatile and highly speculative. These funds are closely influenced by commodity prices and political pressures, and can be a bad dream for the unprepared investor. The rule of thumb in this investment category is: <u>only invest money you can afford to lose</u>. The truth is that it's been many moons since gold has been a good investment. In fact, it has been a rotten investment compared with the stock market. Gold may have seen its day as a strong investment — even as an inflation hedge.

Locating and Investing In the Best Mutual Funds

To make wise choices in mutual fund investing, you'll need a listing of available funds and their long-term performance. And you want this listing to be a comparison of apples to apples.

You'll find useful mutual fund comparisons in *Forbes, Money, Business Week, Barron's* and *Consumer Reports*, among other publications. Each of these magazines publishes an annual mutual fund ranking, comparing the important indicators of each fund's costs and performance. Plus the World Wide Web is ripe with investment sites ready to drown you in useful information about mutual funds.

Each fund family has its own web site, and every brokerage company also maintains a web site with information available on every mutual fund or individual security you could possibly consider investing in. Of course, these brokerage sites may require you to have an account with the firm to have full access to the site's research resources.

These rankings, whether in print or on the Web, usually look back over the last 3- to 10-year period. Just remember that past performance is no guarantee of a mutual fund's future success.

Beware of new funds with no track record, <u>even if they've had spectacular starts</u>.

To find even more detailed information about various mutual funds, check your library for a copy of The Wiesenberger Investment Companies Service. And, in this computer age, you can go to your favorite World Wide Web search engine and search on the words *investing or mutual funds*. This should yield unlimited information sources.

The Automatic Pilot Investing Strategy — Index Mutual Funds

OK...I've given you all the above information about mutual funds, what they are, how they work, and what different kinds there are, so you can develop a basic understanding of them as investment vehicles. But choosing the right fund doesn't have to be complicated, because there's a type of mutual fund that almost guarantees you'll beat the performance of most other funds. It's called the *index fund*.

Index mutual funds track the performance of a specific market by investing in the same securities that make up the corresponding market index. What am I talking about?

Imagine you're sitting in front of your TV watching the news. At some point in the broadcast they come to the financial news and start spouting numbers most people don't understand, like the Dow Jones Industrial Average and the S&P 500. These numbers are indexes calculated to track the performance of a specific group of stocks, bonds, or other securities.

Think of an index as a composite score for that group of securities for that day. Actually, indexes rise and fall minute to minute throughout the day, but the number you most often hear quoted on the news is how an index ended that trading day.

For investing purposes, the most frequently used benchmark index is the S&P 500. Standard & Poor's (S&P) tracks the performance of the 500 largest companies on the New York Stock Exchange. These are generally all large, solid, blue chip companies. And as these companies' stocks rise or fall in value, they push the S&P 500 index up or down correspondingly.

Most Growth and Growth and Income mutual funds track their performance against the benchmark of the S&P 500 index. If they perform better than the S&P 500 index for any period, you'll hear or read them saying they, "beat the market," or "beat the index." Beating the S&P 500 index is the acknowledged measuring stick for all managers who run stock mutual funds. And how do they do on average?

Not very well!

I'm letting you in on what is probably the most under-publicized fact in the investment industry. 70 percent or more of the actively managed Growth and Growth and Income mutual funds return LESS than the S&P 500 index! Another way to say that is the S&P 500 index beats 70 percent or more of the actively managed stock mutual funds. And remember, the S&P 500 is just the composite performance of a fixed group of stocks. There's no high-paid genius (fund manager) buying and selling stocks, in order to add the hot ones and weed out the cold ones. Yet more than 70 percent of the geniuses — picking what they consider to be the winning stocks — can't beat the index.

But the total story is even worse than that, because...

Investors don't generally invest their money and leave it alone. They put it into a mutual fund, watch over it like a mother hen, and pull it out whenever they get nervous — so the average investor's *actual return* from a given mutual fund is always *less* than that fund's overall return, because <u>the average investor doesn't leave their money in the fund long enough to benefit from all the growth runs in any given period</u>. They generally pull their money out when the fund performance moves down for a spell and end up missing subsequent upward trends.

That being said, when investors' *actual returns* are compared to the performance of the S&P 500 index over a reasonable period of time...the index outperforms ALL MUTUAL FUNDS! That's right. If you just invested in the exact same 500 stocks the S&P 500 index tracks — **and left your money there regardless of what the market was doing from day to day** — you would beat the average investor's return on virtually 100 percent of all available mutual funds.

Let that sink in for a moment.

About now you should be saying, "Gee...if only there was a way to invest in all the S&P 500 stocks without having to make 500 transactions."

Well, there is. It's through an S&P 500 index mutual fund.

There are a number of S&P 500 index funds available. These funds buy and hold the exact same 500 stocks the index tracks. So the performance of an S&P 500 index fund closely mirrors the index itself. And since there's no strategy to execute, there's no need for a lot of management and staff to consume part of your returns from the index fund.

In addition to the cost savings from relatively small management fees, index funds offer a tax advantage. Since very few stocks are sold during the year, the fund generates fewer capital gains (taxable events for you) than an actively managed fund would. These savings, compounded year after year within the fund, can make a huge difference in your results.

For example, if you invested $100,000 in a fund that generated just an 8% return, after 15 years you should have $330,692. But if your fund's expenses equal 2.5% per year, that in effect, reduces your annual gain from 8% to 5.5%. This means you'd actually end up with $227.758. Management and other fees would be costing you $102,934 over 15 years.

For the sake of this example let's say your S&P 500 index mutual fund also generated 8% return over those 15 years (even though over the past 15 years the S&P 500 index has actually delivered nearly a 14 percent average annual return). If your S&P 500 index fund's expenses, including management fees, are two percent lower than the other fund — compounded over the 15 years — your effective growth rate would be 7.5%, giving you an account balance of $306,945! The index fund's lower expenses would leave you $79,187 more in your account over 15 years.

Does it really work that well? It sure does...and the big money knows it.

Big institutional investors, like pension funds and insurance companies, keep 30 percent of their assets in index funds at all times and in all market conditions. And they've been doing that for nearly all of the three decades since index funds hit the scene. Beating more than 70 percent of the market all the time is good enough for the big guys, and I recommend that it's good enough for you and me.

The financial press agrees:

> *"Time to face the cold, hard facts, mutual fund fans: over the past 10 years, most people would have been better off trading in their actively managed fund for one that tracks the Standard & Poor's 500. Use a long time horizon or a short one — it doesn't much matter. The results are the same. The indexers cleaned up."*
>
> *Barron's magazine*

S&P 500 index funds only represent that one index. There are also index mutual funds for all the other popular securities indexes. Whether you want to invest in stocks of big companies, stocks of small companies, the whole U.S. stock market, stocks of international companies, bonds, precious metals, or any number of other securities groupings, there are indexes and therefore index mutual funds ready to help you beat the majority of actively managed funds in that category.

This index fund phenomenon dramatically simplifies the Debt-FREE & Prosperous Living® strategy. You could literally pay off your debts, invest in a few index mutual funds, and golf until you're ready to retire. No watching the markets, no moving money around from "hot" fund to "hot" fund, no trying to outguess the experts. Just parking your money in the mutual funds that routinely beat more than 70 percent of their competition — year after year — and not worrying about whether you made the right move.

Now you might be wondering, "What should I do to avoid getting caught in a market crash like the *Tech Wreck of 2000?*" That's a good question, and the answer depends on how old you are, and how actively involved you want to be in managing your investments.

The age question is related to how much time you have before your expected retirement date for your portfolio to recover from a serious correction like the one experienced in 2000. If you're young, you can let your portfolio ride through these corrections with no intervention on your part. The market historically recovers from corrections and begins the climb again. So, over time, you want to be in the market, not on the sidelines.

However, if you're closer to your retirement date, or you're a hands-on investor, you may want to try to get out of the way of significant market retreats. The indicator I use to time moves in and out of the stock market is the Federal Reserve's changing of short-term interest rates. This is because – historically – when interest rates rise, stock values tend to decrease, and when interest rates fall, stock values tend to increase.

If the "Fed" raises interest rates at three consecutive meetings, and especially if some of those raises come between meetings, I consider getting my money out of aggressive stock funds, or even out of stock funds altogether if conditions seem particularly volatile.

The reverse is also true. If the Fed drops interest rates at three consecutive meetings, I'll get back into the market, unless some significant factors tell my gut it's still too risky.

The thing to consider, when trying to time market ups and downs, is that no one is real good at it. My interest rate trigger is the most dependable method I've seen, after more than a decade of closely watching the market move, and it would have helped you avoid the worst of the 2000 correction. But you also have to have your ear to the ground about other factors affecting the market before you commit your funds one way or the other.

Remember, the biggest mistake most non-professional investors make is getting in too late, and getting out too soon. They hesitate investing until they're sure it's a market upturn. By this time much of the gains have already been realized. Then, because they got in too late, they frequently get to ride the next market downturn...and then, to make matters even worse, they bail out just before the next upturn.

If your timeline and stomach will allow it, try to select good funds and just stay with them. Be an "Investor," not a "Trader." Traders try to "time the market," watching the ticker around the clock, on their TV, their computer, their PDA, and whatever other sources they can find. They nervously try to predict exactly when something good or something bad is about to happen, then they jump in and buy or sell stocks accordingly. Studies show that around 98% of them lose money.

Investors, on the other hand, put their money into good securities, hold onto them, and let time increase their value. Over time the average value of the U.S. stock market has continued to rise, year after year, decade after decade. So *investors,* on average, come out much better than *traders*. And experienced investors maximize their portfolio's performance by using what's called "Asset Allocation."

Mixing Asset Allocation With Index Fund Investing

The only remaining component to this automatic pilot investing system is what's called "Asset Allocation." Asset Allocation simply means the percentage of your investment capital you're going to put into each type of index fund.

As I mentioned earlier, stock funds have historically produced the most growth, but with the highest risk of going down in a bad market. Bond funds produce lower growth but generate regular income payments, and they're somewhat less risky than stock funds. Money market funds are much less risky than either stock or bond funds, but generate even lower returns than bonds. So risk and reward move in opposite directions.

What this means in terms of Asset Allocation is that — when you're young, and have time to recover from possible losses — you should accept more risk in order to get the correspondingly higher rewards offered by stock mutual funds. As you age, you should shift more and more of your assets to less risky funds that can produce more and more income for your retirement.

To see what I consider a dependable Asset Allocation model, turn to

Appendix page A17.

This model will give you an idea of how you can allocate your assets if you want to just swing in the hammock and invest practically no time working your investments. Once you've chosen your allocations and selected your index mutual funds, contribute to them regularly, like clockwork, no matter what the market is doing. In other words, use Dollar Cost Averaging.

Dollar Cost Averaging

Investing should be a process, not one adrenaline-packed event after another. One proven method of investing that provides automatic growth through consistency is commonly called dollar cost averaging. What it means is to simply invest the same amount regularly — such as a fixed monthly investment amount. Pick the best funds to be in, based on the current interest rate situation or other pertinent market conditions, then invest the same or an increasing amount, month after month after month. Do not worry whether the market is up or down.

Here's why dollar cost averaging can keep you ahead of the game. Suppose you decide to invest $300 a month. When you first start buying shares in a given fund, they're priced at $15. You get 20 shares for your $300. Now let's suppose the market goes down and the share price slips to $10. You again invest your $300, but this time it buys you 30 shares. When the price gets back up to $15, you have 50 shares worth $750 — **but you only paid $600 for them**. Dollar cost averaging put you ahead by $150.

Dollar cost averaging makes you buy *more* shares when the price drops, so — overall — you come out ahead. The momentum behind dollar cost averaging is that, over time, the stock market has historically continued to rise, despite short-term ups and downs. Since there is every reason to believe this trend will continue into the foreseeable future, your cheaply bought shares will likely be worth more in the future...and you'll have more of them, because you bought some of them cheaply during the market dips.

Follow these basic mutual fund investing rules and you should enjoy a lifetime of successful wealth building — wealth building that is Safe, Simple, and lets you Sleep.

Of course, investing starts **only after all your debt is eliminated**. Until it is eliminated, paying off debt is your best investment.

If all this mutual fund information seems too complicated or like too much work, find a financial professional to help you manage your investment activities. Ask people you trust for recommendations of professionals they trust. You can check to see if a financial professional has had any customer or regulatory problems in the past by calling the Securities and Exchange Commission at 202/942-8090, or the National Association of Securities Dealers at 800/289-9999.

When Can You Retire?

To give you an example of how quickly your investments can add up, and how quickly you could retire on the interest income, turn to the *Wealth-Building/Financial Freedom Calculator* on Appendix page A18.

Determine the amount you'll be investing each month, after all your debts are paid off. This amount should be the total of all your former monthly debt payment amounts, including your mortgage payment, plus your Accelerator Margin™.

Now follow that line across to the number of years you plan to continue putting this amount into your investments. There you'll find the approximate total amount that would be built up in your investment accounts. Now that sounds like real financial independence to me. **You have no debts, you own your home, and you have good money coming in every month whether you work or not.**

A quick look at the numbers on the chart shows that — if you were to maintain a strong monthly investment pattern — you may be able to retire quite comfortably in as few as five years. That is reality, my friend, not the baloney you hear from get-rich programs and schemes. And it certainly beats living on Social Security or working till you die.

You Can Help Those Who Need You

What I consider to be one of the major benefits of getting out of debt is that you are then able to help people in your life who really need it. Whether it's an aging parent, a sibling in trouble, or starving children around the world...you'll have the resources to help.

Many people really want to help others, but they get frustrated when they can hardly take care of their own needs. By following our debt-elimination and wealth-building strategy, you can quickly get to a point where you'll have the option to share as much of your wealth as you please.

After all, you really can't take it with you...but you don't have to leave all your wealth in the hands of credit institutions. *You* should decide how much of your wealth you want to spend on yourself, how much you want to leave behind...and to whom it should go.

Following this program will get you to that point in the shortest possible time.

Being a Part of the Debt-FREE & Prosperous Living® Family

You're really just beginning the process of becoming truly financially free. And, as you continue this exciting transformation of your life, you need never be on your own. We want to be your built-in support group.

Debt-FREE & Prosperous Living, Inc., the publisher of this system, is not just a company that sells books and cassettes. We're a group of people whose sole purpose is helping you achieve financial "un-vulnerability." And we've developed a variety of tools to get the job done. This book is just one of them. It's just a starting point. It's basic training, like boot camp, but it's not the whole picture.

While you can probably take the straightforward concepts taught in this book and apply them successfully without any advanced information, I have found that achieving financial independence is an ongoing process. It involves a continual accumulation of knowledge to maximize your control over all the areas where you use money in your life.

A few examples include buying or selling a house (a mistake here can cost you thousands); buying, selling and maintaining a car; buying insurance; buying investments; buying groceries; buying...well almost anything you might buy. Each transaction will have an effect on your overall Debt-FREE & Prosperous Living® plan. Then there are the legal implications of wealth, bankruptcy, estates, probate, wills, trusts, and so on. All these detailed and constantly changing subjects are beyond the scope of this course.

That's why — as I mentioned earlier — we publish a second component to the Debt-FREE & Prosperous Living® educational system. It's the monthly *Debt-FREE & Prosperous Living®* newsletter. In its pages we fill in all the blanks that may be left by the broad-stroke nature of this course.

If you think you might like more ongoing support in your efforts, then consider this manual your launching pad. Subscribing to the *Debt-FREE & Prosperous Living®* newsletter will provide you with ongoing "mid-course corrections."

The Debt-FREE & Prosperous Living® newsletter will keep you up to date on any changes that might affect the way you should implement your debt-elimination and wealth building plan as time goes on. To find out more about additional tools we produce to help you manage your journey to debt freedom, visit our web site: *www.getdebtfree.com*. It contains our most popular debt-elimination and wealth building books, videos, audio cassettes, newsletters, and PC software and services.

You can also find out more about us and all our products and debt-counseling services at *www.debtfree.com*.

I'm Cheering For You

I lived through a financial crash caused by the misuse of credit. I endured the harassment of collection calls, and the long, hard climb out of the hole. But I also experienced the exhilaration of finding a shortcut to my financial dreams. Today one of life's greatest rewards is the joy of seeing that exhilaration transferred to others...to you. I really care if this works for you.

My goal is to do everything I can to help you through your personal financial deliverance. I know I've challenged you to go against the grain, and that's not easy. So I've also challenged the staff at Debt-FREE & Prosperous Living®, Inc. to be there for you, to help you manage the transition. We'll be there for you when you get disillusioned, or when friends and even family may seem to oppose or frustrate your new financial direction.

> **NOTE: If you do get any flak for taking a radically different financial path, remember that 96 percent of the people in this country <u>do not</u> achieve financial independence (U.S. Department of Health and Human Services study, publication #1311871) — so consider the source...and their likely financial destination.**

We want to share the load of this "against-the-grain" journey with you, so use the Contact Us button on our *www.getdebtfree.com* web site. We're your partners in achieving financial freedom and your resources for the support and tools necessary to get the job done.

We'll win this battle — together. This is more than just a financial system to us...it is our mission. To us it's a crusade to create a debt-free North America!

Valuable Resources in the Following Pages

The following sections of this manual include excerpts from our *Debt-FREE & Prosperous Living®* newsletter (Appendices C, D, and E) to help you follow through with the concepts you've learned up to this point. They offer more specific tactics to implement the strategies we've covered so far.

You'll also find all the tables and charts that have been referenced in the text (Appendix A), a Canadian appendix (B), as well as other resources I thought would be useful for you (Appendix F). Please read through these sections. They contain valuable and *actionable* information that you can put to use starting today.

In this book I've given you all the tools you need to become completely financially free. Now your only foe is inertia, the resistance to actually starting to work out your plan and implement it. So let me put it to you in the form of a question. If you were ever going to begin getting totally financially free...wouldn't <u>today</u> be a good day to start?

Index

Appendix A

Forms and Tables

APPENDIX A

Case Study: Our Average American Family*
Joe and Susan Lucky

1. **Total Annual Household Income:** $47,211 ($3,935/month gross; approximately $2,951 net).

2. **Accelerator Margin:** $390 (10 percent of gross monthly income)

3. **Debts:**

Name of Debt	Balance	Monthly Pmt.	Interest
Mortgage	$87,000	$662	8.24%
MasterCard	$1,425	$36	17.0%
VISA	$1,250	$32	16.5%
Discover	$655	$18	19.8%
His Car	$7,250	$212	12.9%
Her Car	$5,500	$145	13.8%
Home Equity	$5,000	$125	9.6%
Total:	**$108,080**	**$1,230**	

4. **Debt-Free in 7 years and 7 months!** (20 years and 9 months faster than normal.)

5. **They saved $105,407 in interest by following the Debt-FREE & Prosperous Living™ debt-elimination plan.**

6. **Interest Saved Equals Interest Earned: A 31.32 Percent Guaranteed Return!**
   - If the Lucky family would've invested their $390 Accelerator Margin in a mutual fund instead, returning 10 percent annually, they would've received $17,301.24 in interest growth over the same seven year, seven month period. **In order for their investment to give them an equivalent $105,407 in interest growth, they would need to realize a guaranteed, after-tax 31.32 percent annual rate of return, compounded monthly (see page A10)!**

*According to collected data from the U.S. Census Bureau, the National Association of Realtors, Chicago Title and Trust, Bankcard Holders of America, and RAM Research

7. Six-month Cash Reserve: They Can Now Live on 58 percent of Their Income!
- ■ Six months debt-free living expenses: $2,951- $1,230 = $1,721.00 (net pay minus former monthly debt obligations). $1,721 X 6 = $10,326 (compared to $17,706 needed to save with previous debt load). **They now can live on 58 percent of their income because they have no debts!** ($1,721/mo. vs. $2,951/mo.)
- ■ **It would take just six months to save $10,326,** compared to three years and ten months with the previous debt load!

8. Build $1,278,260 in real wealth – using the same money they were paying bills with! After building their six-month ready cash reserve, Joe and Susan can put their $1,620 ($1,230 total monthly payments + $390 Accelerator Margin) into a mutual fund yielding a 10% annual rate of return. This would give them $1,278,260 in real wealth, in the same amount of time it would've taken them to pay off their mortgage the normal way!

"But What if I'm Not 'Average'?"

Although Joe and Susan Lucky are a statistically-average couple, your income may not match up with the Luckys. Here's how the Debt-FREE & Prosperous Living® plan would help you if your income in more or less than typical.

LOWER INCOME
Debt-Free in 1 year and 3 months
Interest Saved $2,591
Wealth Building Potential $247,351

MIDDLE INCOME
Debt-Free in 4 years and 5 months
Interest Saved $146,624
Wealth Building Potential $4,098,777

UPPER INCOME
Debt-Free in 7 years 3 months
Interest Saved $158,273
Wealth Building Potential $3,904,825

"But Shouldn't I Save First?"
A Continuing Study of Our Average American Family

Would Joe and Susan Lucky be better off to save their money instead of paying off their debts? Let's see which strategy is better for the family we looked at on pages A1 and A2. Would it be better for them to save the extra $390 dollars ($4,680 annually) right away, building a cash reserve, and then investing while maintaining their debt load? Or should they apply the money to their debt-elimination plan before starting on their cash reserve and investment plan?

Let's assume we have a mutual fund that pays a 10 percent annual rate of return. The chart below compares both investment strategies over the normal 28 year, 4-month term of their mortgage.

Year	Save First	Year-end Value	Pay off Debt First	Year-end Value
1	Put $17,706 in Cash Reserve		Apply $390/month to pay off debts and mortgage	
2				
3				
4	$1,170	$1,180	Debt-free in 7 yrs. and 7 mos.!	
5	$4,680	$6,204		
6	$4,680	$11,754	Then put $10,326 in cash reserve.	
7	$4,680	$17,885		
8	$4,680	$24,659		
9	$4,680	$32,142	$19,440	$20,356
10	$4,680	**$40,408**	$19,440	**$42,844**

↙ **Break Even Point** ↗

Year	Save First	Year-end Value	Pay off Debt First	Year-end Value
25	$4,680	$341,616	$19,440	$862,266
26	$4,680	$382,287	$19,440	$972,912
27	$4,680	$427,220	$19,440	$1,095,145
28	$4,680	$476,856	$19,440	$1,230,178
28,4m	$1,560	**$494,531**	$6,480	**$1,278,260**

NOTE: For simplicity, we did not include any interest growth on the Cash Reserve accounts. Capital appreciation on cash ready accounts (intended for capital preservation) usually realize an after-tax, annual return of around 1-3 percent, which would insignificantly affect the results of this comparison. These figures are not intended to be a projection of any investment results, and no assurance of any level of investment return can be provided.

In both strategies, Joe and Susan will pay out $550,800 of their lifetime income during this 28 year, 4-month period. But from the previous chart, we see that by following the Debt-FREE & Prosperous Living™ debt-elimination strategy, they will come out $783,729 ahead! You can certainly see the devastating effect that debt has on wealth creation.

The reason the Lucky family came out ahead by paying off their debt first is because more of the money they would've wasted, paying interest to others (they saved $105,407 in interest payments), went to work building wealth FOR them, instead!

How To Compare a Taxable Return vs. a Tax-Free Investment Return

Here is the formula for calculating the taxable return you would need to be equivalent to a tax-free return.

$$\frac{\text{Tax-free return (\%)}}{1 - (\text{tax bracket (\%)})} = \text{Taxable Return Needed}$$

FORMULA

$$\frac{8\% \text{ Tax-free}}{1 - .28 \ (28\% \text{ tax bracket})} = 11.11\% \text{ taxable}$$

EXAMPLE

Your Financial Freedom Lifestyle To-Do List

This is NOT a "To-Do" list in the traditional sense. You are NOT trying to think of all the things you HAVE to do. But rather, you want to create a list of all the things you've always WANTED to do, but never had the time. Within 15 to 20 years, when you achieve <u>true</u> financial independence following the Debt-FREE & Prosperous Living™ Debt-Elimination and Wealth-Building Strategy, <u>you'll have more time than you have ever had before!</u> Some people go crazy when they "retire" because they never bothered to think through what they would do with their new-found time. But you'll be ready, because you'll be able to refer to this list any time you start feeling bored. And you can refer to this list anytime you start losing your resolve to follow your financial plan.

"If I had all the time in the world, and all the money I need, I would..."

_____

_____

_____

_____

_____

_____

_____

_____

_____

_____

_____

_____

_____

_____

_____

_____

NOTE: Use a separate sheet of paper to make this list as long as possible. After all, it's your WANT list.

Monthly Savings Required to Reach Your Financial Freedom Goal

Annual Income Goal (in Today's dollars)	Approximate Nest Egg Needed (in Today's dollars)	Monthly Savings Needed to Reach Your Financial Freedom Goal — Years Remaining Until Financial Freedom —						
		40 years	35 years	30 years	25 years	20 years	15 years	10 years
$10,000	$167,000	$88	$125	$182	$267	$400	$633	$1,101
$20,000	$334,000	$175	$250	$363	$533	$799	$1,263	$2,197
$30,000	$500,000	$262	$375	$544	$799	$1,198	$1,894	$3,295
$40,000	$667,000	$350	$501	$726	$1,066	$1,599	$2,527	$4,396
$50,000	$834,000	$437	$626	$907	$1,331	$1,997	$3,157	$5,492
$60,000	$1,000,000	$527	$751	$1,088	$1,598	$2,397	$3,788	$6,590
$70,000	$1,167,000	$613	$876	$1,270	$1,865	$2,797	$4,421	$7,691
$80,000	$1,334,000	$700	$1,001	$1,451	$2,130	$3,196	$5,051	$8,787
$90,000	$1,500,000	$787	$1,126	$1,632	$2,397	$3,595	$5,682	$9,886
$100,000	$1,667,000	$875	$1,251	$1,814	$2,663	$3,995	$6,313	$10,984

NOTE: The *Approximate Nest Egg Needed* assumes that you can get a six percent return on an "income" fund to generate the *Annual Income Goal* desired. The *Monthly Savings Needed to Reach Your Financial Freedom Goal* assumes an average three percent inflation and 10 percent annual return on savings during investment period. The monthly investment amounts will actually produce a higher accumulated asset amount than shown in the *Approximate Nest Egg Needed* in the second column, because of the inflation factor of three percent. These figures are not intended to be a projection of any investment results, and no assurance of any level of investment return can be provided.

Where Can I Find the Extra Money for My Accelerator Margin?

Note: Finding your *Accelerator Margin* is covered in more detail in the six-cassette *Debt-FREE & Prosperous Living™ Foundations Serie*s, and the <u>101</u> <u>Ways</u> <u>To</u> <u>Increase</u> <u>Your</u> <u>Accelerator</u> <u>Margin</u> book. Both are available by calling 1-888-DEBTFREE.

Start by listing some ways you can cut costs below. Then continue finding your *Accelerator Margin* on the next page.

Don't buy brand new cars

Never buy credit life insurance

Accelerator Margin Finder Form — Part 1

NOTE: Round off all numbers to the nearest whole dollar amount.

STEP ONE: Total Household Income

Income Earner (A) _____ Income Earner (B) _____

INCOME SOURCE	EARNER A	EARNER B
Salary (net, take home)	$	$
Part-time, or Self-employment income	$	$
Home-Based Business Income	$	$
Investment Income	$	$
Social Security	$	$
Pension	$	$
Veteran's Benefits	$	$
Other	$	$
Sub-total	$	$

TOTAL INCOME = (A) $_____ + (B) $_____ = $_____

STEP TWO: Cutting Your Monthly Expenses.

In Part 2 on the next page, list all your "current" monthly expenses in the "Current" column. Now pick those that can be "reduced" and subtract that amount from your current expenditures. Next, total up the money you "found" at the bottom of the page, then enter that amount in the box below. This is your new *Accelerator Margin*! The *Accelerator Margin* you want to shoot for is about 10 percent of your monthly income (25 to 30 percent is preferred if you have no other debt but your mortgage).

YOUR ACCELERATOR MARGIN (From Part 2): | $ | ⬅

Accelerator Margin Finder Form — Part 2

Monthly Expenses	Current	- Reduced	= Accelerator
Retirement Contributions			
Savings			
Dining Out (Lunches at Work)			
Dining Out (other)			
Groceries			
Telephone(s)			
Heating			
Water/Sewer			
Electricity			
Car Maintenance (gas, oil, etc.)			
Parking, Tolls, etc.			
Insurance - Automobile			
Insurance - Health			
Insurance - Home			
Insurance - Life			
Insurance - Other			
Child Care			
Cable T.V.			
Movies and Video Rental			
Other Entertainment			
Sports (Golf, Fishing, etc.)			
Health Club			
Lawn Maintenance			
Laundry			
Pet Food & Care			
Subscriptions (clubs, magazines)			
On-line computer services			
Total *Accelerator Margin*			$

A 31.32% Return On Investment? Here's How...

If we use the statistics from our "average American family" (see pages A1 through A4), you'll see why we agree with Benjamin Franklin when he said, *"A penny saved is a penny earned."*

If they invested $390 a month for 7 years and 7 months...	If they invested $390 a month into paying off debt...
• They put $390 per month into mutual funds for 91 months. TOTAL PAYMENTS = $35,490	• They put $390 per month into debt elimination. TOTAL PAYMENTS = $35,490
• They <u>earn</u> $17,301.24 in interest growth after 91 months.	• They <u>save</u> $105,407 in interest on debt.
• They realize a 10% annual rate of return.	• They realize the equivalent* of a 31.32% annual rate of return.
• Their investment is NOT guaranteed.	• Their investment IS guaranteed.

* Equivalent return is a term we use to quantify savings in interest on debt as an equivalent investment return. This is only used to compare the value of investing your money in debt elimination to putting the same money in a traditional investment vehicle, over the same period of time. For instance, if you were to save $1,000 in future interest on your debts, it's the same as (or "equivalent" to) earning $1,000 in a mutual fund (or any investment vehicle). You're simply "investing" in your debt-elimination instead of a traditional investment vehicle. But the difference is, investing in paying off your debt is guaranteed!

In the case study of our average American family, Joe and Susan Lucky, by investing the $390 in their debt-elimination plan, they saved over six times the gains they would have realized in a mutual fund! Therefore, saving $105,407 in future interest on their debts, in the seven year and seven month time frame, is "equivalent" to getting a 31.32% after-tax, guaranteed, annual rate of return on an investment of $390/mo. for seven year and seven months.

The 31.32% equivalent return on investment is calculated by comparing "future value" of the interest saved on their debts. **Future value = Principal ($390/mo. for 91 months) + interest growth (or savings in this case: $105,407) = $140,897.** Any financial calculator will give you 31.32% as the annual rate of return. This return shows the real power of applying a little money to the average debt load with the Debt-FREE & Prosperous Living™ system. That's leverage!

The Truth About Your Mortgage Interest Tax Deduction

"Traditional" thinking says that you will **benefit** by having a mortgage since, *"the home mortgage interest deduction is the last tax break for the typical American homeowner."*

But let's take a look how this traditional thinking would affect our "average American family" that we introduced you to on pages A1-A4.

	With Mortgage Interest Deduction	Without Mortgage Interest Deduction
Adjusted Gross Income Line 32, 1040	$47,211	$47,211
Itemized Deduction	$7,138 Schedule A — mortgage interest	$6,700 1996 standard deduction
Personal Exemptions (family of four) Line 36, 1040 ($2,550 x 4)	$10,200	$10,200
Taxable Income Line 37, 1040	$29,873	$30,321
Tax (Using IRS rate schedule)	$4,481	$4,549
Difference		**+ $68**

So, by **spending $7,138** in mortgage interest payments, our "average American family" saved a mere **$68** in taxes.

Think what that $7,138 could have produced if it would have been invested in a mutual fund earning just 10 percent.

Note: This example uses 1996 tax tables. For simplicity, this example assumes no other deductions.

IRA Growth Table

This table shows the incredible power of compound interest over time. It also shows the dramatic effect of letting interest compound **WITHOUT TAXES BEING TAKEN OUT**. All the example investors enjoy the advantage of tax-deferred compounding, but the table also shows how much difference it makes to start your tax-deferred investing early in life.

Age	INVESTOR A Contribution	INVESTOR A Year-End Value	INVESTOR B Contribution	INVESTOR B Year-End Value	INVESTOR C Contribution	INVESTOR C Year-End Value	INVESTOR D Contribution	INVESTOR D Year-End Value	INVESTOR E Contribution	INVESTOR E Year-End Value
8	-0-	-0-	-0-	-0-	-0-	-0-	$500	$550	$500	$550
9	-0-	-0-	-0-	-0-	-0-	-0-	750	1,430	750	1,430
10	-0-	-0-	-0-	-0-	-0-	-0-	1000	2,673	1000	2,673
11	-0-	-0-	-0-	-0-	-0-	-0-	1250	4,315	1250	4,315
12	-0-	-0-	-0-	-0-	-0-	-0-	1500	6,397	1500	6,397
13	-0-	-0-	-0-	-0-	-0-	-0-	1750	8,962	1750	8,962
14	-0-	-0-	-0-	-0-	$2,000	$2,200	-0-	9,858	2,000	12,058
15	-0-	-0-	-0-	-0-	2,000	4,620	-0-	10,843	2,000	15,463
16	-0-	-0-	-0-	-0-	2,000	7,282	-0-	11,928	2,000	19,210
17	-0-	-0-	-0-	-0-	2,000	10,210	-0-	13,121	2,000	23,331
18	-0-	-0-	-0-	-0-	2,000	13,431	-0-	14,433	2,000	27,864
19	-0-	-0-	$2000	$2,200	-0-	14,774	-0-	15,876	2,000	32,850
20	-0-	-0-	2,000	4,620	-0-	16,252	-0-	17,463	2,000	38,335
21	-0-	-0-	2,000	7,282	-0-	17,877	-0-	19,210	2,000	44,369
22	-0-	-0-	2,000	10,210	-0-	19,665	-0-	21,131	2,000	51,006
23	-0-	-0-	2,000	13,431	-0-	21,631	-0-	23,244	2,000	58,306
24	-0-	-0-	2,000	16,974	-0-	23,794	-0-	25,568	2,000	66,337
25	-0-	-0-	2,000	20,872	-0-	26,174	-0-	28,125	2,000	75,170
26	$2,000	$2,200	-0-	22,959	-0-	28,791	-0-	30,938	2,000	84,888
27	2,000	4,620	-0-	25,255	-0-	31,670	-0-	34,031	2,000	95,576
28	2,000	7,282	-0-	27,780	-0-	34,837	-0-	37,434	2,000	107,334
29	2,000	10,210	-0-	30,558	-0-	38,321	-0-	41,178	2,000	120,267
30	2,000	13,431	-0-	33,614	-0-	42,153	-0-	45,296	2,000	134,494
31	2,000	16,974	-0-	36,976	-0-	46,368	-0-	49,825	2,000	150,143
32	2,000	20,872	-0-	40,673	-0-	51,005	-0-	54,808	2,000	167,358
33	2,000	25,159	-0-	44,741	-0-	56,106	-0-	60,289	2,000	186,294
34	2,000	29,875	-0-	49,215	-0-	61,716	-0-	66,317	2,000	207,123
35	2,000	35,062	-0-	54,136	-0-	67,888	-0-	72,949	2,000	230,035
36	2,000	40,769	-0-	59,550	-0-	74,676	-0-	80,244	2,000	255,239
37	2,000	47,045	-0-	65,505	-0-	82,144	-0-	88,269	2,000	282,963
38	2,000	53,950	-0-	72,055	-0-	90,359	-0-	97,095	2,000	313,459
39	2,000	61,545	-0-	79,261	-0-	99,394	-0-	106,805	2,000	347,005
40	2,000	69,899	-0-	87,187	-0-	109,334	-0-	117,485	2,000	383,905
41	2,000	79,089	-0-	95,905	-0-	120,267	-0-	129,234	2,000	424,496
42	2,000	89,198	-0-	105,496	-0-	132,294	-0-	142,157	2,000	469,145
43	2,000	100,318	-0-	116,045	-0-	145,523	-0-	156,373	2,000	518,269
44	2,000	112,550	-0-	127,650	-0-	160,076	-0-	172,010	2,000	572,286
45	2,000	126,005	-0-	140,415	-0-	176,083	-0-	189,211	2,000	631,714
46	2,000	140,805	-0-	154,456	-0-	193,692	-0-	208,133	2,000	697,086
47	2,000	157,086	-0-	169,902	-0-	213,061	-0-	228,946	2,000	768,995
48	2,000	174,995	-0-	186,892	-0-	234,367	-0-	251,840	2,000	848,094
49	2,000	194,694	-0-	205,581	-0-	257,803	-0-	277,024	2,000	935,103
50	2,000	216,364	-0-	226,140	-0-	283,358	-0-	304,727	2,000	1,030,814
51	2,000	240,200	-0-	248,754	-0-	311,942	-0-	335,209	2,000	1,136,095
52	2,000	266,420	-0-	273,629	-0-	343,136	-0-	368,719	2,000	1,251,905
53	2,000	295,262	-0-	300,992	-0-	377,450	-0-	405,591	2,000	1,379,295
54	2,000	326,988	-0-	331,091	-0-	415,195	-0-	446,150	2,000	1,519,425
55	2,000	361,887	-0-	364,200	-0-	456,715	-0-	490,766	2,000	1,673,567
56	2,000	400,276	-0-	400,620	-0-	502,386	-0-	539,842	2,000	1,843,124
57	2,000	442,503	-0-	440,682	-0-	552,625	-0-	593,826	2,000	2,029,636
58	2,000	488,953	-0-	484,750	-0-	607,887	-0-	653,209	2,000	2,234,800
59	2,000	540,049	-0-	533,225	-0-	668,676	-0-	718,530	2,000	2,460,480
60	2,000	596,254	-0-	586,548	-0-	735,543	-0-	790,383	2,000	2,708,728
61	2,000	658,079	-0-	645,203	-0-	809,098	-0-	869,421	2,000	2,981,800
62	2,000	726,087	-0-	709,723	-0-	890,007	-0-	956,363	2,000	3,282,180
63	2,000	800,896	-0-	780,695	-0-	979,008	-0-	1052,000	2,000	3,612,598
64	2,000	883,185	-0-	858,765	-0-	1,076,909	-0-	1,157,200	2,000	3,976,058
65	2,000	973,704	-0-	944,641	-0-	1,184,600	-0-	1,272,930	2,000	4,375,864
Less Total Invested:	(80,000)		(14,000)		(10,000)		(6,750)		(110,750)	
Equal Net Earnings:	893,704		930,641		1,174,600		1,266,180		4,265,114	
Money Grew:	11-fold		66-fold		117-fold		188-fold		38-fold	

Additional Principal Prepayment Forms

> **Make as many copies of these coupons as you will need to pay off your mortgage.**

Use these coupons to make the *Accelerator Margin* payments on your home mortgage loan. WRITE TWO CHECKS: one for the regular mortgage payment amount and one for the extra amount. Staple the regular payment check to the regular payment coupon. Staple the *Accelerator Margin* check to a copy of one of these coupons with the appropriate information filled in.

NOTE: Your mortgage lender may already have a system for you to follow in making prepayments. Check your normal payment coupon to see if there is a location on it for an extra amount to prepay principal. Also, call your lender to find out if there are any specific guidelines they want you to follow in making prepayments.

Apply this amount $ [ ]   Check # _____

To prepay the balance of loan number _____

NOTE TO FINANCIAL INSTITUTION: Extra payment is to go on the principal of the next (not the last) payment and sequential adjacent payments until all of the extra payment is used.

Names(s) on Loan _____

Address _____

City _____ State _____ Zip _____

If you have questions, call me at _____

Apply this amount $ [ ]   Check # _____

To prepay the balance of loan number _____

NOTE TO FINANCIAL INSTITUTION: Extra payment is to go on the principal of the next (not the last) payment and sequential adjacent payments until all of the extra payment is used.

Names(s) on Loan _____

Address _____

City _____ State _____ Zip _____

If you have questions, call me at _____

Apply this amount $ [ ]   Check # _____

To prepay the balance of loan number _____

NOTE TO FINANCIAL INSTITUTION: Extra payment is to go on the principal of the next (not the last) payment and sequential adjacent payments until all of the extra payment is used.

Names(s) on Loan _____

Address _____

City _____ State _____ Zip _____

If you have questions, call me at _____

Debt-Elimination Time Calculator

Total Debt Amount	1 year	2 years	3 years	4 years	5 years	6 years	7 years	8 years	9 years	10 years
$ 1,000	$ 87	$ 46	$ 32	$ 25	$ 21	$ 18	$ 16	$ 15	$ 14	$ 13
3,000	262	137	95	75	62	54	48	44	41	38
5,000	437	228	159	124	104	90	80	73	68	63
7,000	612	320	223	174	145	126	113	103	95	89
10,000	875	457	318	249	208	180	161	147	135	127
15,000	1,312	685	477	373	311	270	241	220	203	190
20,000	1,749	914	636	498	415	361	322	293	271	253
30,000	2,624	1,371	954	747	623	541	483	440	406	380
40,000	3,498	1,827	1,272	995	830	721	644	586	542	507
50,000	4,373	2,284	1,590	1,244	1,038	901	804	733	677	633
75,000	6,559	3,426	2,385	1,866	1,557	1,352	1,207	1,099	1,016	950
100,000	8,745	4,568	3,180	2,489	2,076	1,803	1,609	1,465	1,354	1,267
125,000	10,931	5,711	3,975	3,111	2,595	2,253	2,011	1,831	1,693	1,583
150,000	13,118	6,853	4,770	3,733	3,114	2,704	2,413	2,198	2,031	1,900
200,000	17,490	9,137	6,360	4,977	4,152	3,605	3,218	2,930	2,709	2,534
250,000	21,863	11,421	7,950	6,221	5,190	4,506	4,022	3,663	3,386	3,167
300,000	26,235	13,705	9,540	7,466	6,228	5,408	4,827	4,395	4,063	3,800
350,000	30,608	15,990	11,130	8,710	7,265	6,309	5,631	5,128	4,740	4,343
400,000	34,981	18,274	12,720	9,954	8,303	7,210	6,436	5,860	5,417	5,067
450,000	39,353	20,558	14,310	11,198	9,341	8,111	7,240	6,593	6,094	5,700
500,000	43,726	22,842	15,900	12,443	10,379	9,013	8,045	7,325	6,771	6,334
550,000	48,098	25,127	17,490	13,687	11,417	9,914	8,849	8,058	7,449	6,967
600,000	52,471	27,411	19,080	14,931	12,455	10,815	9,653	8,790	8,126	7,601
650,000	56,843	29,695	20,670	16,175	13,493	11,717	10,458	9,523	8,803	8,234
700,000	61,216	31,979	22,260	17,420	14,531	12,618	11,262	10,255	9,480	8,867
750,000	65,589	34,264	23,850	18,664	15,569	13,519	12,067	10,988	10,157	9,501
800,000	69,961	36,548	25,440	19,908	16,607	14,420	12,871	11,720	10,834	10,134
850,000	74,334	38,832	27,030	21,152	17,645	15,322	13,676	12,453	11,511	10,767
900,000	78,706	41,116	28,620	22,397	18,683	16,223	14,480	13,185	12,189	11,401
950,000	83,079	43,401	30,210	23,641	19,720	17,124	15,285	13,918	12,866	12,034
1,000,000	87,451	45,685	31,800	24,885	20,758	18,026	16,089	14,650	13,543	12,668

Total Monthly Accelerated Payment Amount

Calculating Your Debt Payoff Priority

A: **Your** *Accelerator Margin* (from page A8)
Usually 10% of your monthly gross income: $

B: Write down each debt in the first column below, total balance in Column 2, the bill's minimum monthly payment (exclude tax and insurance) in 3, then divide the total balance by the monthly payment, putting the answer in Column 4. Prioritize your debts in Column 5 by starting with the lowest division answer in Column 4, until all are numbered. Column 6 is used to show the accumulated *Accelerator Margin* roll-up from debts 1,2,3, 4,... as they are paid off (including monthly payment). Column 7 is Column 2 divided by Column 6. Column 7 is an approximation.

Name of Debt	Total Balance	Monthly Payment	Division Answer	Pay-off Priority	Margin Roll-up	Months to Pay off
1	2	3	4	5	6	7
TOTALS						

C. Total Debt (total Column 2): $

D. Total Monthly Payments (total Column 3): $

E. Total Accelerated Payments (A + D): $

To order DebtFree™ for Windows®, the Debt-Elimination and Wealth-Building PC software, that automatically performs all of these calculations — and much more — for you, call 1-888-DEBTFREE.

John Cummuta's Favorite Index Mutual Funds

U.S. Stock Market

Fund	Expense Ratio	Objective	800#
Vanguard Index 500 Portfolio	.20	Grwth&Inc.	635-1511
Vanguard Index Total Stock	.22	Grwth&Inc.	635-1511
Vanguard Index Small-Cap	.25	Aggr Grwth	635-1511
Schwab Cap Tr:S&P 500/E	.28	Grwth&Inc.	266-5623
Schwab Inv: 1000	.49	Grwth&Inc.	266-5623

Bonds

Fund	Expense Ratio	Objective	800#
Vanguard Fxd:Intmed-Treas	.25	Inc-Treas	635-1511
Vanguard Fxd:Sh Tm-Treas	.25	Inc-Treas	635-1511
Fidelity U.S. Bond Index	.31	Inc-Treas	544-6666

Flexible (contains both stock and bond indexes in one fund)

Fund	Expense Ratio	Objective	800#
Vanguard Balanced Index	.20	Bal-U.S.	635-1511

International Stock

Fund	Expense Ratio	Objective	800#
Vanguard Intl Eq: European	.35	Growth	635-1511
Vanguard Intl Eq: Pacific	.35	Growth	635-1511
Schwab Cap Tr: Intl Index	.69	Total Retrn	266-5623

* Before investing in any of these funds, call their 800# and ask for a prospectus. Make informed decisions.

Asset Allocation Model

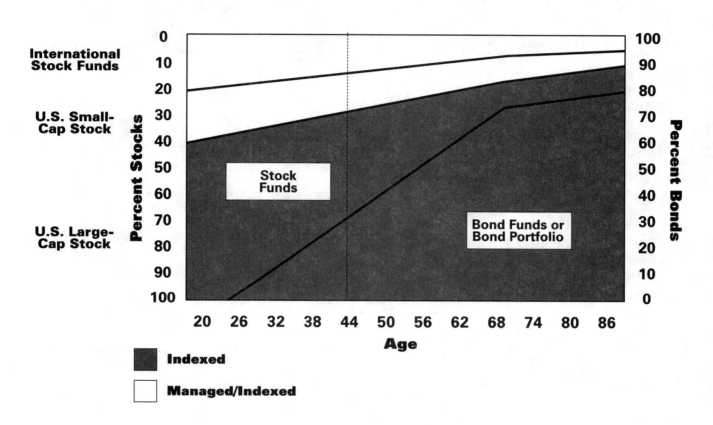

Using the above table, if you were 44 years of age, for instance, you would allocate approximately 70 percent of your investment portfolio to stocks and 30 percent to bond funds. Of the 70 percent of your assets invested in stock funds, approximately 13 percent should be in managed or indexed International Stock Funds, approximately 29 percent should be in managed or indexed Small-Cap funds, and the balance in Indexed Large-Cap Funds.

As a general rule, as you approach retirement age, more of your assets should be moved from the more volatile Stock Funds to the more stable Bond Funds.

Wealth Building/Financial Freedom Calculator

Monthly Investment Amount	5 years	10 years	15 years	20 years	25 years	30 years
$ 100	$ 7,744	$ 20,484	$ 41,447	$ 75,937	$ 132,683	$ 226,049
200	15,487	40,969	82,894	151,874	265,367	452,098
300	23,231	61,453	124,341	227,811	398,050	678,146
400	30,975	81,938	165,788	303,748	530,733	904,195
500	38,719	102,422	207,235	379,684	663,417	1,130,244
600	46,462	122,907	248,682	455,621	796,100	1,356,293
700	54,206	143,391	290,129	531,558	928,783	1,582,342
800	61,950	163,876	331,576	607,495	1,061,467	1,808,390
900	69,693	184,360	373,023	683,432	1,194,150	2,034,439
1,000	77,437	204,845	414,470	759,369	1,326,833	2,260,488
1,200	92,924	245,814	497,364	911,243	1,592,200	2,712,586
1,400	108,412	286,783	580,258	1,063,116	1,857,567	3,164,683
1,600	123,899	327,752	663,153	1,214,990	2,122,933	3,616,781
1,800	139,387	368,721	746,047	1,366,864	2,388,300	4,068,878
2,000	154,874	409,690	828,941	1,518,738	2,653,667	4,520,976
2,200	170,362	450,659	911,835	1,670,611	2,919,033	4,973,073
2,400	185,849	491,628	994,729	1,822,485	3,184,400	5,425,171
2,600	201,336	532,597	1,077,623	1,974,359	3,449,767	5,877,269
2,800	216,824	573,566	1,160,517	2,126,233	3,715,134	6,329,366
3,000	232,311	614,535	1,243,411	2,278,107	3,980,500	6,781,464
3,200	247,799	655,504	1,326,305	2,429,980	4,245,867	7,233,561
3,400	263,286	696,473	1,409,199	2,581,854	4,511,234	7,685,659
3,600	278,773	737,442	1,492,093	2,733,728	4,776,600	8,137,757
3,800	294,261	778,411	1,574,987	2,885,602	5,041,967	8,589,854
4,000	309,748	819,380	1,657,881	3,037,475	5,307,334	9,041,952
4,200	325,236	860,349	1,740,775	3,189,349	5,572,700	9,494,049
4,400	340,723	901,318	1,823,670	3,341,223	5,838,067	9,946,147
4,600	356,211	942,287	1,906,564	3,493,097	6,103,434	10,398,244
4,800	371,698	983,256	1,989,458	3,644,970	6,368,800	10,850,342
5,000	387,185	1,024,225	2,072,352	3,796,844	6,634,167	11,302,440

Example: If you invest $1,000 each month for 25 years, you'll have $1,326,833 in total principal — and you'll be able to retire at an income of $11,056 per month for the rest of your life without putting another penny in. Based on an average 10 percent Return on Investment.

■ **Number of Years until I'm Debt Free:**
(using chart on page A14)

	years

■ **Number of Years I Want to Save:**

	years

■ **Total Amount of Investment each Month:**

$

■ **Total Investment Nest Egg:**

$

NOTE: These figures are not intended to be a projection of any investment results, and no assurance of any level of investment return can be provided.

Appendix B

Debt-FREE & Prosperous Living™ in Canada

APPENDIX B

Debt-FREE & Prosperous Living™ in Canada

Too often we fail to recognize history, fail to identify ourselves as influential parts in the historical narrative. History is more than just grainy pictures in an old, dusty textbook. History is active, a statement made in the present to be looked upon by the next generation (and generations thereafter) as wise or foolish, innovative or inane.

History is being made right now in Canada.

The Canadian federal government is acting with one wary eye focused on the past and the other cast to the future, determined to make it a prosperous one. And, for the first time in years, that future is characterized by potential wealth and prosperity rather than an economy stifled by excessive borrowing and suffocating interest payments. Canada has made getting out of debt its number one priority, and in doing so has given its constituents an example to follow.

Like many industrialized countries (including the United States), Canada's recent economic history is marked by irresponsible borrowing sprees. The Canadian national debt has exploded, and interest payments have spiraled out of control. Like the individual consumer who uses credit cards to finance extravagant purchases, the entire nation has discovered how interest charges can transform a seemingly manageable debt amount into a wealth-siphoning monster. Canada, like most debtor countries, originally borrowed to bolster its economy, but its credit habit instead has proven to be a factor that's inhibiting growth.

The Canadian federal government, however, has made a decision upon which history is likely to look kindly. A decision to right the country's economic outlook before further damage is wrought. A decision to rid themselves and their citizenry of the debt that was crippling each and every one of their lives.

How was this accomplished? Canadians are certainly aware their government chose to solve their debt dilemma with what seems to be any government's only recourse when confronted by a self-imposed, cloudy economic horizon — taxes have to be raised and certain programs cut. Such is the nature of debt.

This section of the *Debt-FREE & Prosperous Living™ Basic Course* is here to tell you there appears to be light at the end of the tunnel, for the country as a whole and for the individual Canadian consumer. The Canadian national debt is fast dissipating. Many believe it will be completely eradicated by the turn of the century, or soon thereafter. In fact, the *Vancouver Sun* pointed to governmental policy as an influential factor in the country's changing economic tides, writing, *"Economists credit low interest rates, high commodity prices, government-spending restraint and positive economic growth for the stunning turnaround in the country's fiscal health."* In the very same story, British Columbian economist Craig Riddell commended the Canadian citizenry for its willingness to welcome *"some massive changes and to elect governments that would make these changes."* The debt has dropped dramatically, the economy is growing, and government spending has steadily declined.

"Big deal," you say. *"It doesn't affect my life."*

You couldn't be more wrong. Consider the national deficit currently saddling the United States. Every dollar pledged to reducing America's debt (and American taxpayers, like their Canadian counterparts, think they're already paying too steep a price in this regard) does nothing to reduce the size of the debt, not even by a penny. The national debt of the U.S. is so massive, so out of control, at this point every available tax dollar puts a dent in only the interest payments. Tax rates, in fact, would have to be considerably higher to make any real progress against the debt itself. The monetary habits of the United States' government have created a vicious, endless circle in which taxpayers contribute an ever-greater portion of their earnings, yet the bulge of the deficit widens.

Canadian leaders, it seems, have recognized the folly of this "one step forward, two steps back" approach to economics. Although the battle against debt is not yet finished, Canadians are envisioning a future of reduced taxes (read: increased income) and improved governmental services such as health care and education. Debt elimination on a nation-wide scale frees funds...funds that can be used (by the prudent government) to improve the quality of its citizens' lives.

Still, you may wonder what in the world this has to do with you personally. Certainly you, like any consumer, enjoy the sound of reduced taxes and increased wealth. But other than having a few extra dollars lying around, you may think your life stands to change very little. We would like to devote the rest of this space to correcting that line of thinking. In fact, your approach to personal finance should, in some respects, emulate the fiscal philosophy of your government. The elimination of credit debt, be it from credit cards, home mortgages, or car loans, should be the number one financial priority of you and your family.

What is credit's major draw (some say advantage, but it really isn't an advantage)? It allows a consumer to purchase things he or she normally wouldn't be able to afford — or, more likely, things he or she could eventually afford…just a little sooner. The big screen television, the stereo system, the sporty new car — credit gives them to you immediately. But are these items really yours? In reality, a reliance on credit only propagates a facade of wealth, a lifestyle beyond your true means. It's a lie, and one that will prevent you from building the personal wealth needed to insure a comfortable retirement. The first step, then, on the path toward true financial independence is relieving yourself and your family of this tiresome burden. How? The *Debt-FREE & Prosperous Living™ Basic Course* advises you to know your enemy.

Why is credit such a tenacious foe?

Like any other vice, credit use is a habit that starts small and grows almost invisibly. You start by using your credit card "only when it's most convenient," and soon are relying on it to purchase high-cost items you'd otherwise be unable to afford. What was once merely a trickle becomes a violent downpour. The lure of the "buy now, pay later" lifestyle appeals strongly to a generation accustomed to instant gratification, and many consumers are unable to resist "owning" big-ticket items they once thought beyond their wildest dreams.

Adding to the difficulty is credit's pervasiveness. Credit card offers are literally an everyday occurrence for many Canadians, and banks try to further spur credit card applications by offering special, low interest rates. In a Canadian Bankers Association report, CBA President and CEO Raymond Protti told the House of Commons Industry Committee, *"Interest rates on bank credit cards are at their lowest rates in over 20 years." Protti continued in his praise for banks' apparent generosity. "Not only have banks been leaders in offering the lowest-priced cards, they have been the most innovative," he said to* the Committee. *"Banks offer a wide range of card products to meet the needs of different consumers."*

Rather than accepting Protti's self-congratulatory rhetoric, you need to ask yourself why the banks would go to such lengths. Are banks the arbiters of fiscal dreams they claim to be or simply opportunists in a world where a person's worth is too often measured by what they have (not necessarily what they own)? The evidence points to the latter. The *Vancouver Sun* quoted a Statistics Canada report stating household debt in Canada has never been greater, despite the fact Canadian investments in mutual funds and RRSPs are on the rise.

Statistics Canada says households *"are feeling wealthier and wealthier,"* but many experts are pessimistic for the long term, and with good reason. Credit's methods are subtle — it gives the **appearance** of wealth without actual wealth itself. In the end, after paying sometimes two and three times more for a purchase than necessary (after factoring in interest payments), the credit dependent winds up with little or nothing to show for his or her money. Ownership is an expensive proposition when dealing on credit's terms. Too often the price is too high and, after a few months or a year, the consumer has to relinquish all use and ownership (this happens all the time when leasing a car — the lessee is unable to keep up with the payments and forfeits not only the vehicle but also all the cash he or she has already paid plus any penalties included in the lease for breaking its terms).

It becomes quickly apparent the "reasonable credit terms" do more to harm the consumer than help. The *Weekend Sun* reported 1996 was a high water mark for British Columbian personal bankruptcies. An incredible 6,437 British Columbians filed for bankruptcy, a full 32 percent more than 1992's previous record. Canada on the whole experienced a 22 percent increase in personal bankruptcies, and Toronto bankruptcy trustee Frank Kisluk had no problem pinpointing the reason. *"People are living with a much higher level of credit now and they're in a much more precarious position,"* he told the *Sun. "When the slightest thing happens, like getting sick or separated, that throws them over the edge."*

Kisluk's words identify the danger of an exaggerated reliance upon credit. The appearance of wealth can only be nebulously maintained when everything's going right and personal finances are functioning at an optimum level. Banks that went out of their way to make credit accessible to the consumer aren't nearly as cordial when payments are late. Penalties are assessed, and the credit hole deepens. An already difficult situation becomes even less tenable.

What's a Canadian to do?

So how is the average Canadian consumer supposed to battle this seemingly endless downward financial spiral? Like many problems, the credit dilemma is simple to solve in theory but encounters a few stubborn snags in execution. That's where the *Debt-FREE & Prosperous Living™ Basic Course* comes in. Having already helped tens of thousands of Americans out of debt and on to the path of true financial independence, we look to apply the same sound financial principles to Canada, and expect the same kind of success for you. The Debt-FREE & Prosperous Living™ strategies stem the tide of credit reliance by demanding, first and foremost, that you pledge your most recent credit purchase was your last. Your first step toward financial freedom is destroying all of your credit cards, followed by a fail-safe strategy to eliminate any credit debt you have already accrued.

We believe most readers can pay off their credit debt using the money they already earn, and the *Debt-FREE & Prosperous Living™ Basic Course* devotes many of the book's early pages to unearthing funds you never suspected you had, which can be applied to your credit debt. Don't worry. This is not an austerity program. We won't ask you to stop driving to save on gas or reduce your intake of food by a factor of two. You don't have to live like a pauper to save money. Some of the savings methods you already know about (using coupons, for example). Others aren't so obvious, and Debt-FREE & Prosperous Living™ assists you in exploring certain cost-cutting avenues of which you might not be aware.

A good example of this is Hiyaguha Cohen's "Consumer Cost-Cutting" column published monthly in the *Debt-FREE & Prosperous Living™* newsletter. Ms. Cohen is a published contributor to <u>Cut</u> <u>Your Spending</u> <u>in</u> <u>Half</u> <u>without</u> <u>Settling</u> <u>for</u> <u>Less</u>, a Rodale Press book which teaches you how to expand your budget and value your spending dollar, and each month she passes her expertise on to newsletter subscribers. Her advice can be applied immediately to your life, and the financial benefits are expressly apparent. A quick read will show you how to save money when going out for a night on the town, how to uncover a bargain-basement gem at a yard sale (or have a yard sale of your own, for that matter), how to sift through all the promises and promotions and really save on your phone bill – all issues that affect the Canadian consumer. The amounts you save may seem small, but as time passes and you become privy to more and more of Ms. Cohen's counsel, you'll be surprised to realize how much money you've needlessly wasted. When utilized within the dictates of the Debt-FREE & Prosperous Living™ system, "Consumer Cost-Cutting" will allow you to realize the full potential of your income.

Many of the columns found in the *Debt-FREE & Prosperous Living™* newsletter are dedicated to saving you money. Jim Gaston's column, "Your Automobile," is filled with maintenance tips to prevent expensive break-downs as well as information on how to find the best used car value and why it's financially unwise to lease a car. "Buying, Maintaining, and Selling Your Home" gives exactly what its title promises — ways to find the best price when buying or selling, and techniques to improve energy efficiency and re-sale value while you're living in your home. And "Living Where It's Cheap," written by Mike DiFrisco, provides a wealth of infor-mation for anyone looking to relocate to a more affordable area. The *Debt-FREE & Prosperous Living™* newsletter is published to build upon the foun-dation of the Basic Course. Financially speaking, your goal has to be to eliminate all your debts and begin building toward a stable economic future. To accomplish this, you need to stop wasting money on posses-sions you don't need and stop paying too much for those crucial to your everyday existence. The *Debt-FREE & Prosperous Living™* newsletter will help curb your wasteful spending habits, and you'll have more income to work with as a result.

Of course, what you do with your newly discovered wealth is perhaps more important than the wealth itself. If, by your own means and the advice of the *Debt-FREE & Prosperous Living™* newsletters, you've managed to squeeze an additional $250 from your monthly income, it's crucial to your financial health to use it wisely. The temptation will be great to blow this $250 windfall on something that is more of a luxury than a necessity. At this point, you must resolve to stay on track. Too often the consumer thinks of financial independence as something that belongs to the distant future. But the future is only the culmination of the decisions you make between now and then, and the degree of success you achieve in your financial future depends heavily on your current financial decisions. Instead of spending frivolously, the *Debt-FREE & Prosperous Living™ Basic Course* suggests you use your money to continue to reduce your credit debt. Or, if that's a hurdle you've already cleared, use it to start building and accumulating wealth. Motivation and determination are the keys to continuing on the prosperous path you've begun to travel. Complacency, as much as credit, should be recognized and avoided.

Let's now assume you've completely eliminated your credit debt

Everything you have is really yours, and you owe no man. Is the process complete? Has the fight been won? E. Raymond Pastor (who contributes to the *Debt-FREE & Prosperous Living™* newsletter with his monthly column, "Your Retirement") flatly states in his book, <u>The 401(k)</u> <u>Success</u> <u>Plan:</u> <u>How</u> <u>Not</u> <u>to</u> <u>End</u> <u>Up</u> <u>Broke</u> <u>and</u> <u>Embarrassed</u> <u>When You're</u> <u>65</u>, that 96 percent of all retirees have incomes inadequate to support them through their retirement years. Being debt free is a good start but it doesn't guarantee a retirement in which you can sustain the standard of living to which you are accustomed. You now must make your money grow, and the most efficient way to accomplish this is investing.

The world of investments, like the world in general, is becoming increasingly complex. The *Debt-FREE & Prosperous Living™ Basic Course* acknowledges most consumers, be they American or Canadian, have precious little free time, and they don't want to spend the free time they have researching the stock market. But we've formulated a simple solution that will allow you to reap the rewards inherent in stock investments without having to become an unlicensed market specialist: mutual funds.

The advent of the mutual fund has opened a completely new window of opportunity for Canadians and Americans alike, and the mutual fund market in Canada is expected to expand further. In an article entitled, "Smart Funds 1997: A Fund Family Approach to Mutual Funds," Jonathan Chevreau writes, *"Industry observers expect that by the end of this century, there will be more than 1,500 mutual funds in Canada."* Your task, then, is to pick a winner, and although the sheer number of mutual funds available to the Canadian investor can be overwhelming, it's not as difficult as you might think. The rules for selection are the same no matter if you're north or south of the Canadian.

Deciding on a mutual fund is dictated by the fund strategies with which you do or do not feel comfortable. Your best course of action is to read the mutual fund prospectus published by the respective mutual fund companies. Take your time. Some prospectuses speak in tongues not familiar to the general populace. A little patience, however, will reveal to you the fund's features, objectives, policies, and history. As the list of potential funds narrows, ask around. Perhaps a friend or relative has some experience with a mutual fund that has piqued your interest. Also, if you are a newsletter subscriber, refer to the Mutual Fund Update in the "Building Your Wealth" section of the *Debt-FREE & Prosperous Living™* newsletter. The phone numbers of funds recommended by a minimum of six of America's top financial newsletters are listed, and future issues of *Debt-FREE & Prosperous Living™* will include research of the Canadian mutual fund picture by the *Debt-FREE & Prosperous Living™* editorial staff. Keep abreast of both Wall Street and the Toronto Stock exchange — a successful portfolio is diverse, and refusing to diversify properly is akin to throwing money to the wind. Be sure you read the section of this *Basic Course* on Index Mutual Funds.

With its generous laws regarding investment taxation, the federal government has made available to the Canadian consumer an investment option similar to the American IRA. RRSPs offer tax deferred earnings, $2,000 over-contributions, phenomenally large tax returns, and the ability to easily shift funds from other investments into RRSPs. Investments in RRSPs effectively eliminate one of the two major investment deterrents: excessive taxation (the other deterrent, risk, can never be completely skirted). And RRSPs fall directly in line with the Debt-FREE & Prosperous Living™ investment strategies. The owner of an RRSP controls the direction of the investment. If you want your entire RRSP invested in mutual funds, it's completely within your rights (although Canadian federal law mandates no more than 20 percent of said funds be invested in foreign or international stock).

Do the *Debt-FREE & Prosperous Living™ Basic Course* and financial philosophy translate to Canada? The answer is yes, and flawlessly. In fact, it doesn't matter if you live in Washington, D.C.; London, Ontario; or London, England, for that matter. Intelligent financial planning, the kind that allows you to live your life the way you want to live it and retire comfortably when you're ready, knows no geographic boundaries. Debt-FREE & Prosperous Living™ defies government restriction and convention and challenges your preconceptions of wealth and security. The Debt-FREE & Prosperous Living™ system is unique, but only in that it provides a plan to reduce debt and build wealth that doesn't depend upon bells and whistles or tricks and mirrors. Its uniqueness lies in its rate of success, and it applicability to any country or person.

Appendix C

Debt-Elimination Newsletter Articles

Consumer Cost-Cutting
Staying on Track to Debt-Freedom
Living Where It's Cheap

APPENDIX C

Selected *Debt-FREE & Prosperous Living™* Newsletter Articles Dealing With Debt Elimination

The following articles have been organized according to the column under which they appear in the *Debt-FREE & Prosperous Living™* Newsletter, making access to a specific topic more convenient for the reader. To subscribe to the *Debt-FREE & Prosperous Living™* Newsletter, call 1-888-DEBTFREE.

Consumer Cost-Cutting:
The easiest way to add to your *Accelerator Margin* is to start cutting costs. Everyday household expenses often seem minuscule when you are confronted by large amounts of debt or are saving money to be applied to a car or house or retirement fund, but these smaller expenses can make a big difference. Hiyaguha Cohen, contributing author of <u>Cutting Your Spending in Half Without Settling for Less</u>, and Lois Cummuta, share with you methods to reduce expenses without sacrificing your quality of life. This is not an austerity program but simple, effective ways of increasing your *Accelerator Margin*. Phone bills, groceries, a night out on the town — all are ordinary expenses that can be cut drastically by following the advice of Ms. Cohen and Mrs. Cummuta.

Staying on Track to Debt-Freedom:
Everyone can use a little encouragement when pursuing a goal as important and worthwhile as complete debt elimination. When ultimate success is not quickly attained, it's far too easy to fall back into the poor spending habits and reliance on credit that started all your financial trouble in the first place. Maureen Wild offers sensible advice and useful ways to keep motivated in her column, "Staying on Track to Debt-Freedom." Eliminating all personal debt, after all, requires both sound financial strategy and the proper frame of mind. Mrs. Wild lends a reassuring voice and helping hand to those who have dedicated themselves to debt freedom.

Living Where It's Cheap:
"Living Where It's Cheap" is tailor-made for the family tired of forfeiting a large percentage of its income to big-city living. Mike DiFrisco, former author of a respected travel newsletter, informs the reader of places boasting affordable housing and low crime rates. Places, in short, where you can raise a family safely without mortgaging away your entire financial future. Mr. DiFrisco also highlights the positive and negative qualities of states represented in the following selections. Anyone considering relocation would be well-advised to use "Living Where It's Cheap" as a resource.

Consumer Cost-Cutting:

Simple Home Remedies

In 1995 American consumers spent $16.1 billion on over-the-counter medications, a good portion of which paid for the more than $600 million worth of commercials for cold and sinus remedies alone. Do we really need all those costly drugstore goodies, or have we been hoodwinked by the great advertising blitz? Dollar-conscious consumers can make their own equally effective treatments for a fraction of the cost using items commonly found at home.

In fact, many simple and cheap home remedies work just as well (or better) than their pricey drugstore counterparts. Plus, home remedies rarely have toxic side effects, as store-bought treatments often do. So unless you have severe or prolonged symptoms — in which case you should consult your doctor right away — try the cheaper, home-made alternative first.

We've included some of our favorite home remedies below:

COMMON COLDS
Although decongestants and nasal sprays might give you temporary relief, commercial cold remedies come no closer to curing colds or shortening their duration than did folk treatments thousands of years ago, says the Consumer Reports TV News medicine show. Don't waste your money on high-priced cold medications with

warnings on the label. Try one of these harmless, time-honored cures first:

NATURAL DECONGESTANTS FROM THE CUPBOARD
Spicy foods containing cayenne, chili peppers, Tabasco, and horseradish trigger the flow of mucous. Try popping a hot tamale in your mouth instead of a pseudoephedrine cap (but remove the cheese: dairy is a no-no for cold sufferers).

GARLIC SECRETS
Garlic has a natural antibiotic effect. If you want to knock out your cold within 24 hours, try this cure. Friends swear it works! Take a clove of fresh garlic and place it in your mouth between your gums and your cheek. Keep it there all day, biting into it occasionally. (Warning: Do not try this remedy at work, unless you want to get demoted.)

For a similar but less pungent cure, make a blend consisting of one crushed garlic clove, half a teaspoon of cayenne pepper, a teaspoon of honey, and one crushed 1,000 mg tablet of Vitamin C. Take three times daily with meals.

NASAL SPRAY THE CHEAPER WAY
Commercial nasal sprays can easily become addictive, plus they make the stuffiness come back with a vengeance each time you use them. Instead of buying the commercial spray, make a spray at home in minutes with no negative aftereffects — and it costs pennies. Add one-third of a teaspoon of non-iodized salt and a pinch of baking soda to an eight-ounce cup of warm water, and

dispense it from a spray bottle.

SINUS INFECTIONS
According to a 1993 study at the University of Virginia, sinus infections may have replaced the common cold as our most frequent illness. Before you run to the doctor for an antibiotic, try a combination of these natural and less expensive alternatives. We have personally found them highly effective. Always be sure, however, to consult a physician if your symptoms worsen or continue to persist. Sinus infections can get nasty.

ANTI-INFECTION DIET
For several days, restrict your diet to a thick broth made mostly of leafy greens (chard, kale, collards), plus lots of carrots, onions, and garlic. You also can add a little rice, tofu, or chicken if desired. Avoid all dairy products, wheat products, and sugars. All produce mucous.

SINUS HERBS
Go to your health food store and get a mixture of the herbs goldenseal and echinacea, preferably in liquid form. These herbs fight respiratory infection. Your cost will probably be around $10, which certainly beats the price of an office visit and prescription.

CONSTIPATION
Commercial laxatives weaken the digestive system and can become habit forming. Save money — and your intestines — by eating two small apples first thing in the morning. Follow with a glass or two of boiled water with a teaspoon of honey mixed in.

POISON IVY AND OTHER ITCHY IRRITATIONS
Apply a paste of baking soda

mixed with water to blistering skin. Or, soak gauze in ice-cold milk and apply to the itchy area for three minutes. Repeat for a total of 15 minutes.

HAY FEVER

Try mincing the peels and inner rinds of grapefruits and lemons, and simmering with a bit of water for about 10 minutes. Add honey to sweeten, and take one teaspoon three times daily. You can also try taking regular doses of locally produced honey to desensitize yourself to pollens in your environment.

COUGH

Commercial syrups typically work on the cough center in your brain to suppress the cough reflex. If you have a superficial cough, try this brew, which doesn't mess with your head. Combine two tablespoons of diced onion with a half-cup of honey, and cook over a double boiler for a few hours.

Strain through a coffee filter before using, and then take a few tablespoons every four hours.

For more extensive listings of home cures, read magazines like *Prevention* or *Natural Health,* where you'll find regular articles on folk remedies of all types. Also, consult your library. You'll find numerous books listing alternative remedies for everything from blisters to obesity. ■

Saving on Your Phone Bill

Big telephone companies such as AT&T, Sprint and MCI spend millions of dollars on advertising each week. Their compelling commercials tell us we'll save a bundle if we switch to their service. They offer us gifts and hefty checks, if only we will choose them. But what's the real story? Does one company really offer considerably better rates than the next?

Unfortunately, we the consumers pay dearly to support the huge promotional budgets of the big phone companies. In the end, the differences in rates among these companies are minimal, though each offer some advantages the others don't. The secret to cutting your phone bill begins with truly understanding your charges.

CALCULATE WHAT YOU PAY PER MINUTE OF CALLING

In order to compare rates, you need to know exactly what you currently pay per minute for long-distance service. Here's how to figure it out:

On your most recent phone bill, total the number of minutes of long-distance calls. Then look at your total charges for long-distance calls. Divide the total number of minutes into the total cost. This will give you your cost per minute.

You can also determine how much you spend per minute by category. Simply look at your time and charges for domestic calls, international calls, 800-number calls, daytime calls, and evening and weekend calls. Then divide the number of minutes for each category into the total cost for that category.

When you compare rates from company to company, look at what you currently spend overall and by category, and compare it to the rate charged by the competitor.

FINDING THE CHEAPEST PER-MINUTE RATE

Over 40 independent phone companies compete with the Big

Three. These companies save you money because they buy services in bulk from the major providers and connect their customers at wholesale rates. Also, they keep their advertising budgets low. They typically spread word of their services through network marketing channels or through inexpensive means such as ads on the Internet. This lets them charge considerably lower per-minute rates.

Alternative companies usually bill your calls in six-second increments, rather than in the one-minute increments typical of the major carriers. This means that you don't pay for time you don't use, which can add up to big savings by the end of the month.

Each independent company offers its own discounts and advantages, but one benefit typical to most is a drastic reduction in the cost of calling-card calls. Some even completely waive the surcharges for calling cards.

BEWARE THE PHONE USERS BERMUDA TRIANGLE

Several types of calls can drive phone bills into the realm of the exorbitant. Calling-card calls are probably the worst offenders. The big phone companies bill you a surcharge of 79 cents to one dollar for each calling-card call, plus sky-high per-minute rates. If you make a lot of calls while on the road, you'll end up paying outrageous amounts.

The solution? Get a phone service that waives the calling-card surcharge. If you can't do that for some reason, at least buy prepaid calling cards at your local convenience store. Before you buy,

though, find out how much you'll pay per minute of calling time.

You can also incur huge expenses by inadvertently making 900-type calls. We recently found an extra $65 in charges tacked onto our bill for calls to a seemingly local weather number — which turned out to be a pay-per-call service. Beware: 900 numbers aren't the only ones that charge huge fees for access. Watch out for any numbers in your area code with 976 or 550 as the first three digits.

Call your local phone company to find out what other numbers to watch out for in your region.

ALWAYS EXAMINE YOUR BILL CAREFULLY
Phone companies are hardly infallible. Check your bill! If you do find charges on your bill for calls you didn't make, or for accidental 900-number calls, dial your phone company and ask them to remove the charges from your bill. They'll usually do so without argument. ∎

How Super-markets Work Hard to Get Your Dollars

The aisles of your local supermarket are more than a random organization of products. When the consumer walks these aisles, he or she is the target of a shrewd, subtle marketing campaign designed to encourage unnecessary spending.

SUPERMARKET DESIGN: PSYCHOLOGICAL POCKET-PICKING
The supermarket is designed to get you to put more than you

intended or needed into your shopping cart.

Have you ever noticed that when you run to the store just to get a gallon of milk, you have to walk all the way to the back of the building to find the dairy products. This is no accident. It's a carefully considered plan to get you to traverse a variety of specific aisles, hoping you'll walk out with much more than milk.

This tactic is crafty enough, but sometimes the store will actually try to slow your pace through the store by putting obstacles, such as merchandise displays, in your way. This gives them more time to visually entice you to buy things that weren't on your mind when you walked in the door. Most of the time it works.

OTHER STORE-LAYOUT TACTICS
• The produce department is usually located close to the entrance. Fresh fruits and vegetables are often an impulse buy, so grocery stores want to make sure everyone passes them. They are color-

ful, natural, and difficult to resist for a body that craves instant gratification.

• Attractive floral displays are usually close to the greeting cards. This obvious tactic gets card buyers to add flowers to the purchase. It works particularly well on husbands who know they haven't been attentive enough to their wives.

• The bakery serves up more than bread. The delectable aroma wafts throughout the store, encouraging a bakery purchase.

• Have you ever wondered why the refrigerated cases are so wide open? I used to think they were created by an idiot who never had to pay an electric bill in his life, but the reason is now clear to me. The more you can see, the more you will buy. Those electric bills are funded by your extra purchases.

• Related products are almost always displayed together. This is done not only for convenience but also to plant a seed in your mind. Seeing related products makes your subconscious crave both the product you came for and whatever is near it. A classic alignment is the soft drink section, which is in the same aisle as the chips and other snacks.

THE SUPERMARKETS CONTROL THE GROCERY GAME

Product placement in the store can make or break a product, especially a new product. Some store chains actually require manufacturers to pay huge slotting allowances to stock a new item. Shelf space sometimes goes to the highest bidder, squeezing out smaller manufacturers. And who do you think pays the slotting allowances in the end?

In a typical store, the high-traffic prime areas are the dairy and meat sections, end-of-aisle displays, and checkout stands. The top and bottom shelves in the inner aisles, where the canned goods are displayed, are less desirable.

CLOSE YOUR EYES AT THE CHECK OUT COUNTER

The checkout area is loaded up with high-margin, impulse items like magazines, batteries, gum, and candy. These small, inexpensive purchases are often grabbed without thought or consideration.

The utilization of a check-cashing card clues the supermarket in to the shopping habits of you and your fellow shoppers. The products you purchase are being scanned at the cash register, which provides the store with a volume of information about your shopping choices. It's called micro-marketing.

Micro-marketing is the electronic targeting of individual consumers. Information about your shopping habits is gathered from electronic scanners, shopper surveys, and information you provide when you apply for a check-cashing card or preferred-shopper card.

The result: they know if you are

an occasional or frequent shopper; whether you buy store brands or only brand-name products; if you buy prepared food items such as frozen waffles or dinners; whether or not you own a pet, and so on. From this information they can let manufacturers know who is most likely to buy similar, competitive items.

Stores also use checkout scan data to keep track of which products are in greatest demand, changing their product mix to add more high-profit perishables and to eliminate slow-moving products.

So, as you're wheeling your cart down the aisles of your favorite supermarket, be aware and keep your defenses up.

The best defense: make a list and stick to it!

Oh, yes — don't forget your coupons! ■

Auction Savvy

If you want to find incredible bargains and make your friends swoon with disbelief, try attending auctions. It does take a bit of know-how to score at an auction, but don't be afraid to give it a try. These pointers will help you.

What types of auctions offer rock-bottom deals?

LOOK FOR BANKRUPTCY AUCTIONS

At these auctions, companies

going out of business sell off their property for whatever they can get. Bankruptcy auctions are usually held at the site of the defunct company. You can also do quite well at auctions sponsored by government agencies like the GSA, the Customs Office, or the Department of Defense. Expect to pay a 10 percent commission to the auctioneer on any purchases you make.

MAKE SURE THAT THE AUCTION WILL HAVE NO RESERVES

This means that no matter how low your winning bid, you get the item. Avoid auctions that have a pre-set floor, at which you must

bid above whatever starting price the auctioneer sets. This makes it much more difficult to get the amazing deal you seek.

BE WARY OF AUCTIONS HELD REGULARLY AT THE SAME LOCATION

Some auctioneers buy and sell their own property, and since they need to recoup what they paid for their merchandise, you'll end up paying more for it.

THE WORST AUCTIONS SPECIALIZE IN ANTIQUES OR COLLECTIBLES (FROM A COST-CUTTING POINT OF VIEW)

At these auctions, you can end up paying far more than retail value for an object you desire. At an auction of Jackie Onassis property, for instance, a $500 fake pearl necklace sold for $211,500, and a few faded pillows worth $50 sold for $25,000.

PREPARE FOR THE AUCTION AHEAD OF TIME

Most auctions have an inspection period before the bidding begins. Go early and thoroughly check anything you may desire. Be skeptical of merchandise sold in "as is" condition, which can indicate defective objects, cars without engines, and houses without plumbing.

Shop around before the auction so you know comparable retail prices for the items that interest you, and bring your research material with you. Also, bring a flashlight in case the showroom lacks adequate lighting. And definitely attend a few auctions as an observer before ever placing a bid.

What about auction protocol? You'll need to bring cash or a cashier's check with you. Most auctioneers will not accept credit cards or personal checks.

Sit where the auctioneer can see you, and don't be timid when you make your bid or you might lose out.

SPECIAL PRECAUTIONS: MAKE SURE YOU KNOW WHAT YOU'RE BIDDING FOR

At the start of most auctions you'll receive a written list of the items being sold by number.

When the bidding begins, the auctioneer's assistant will hold up each item in turn. Make certain that the object being displayed matches the number for that item on your list. Otherwise, you might find yourself bidding $500 for a plastic garbage can.

WATCH FOR AUDIENCE SHILLS

These are people hired by the auctioneer to keep bidding the price up. You'll stay out of trouble if you write down how much you want to spend ahead of time, and then stick to your limit. Also, don't let your enthusiasm for a particular object be too apparent or the shills will target you.

ALMOST EVERY AUCTION HAS A COLORFUL INCIDENT

The auctioneer yells and curses, or fights may break out between people bidding against each other. This shouldn't concern you — you don't need to get involved, and flare-ups usually last only seconds. Auctions rarely offer a classy atmosphere.

HOW AND WHEN SHOULD YOU START BIDDING?

If you place the first bid of the sale, you might pick up a great deal. It usually takes the other bidders a few minutes to get into the swing of things. Plan to start the bidding at about 15 percent of the object's retail price.

HOW MUCH CAN YOU SAVE?

Plenty. At a recent electronics auction, a friend picked up a brand-new Sony camcorder and a top-

quality Walkman for a total of $50. Another friend bought an accounting machine for $50, then sold it for $1,500.

REAP SAVINGS — BUY IN LOTS

At a recent clothing auction, I found top-quality suit jackets with retail values up to $250 going for $17 apiece. The only catch was you had to buy eight of them to get the deal — a typical scenario at auctions of all types. If you have a big family or many friends, you can outfit them all for a song.

HOW CAN YOU FIND OUT ABOUT UPCOMING AUCTIONS?

Most larger newspapers have a special section that lists auctions. Once you find an auction that interests you, check the auctioneers reputation by calling the Better Business Bureau. You want to make sure that you can trust claims that electrical objects will work, or that 18-karat jewelry won't turn out to be a cheap alloy.

For information about government auctions, simply call the relevant regional office. Try the General Services Administration in your area for starters. To bid on luxury items, like boats and jewelry seized from felons, contact the U.S. Marshals Office, U.S. Department of Justice, 600 Army-Navy Drive, Arlington, VA 22202-4210. ■

Doing Up the Town for Less

You don't need to spend a fortune to go out on the town. For little more than the price of pizza and a video, you can enjoy a wealth of cultural activities and even have an elegant evening out — no matter where you live. Follow these tips to have twice the fun for as low as half the usual price.

USE COUPONS

You can save up to 50 percent on meals and admissions simply by using coupons. If you live in a tourist area, start by going to your local travel bureau and looking for seasonal booklets and newspapers. These publications almost always have coupons inside. Other good sources for coupons include tour books (like the Mobil Travel Guide) and local newspapers. You might even find relevant discount coupons in your local Yellow Pages. Many now include an extensive coupon section.

BUY A TRAVEL DISCOUNT MEMBERSHIP

Why pay full price at restaurants when you can get two for the price of one meals simply by presenting a travel discount card? For a nominal investment, you'll reap two-for-one dining deals at scores of restaurants and deeply discounted admissions to local events. You might even find half-price parking deals. If you decide to stay overnight, your card can get you a 50 percent discount at top-notch hotels.

For example, the *Great American Traveler Discount Hotel Program and Hotel Directory* offered by DF&PL gives you 50 percent off standard rates at more than 1,400 hotels nationwide! Many of these hotels also offer 25 percent discounts at their restaurants. The directory includes hotels from all major chains in the most desirable locations in the country. (To order call 1-800/332-3465 and ask for product #GAT.)

THE EARLY BIRD EATS BETTER FOR LESS...

Many restaurants offer great discounts on meals if you dine early, usually before 7:00 p.m. Try calling the local Chamber of Commerce or the Visitors Bureau to find out which restaurants in your area offer early-bird specials. You can also check the local papers for advertisements, or call the restaurants of your choice and ask them directly.

BUT THE LATE BIRD GETS HALF-PRICE TICKETS

Most cities have a central place where you can buy rush tickets for shows and concerts at half-price. Go to the half-price booth a few hours before the show, and you can buy any unsold ticket for 50 percent off. (Contrary to what most people think, rush seats aren't necessarily obstructed view seats. It's often the more expensive tickets that go unsold.) Call the local Chamber of Commerce or Arts Council to find out where to get half-price tickets in your area.

GET FREE PASSES

Next time you go to the library in search of a good detective novel, ask if they provide free passes to area museums and sights. Many libraries do, and all you have to do is ask. Also, public schools often have free passes, and you don't necessarily have to be a student to use them. Call your local Parent-Teacher Association for information.

SEE SHOWS ON A SHOESTRING

Enjoy top-notch theater and music for a fraction of the price by attending a rehearsal or preview instead of a regular performance. Call the box office or your local Arts Council for information about these options. Also, watch for cheap, or even free, productions at local colleges and experimental theaters. Many colleges offer year-round student performances. You might even luck out and discover the next Pavarotti.

GO GALLERY HOPPING

Most cities have a gallery district, where you can view a wide range of art for free. Some places specialize in low-end local work, but others carry masterworks priced at more than $100,000. A recent trip through several Boston galleries, yielded works by Renoir, Picasso, and John Lennon. An added advantage: many galleries offer free refreshments to browsers. How can you go wrong?

GET LITERARY

Most larger bookstores host an ongoing series of readings by well-known authors, almost always for free. Call your local bookstores for a schedule. You can also find free lectures almost any night of the week at local universities. If you want to splurge, you'll find poetry readings at cafés, often for no more than the price of a cup of coffee. ■

Saving on Prescription Drugs

Don't assume all pharmacies charge the same amount for standard medications. In fact, the amount you pay for your prescription can vary by 500 percent or more, depending on where and how you shop. Follow these guidelines to cut your prescription bills dramatically:

THE BEST PRICE BUSTER: INSURANCE COVERAGE

If you're single and relatively healthy, you probably don't worry much about the cost of prescription drugs. But if you ever develop a serious illness or have kids who are chronically ill, you're in for a shock about the price. You can easily pay $200 or more a month on medications. Many elderly and chronically ill people do.

You can protect yourself from the nightmare of outrageous medication bills by making certain that you get a health insurance policy with a prescription drug rider. This means that your health insurance either totally or partially covers the cost of any prescription medications you purchase. Don't overlook this important benefit when shopping for a health insurance plan: it can save you thousands of dollars!

ELAVIL BY ANY NAME IS STILL A PILL: GOING GENERIC

As you know, two pairs of jeans that look identical can differ greatly in cost if one pair has a Guess label and the other has a Wal-Mart tag. In the same way, most medications come in both expensive brand-name versions and cheaper generic renditions. Price differences can be astonishing. By purchasing the generic, you'll usually save at least 50 percent — often substantially more than that. For instance, at the Shop-N-Save Pharmacy in Lunenberg, Massachusetts, the name-brand antihistamine Entex LA costs $44.71 for 40 tablets, but the generic version costs only $4.99!

Generic drugs have the same active ingredients as their more expensive brand-name equivalents; they just use different binders and fillers. Do the binders and fillers affect performance of the drug? No! The generic version may smell more unpleasant or melt more easily than the name brand, but the FDA monitors them to make sure they work as effectively as name-brand medications.

Why do brand-name medications cost so much more if they don't work better than their generic counterparts? Because drug companies charge you for the millions of dollars they spend researching and developing the medications and then promoting them to doctors and pharmacists. The generic companies don't incur such large research or advertising expenses.

When your doctor writes you a prescription, always ask if you can have the generic version. Some doctors automatically write the prescription for the brand-name drug because they don't know the name of the generic equivalent, or they just don't like generic drugs. Even so, in some states, pharmacists can substitute generic drugs for brand-name ones without getting the doctor's permission. So, remember to also ask the pharmacist to give you the cheaper generic version. In fact, in a few states, pharmacists must use the generic equivalent if it's available unless the doctor specifies no substitutions on the prescription.

COMPARISON SHOP

Medication prices vary dramatically from one pharmacy to the next. You may assume that the big discount chains have lower prices, but don't be fooled! Our research shows that small, independent stores sometimes beat the prices of the chains. Because most of us don't shop around for medications, pharmacies pretty much charge us what they want and assume we won't question the price of a prescription. In fact, one New England discount chain had the highest medication prices in our survey.

One note of caution: in buying medications, price isn't everything. Considering that the typical pharmacist catches at least two errors in physician prescriptions each week — and such errors can be fatal — it may be worth it to patronize a more expensive store in order to get a pharmacist you can trust. A good pharmacist keeps accurate records of your prescription history, answers your questions thoroughly, and is cautious when switching you from one medication to another.

MAIL ORDER MEDICATIONS

If you don't need your medication immediately, you might save a bundle by using a mail order service. Several organizations provide drugs by mail at very low prices. ∎

Hosting a Yard Sale

Yard sales have become a national institution and an easy way to clean house and make money at the same time. When the basement overflows with junk, you simply put a few signs on trees announcing your upcoming sale, then set up shop for the day. You don't need any special entrepreneurial gift to host a yard sale.

In fact, most people who hold yard sales could increase their profits substantially by practicing some insider secrets. Why make only $150 when you might reap as much as $1,200 from the same merchandise by applying a little yard sale know-how? Follow these pointers:

PREPARATION

Get experience. Before having your sale, volunteer a few hours at a friend's or neighbor's sale. Spend the time observing the shoppers and take note of which items and types of displays attract attention. Also, frequent local yard sales to pick up tips (and good deals in the process).

Choose a date for your sale. Weekends usually are best, but avoid holiday weekends because too many people go away. Saturday and Sunday work equally well.

Start your yard sale early in the morning. Most yard sales begin around 9 a.m., but consider opening as early as 7 a.m. Why? Bargain hunters often come early to find the best deals and best merchandise. If you schedule your sale early, those early birds will come to see you before checking out the other neighborhood sales.

Location. If you have a choice, set up in a ritzy (but heavily-trafficked) part of town. Make sure the site is easy to get to and has plenty of parking. Locations a block or two off a main street work best.

Gather your merchandise. You need to assess how much you have to sell, because a large quantity of merchandise is essential in making a decent profit. If you don't have enough for a big sale, ask some neighbors to join forces with you.

Clean and repair items you intend to sell. Clothing should be washed and ironed, jewelry polished, furniture dusted. It seems obvious, but lots of people seem to think anything sells at a yard sale, no matter the condition.

Price items ahead of time. Many shoppers hate to ask about price, so make it easy for them. Clearly mark prices on all items, using easily removable tags. Ask for about 30 percent more than you expect, so you'll have negotiating room if customers try to bargain (and they will).

PROMOTION

Newspapers. It pays to advertise in the local paper a few days before the event. Dedicated yard sale shoppers comb the ads to plan their shopping strategy, so even a small ad brings lots of customers.

In your ad, mention a few of the more exciting items you'll be selling. Computers, antiques, sporting equipment, and furniture usually draw crowds.

Posters. Make your own posters on standard-size paper and put them up on bulletin boards and telephone poles. Use the same strategy in your poster as in your ads, mentioning your hottest items. If you plan to have a big sale, say something like "Huge yard sale..." to entice shoppers.

Signs. The more attractive and fun you make your signs, the more likely you'll attract impulse shoppers from their passing cars. Use clip art, transfer lettering, and bright colors, but stay simple. Your signs should be extremely easy to read. Large arrows pointing the way to your house work better than written directions. Experts say you should have a sign up at every intersection within a two-mile radius of your house.

THE DAY OF THE SALE
Personnel. Don't try to hold the yard sale by yourself. You'll need at least two people to deal with the heavy traffic. Also, theft can be a big problem at yard sales, so you'll need extra people to police the goods.

Drawing in the drive-bys. Many cars slow down, look, and then keep on going. To minimize drive-bys, put up a sandwich-board sign announcing the sale in front of your house or on your car. Make your sale look attractive from the road. String crepe paper runners or colorful ribbon in front of your house, put up balloons, and make sure the most appealing items can be seen from the road.

Display. Presentation can make

or break sales, yet most yard salers just pile stuff up in ugly heaps. Make your merchandise look good. Cover tables with brightly colored cloths, group similar merchandise together, attach balloons to tables, hang clothing up, and display jewelry against a dark background.

Be friendly. Make potential buyers like you. Offer a handshake and a smile, tell shoppers about special items, and point out items related to their interests. Your profits will skyrocket if you treat people like guests in your home.

Make it fun. People shop at yard sales not only for bargains, but also for recreation. If you make your sale fun, people will stay longer and spend more money. Plus, you'll enjoy the experience more.

For instance, you can create colorful grab bags with low prices, or offer special mystery bags. Try offering a free box of stuff you really don't care about. Play music in the background.

Some people put cute sayings on the price tags or put up fun posters. You can bag delicate items in colorful wrap, provide free or low-cost drinks and refreshments, or have a raffle. Use your imagination, and watch the profits roll in.■

The Lost Art of Bargaining

Several years ago, while shopping in New York, a friend from India saw a musical instrument he liked. To our shock and embarrassment, he offered the shopkeeper 50 percent of the asking price. *"This is America,"* we tried to tell him. *"We DON'T bargain with store owners here."* As it turned out, our friend taught us a lesson. After an hour of loud dickering, he managed to wrangle a 30 percent reduction in price.

It's said, *"Everything is negotiable."* We Americans, however, have little stomach for negotiating. We think it's rude and uncouth to try to bargain; we consider the price-as-marked holy. That's unfortunate, because you can get at least some concession on price if you try, and sometimes you can save incredible amounts of money. You just need to be persistent (perhaps a little bit brazen), maintain a sense of humor, and practice these tactics:

DON'T FEEL GUILTY
Our friend wondered, *"Why give them so much money unnecessarily?"* Most retail stores mark up merchandise by at least 50 percent, so even if you get 40 percent off the sticker price, the store's owner won't have to file for bankruptcy.

DON'T BE SHY
If you don't ask, you don't get. And if you back down at the first sign of resistance, you don't get, either. The shop wants your business, so conduct it on your terms.

Some experienced hagglers make an offer far below the sticker price. If the shopkeeper resists, the following counter-offer is even lower. This technique yields both healthy discounts and interesting reactions.

TAKE AS LONG AS YOU POSSIBLY CAN
The more you drag out the sales process, the more anxious the shopkeeper will be to get rid of you (and possibly agree to your price). Ask every question you can dream up — how the item works, how it was made, how it compares to similar items — before making your first pitch for a more affordable price. Hem and haw, and maybe even leave to think it over. Come back the next day and start the process all over again, making sure you deal with the same person.

Stalling is a classic negotiating tactic. Remember, as long as the salesperson is helping you, he or she can't make sales to other customers. If the salesperson works on commission, he or she will do anything to get you out the door.

Shopper Reid Kneeland reports using the stalling technique to earn a 30 percent reduction on a $2,500 guitar. *"It took me six hours,"* he says, during which time he held onto his calculator and spent a lot of time punching the keys. Kneeland advises, *"It doesn't matter what numbers you are punching. This is for effect."*

FLASH THE CASH

An acquaintance recently got a huge discount on a diamond necklace for his wife by simply showing the salesperson the money. *"Most customers pull out the credit card to pay for expensive items,"* he says. *"The store owner has to wait to get payment. I tell the clerk, 'I'll pay cash right now if you give me a 30 percent discount.' The store owner wants the money in his pockets."*

Credit card companies also take an eight percent cut from the store for every credit purchase. Every time you pay cash, you save the store that eight percent surcharge, which you should unabashedly point out when lobbying for your discount.

CHOOSE YOUR TIME AND PLACE

Although you can bargain in large chain stores, you first need to find someone who makes decisions, and that can take some doing. In smaller stores, you'll probably find the manager or assistant manager behind the counter, and either has the authority to cut you a deal. Novice bargainers will probably find smaller, independent shops easier targets.

TRY FOR A VOLUME DISCOUNT

If you plan to buy more than one item, ask for a discount. This works well if you have a friend with you who is also interested in buying. If you're both in the market for a puppy, tell the salesperson you want a reduced price because you'll be purchasing two. Think creatively. If you meet resistance, ask for whatever extras you can think of — free grooming, a bag of dog food, a book on dog care, or maybe some rawhide bones.

In her article, "Dickering for Dollars," Deborah Diamond tells of a woman who asked a salesman to throw in a box of paper with the printer she was buying. When he gave her a hard time, she said, *"Why are you being so cheap about it? I'm buying a printer for $250, and I'm asking for a lousy box of paper."* She got the paper, free of charge.

USE ANY EXCUSE TO ASK FOR A DISCOUNT

First, ask if the item is available at sale price (even if the sale hasn't started). Then examine the item. Bring even the slightest defect to the salesperson's attention and ask for a price reduction.

If that doesn't work, remind the store owner of any impending holidays, or quote a competitor's price. Use anything at your disposal to lower the price of the item in which you're interested. It's your money, and you shouldn't spend any more than you have to. ■

Staying on Track to Debt-Freedom:

Ten Keys to Sticking with Your Debt-Elimination Plan

Most of us are familiar with the claustrophobic phenomena of cabin fever. In relationship to your debt-repayment plan, there is a symptom of cabin fever that could cause you to wander off your plan and lose sight of your ultimate goal — to be financially "un-vulnerable." This is the desire to spend money.

The spending impulse comes on strongly in the spring. Warmer temperatures often lead to a sharp decrease in discipline. As the warm weather approaches, our minds catalog the many summer items we'd like to buy and the things we'd like to do.

A new patio set for summertime entertaining. A bigger tent for improved accommodations on family camping trips. A new summer wardrobe to replace older styles. The mounting expenses imposed by all of these desirables can tempt even the disciplined consumer to stray into his or her wallet or purse for a credit card. It's easy to tell yourself you'll pay it off a little later.

These are normal feelings, but they can ultimately destroy your plans to be out of debt and on your way to real prosperity. Here are a few tips to help you resist temptation and avoid wandering.

1. Review your debt-repayment schedule. Remind yourself of when you will pay off each debt. Consider how much cash you will be able to spend when you are no longer paying these debts. Let yourself get excited about owing no man and being in total control of your own finances. Remember just how real and possible this goal is. You can do it.

2. Go over your Retirement Lifestyle To Do List. These are all the things you would buy or do if money were no object. Add some of your cabin fever items to this list. Let them be your reward for reaching your goal rather than something that prevents you from reaching your goal.

3. Give in to some smaller impulses. Only those not interfering with your debt-repayment schedule. If you deprive yourself completely, you may be more tempted to quit. Treat yourself every now and then, but don't use money from your accelerator margin. Stay on your repayment schedule.

4. Share the Financial Independence strategy with other people. Tell them about your own goals and success. You'll be amazed at how much this will encourage you. And, if you convince them to try it, you can sell them a Basic Course and earn a little extra money to apply toward some of your smaller impulses or toward your bills!

5. Get some new hobbies. It's surprising how often our thoughts turn to spending when we are bored. The more you occupy your time with activities you enjoy, the less likely you are to lament your temporary freeze on unnecessary spending. The secret of patience is doing something else in the meantime.

6. Try going to garage sales and auctions. You may find some great bargains without adversely affecting your budget and might even supply a few of those things you've been wishing you could buy.

7. Have a garage sale yourself. Clear out some of the clutter you've been sitting on all winter and make some extra cash.

8. Barter and trade, if possible. You may have a friend who can easily whip up those curtains you've been wanting in exchange for something you can do for them. This not only saves money, but also enriches your relationships.

9. Try rewarding yourself in small ways as each debt gets paid off. You might go out to dinner, buy yourself a small treat, or take a day off work just for yourself. Focus on each little success and don't fixate on the long-term picture.

10. And finally, if nothing seems to help you resist the temptation to spend, try calling the DF&PL office. There is always a friendly person willing to encourage you to re-commit yourself to your debt-repayment goal. It is truly the desire of everyone at DF&PL to see you succeed in becoming financially free. ■

Teaching Your Kids Good Money Habits

Maintaining a responsible budget is not easy. It takes persistence, self-discipline, and determination, and can be made easier by the support and cooperation of those closest to you.

Though most people will sit down with their spouse and work together to plan their household budget, few parents remember or think to include their children in the process. Yet your children may be the key to the failure or success of your plan.

Children need to be taught the correct way to manage their money because bad spending habits are learned early in childhood. Good money management is one of the most important lessons you can teach your children.

The first and most important step in teaching your children good financial habits is to be a good example. They'll learn more from what they see you do than from what you tell them. Be consistent in living on a strictly cash basis and don't ever let your kids see you using credit, which would "dis-credit" everything you've taught them about staying debt-free.

The next step is to talk to your children about your debt elimination plan. Let them see how you plan your budget. Also let them sit in on some of the decision-making processes for major expenditures. They need to hear how you decide something is worth the investment and what criteria is used to determine the acceptability of a large purchase. As they listen to the pros and cons, they'll begin understanding how to make buying a mental process instead of an emotional one.

Lastly, sit down with your children and help them make a budget of their own. Most children begin receiving an allowance by grade school. They may also be doing odd jobs from which they earn money at home or elsewhere. It's important, as they begin to earn disposable income, to provide counsel on the correct way to handle their money.

Here are some principles to follow to help your children make a budget.

KEEP IT SIMPLE
Keep it at their age level. With young children, simply break their earnings down into three categories: saving, spending, and giving. For saving, it's a good idea to buy them some kind of piggy bank. They should understand savings are kept for a specific purpose and are not for general spending. This is also the time to teach them the benefits of giving, whether it be to the church or some type of charity.

As they get older, they'll begin to break these categories down into more specific areas. Use this time to teach your children about shopping for the best bargains

and reading the labels. Let them begin to make some purchases for themselves, such as those big-name athletic shoes they want. This will help them begin to recognize the part advertising plays in their shopping habits. Teach them to think carefully about the wisdom of a purchase and to avoid purchases based strictly on emotions.

As they approach adulthood, your children should begin to account for expenses that come at regular intervals, such as paying their own phone bill or car insurance. You should be aware that you're not doing your children a favor by taking care of these commitments for them. Help them understand the importance of living within their means and functioning on limited resources. Let them make their own choices. By doing so, you'll help them move into the adult world in which they'll be on their own.

LET THE BUDGET REFLECT THEIR DESIRES.
Help your children make a workable budget, but be careful not to force them to spend their money the way you think they should. Help them to set savings goals that reflect their plans for the future. It's important for you to help your children at every stage to move toward independence and responsibility.

Work out a budget with each child separately. Each child's budget should reflect his or her age, interests, and priorities. Give your child some freedom once the budget is made. We all make mistakes. Even as adults, we mess up on our budget. This is an important part of the learning process.

Use a budget as a tool to teach your children important financial principles and concepts. For instance, if they end up with a shortage of money when they complete their budget, ask them where they can make adjustments or eliminate waste. If they come out ahead, ask them where this extra money can go. And be sure to teach them the important principles of staying debt-free.

Teaching your children good money habits will help prepare them for a lifetime of financial freedom. ■

Put it in Writing

The written word is persuasive. A spoken word is quickly forgotten, but put the same words in writing and the phrase is instantly given new credence and respect. For that reason, putting it in writing is a wise business practice. When everything is written out, you're able to see clearly what needs to be accomplished, how it will be done, and what your responsibility is. By putting it in writing, you're making a commitment.

Putting it in writing will also motivate you and keep you on track financially. By writing down your financial goals, you make a commitment to them. Written goals urge us to action and determine our direction.

Here is a list of financial goals as stated in The 15-Minute Money Manager, written by Bob and Emilie Barnes. These are merely generalized. You must personalize them. Decide for yourself what your goals are, and when and how you wish to reach them.

• **Income goal** — your desired increase in yearly income. You need to be realistic in this area. All other financial goals are based on this one. If your yearly income doesn't grow by at least four to five percent, you're losing ground

to inflation.

• **Career goal** — the type of work you want to do, the position you want to attain, or the business you want to create. Make a list and give yourself a one-year goal and a five-year goal for each.

• **Acquisition goal** — the things you want to buy and own. Make a list of all the things you would like to own, how much they cost, and the date by which you hope to acquire them.

• **Travel goal** — the places, nationally and internationally, you want to visit and experience. Make a list of the top 10 places you'd like to visit. Set a target date for each. Your list can include specific names of countries, states, cities, monuments, and other attractions.

• **Accomplishment goal** — things you want to do and become. Make a list of all the things you want to achieve. Include positions you would like to hold in clubs, groups, church, and your community. Include sports in which you would like to be involved. Also list any awards you want to win or other forms of recognition you want to earn.

• **Educational goal** — the knowledge you want to acquire for personal, financial, or career advancement. Make a list of the courses or programs you'd like to take and the estimated cost. Some examples are speed-reading courses, night school, courses to complete your

degree, real estate courses, and anything that may assist in attaining your career or income goals.

• **Recreational goal** — the fun things you want for recreation and sports. Make a list of the recreational vehicles you'd like to own, the date by which you hope to acquire them, and the estimated cost of each. These may include a sports car, motorcycle, bicycle, snowmobile, sailboat, jet ski, fishing boat, or camper.

• **Investment goal** — the income-producing, tax-reducing, or net-worth-increasing investments you want to own. Make an investment chart to identify where you are now, and where you want to be next year, five years from now, and at the age of 65. Some suggestions that may help you fill in your income goals are cash in the bank, investment accounts, retirement accounts, your home, real estate investments, and other assets.

By focusing on these financial goals now, you will begin to think about ways to achieve them. The first step, if you have not done so, is to get completely out of debt and begin functioning on a strictly cash basis. Let these goals motivate you to get out of debt, so your cash will be your own to do with as you please.

Put it in writing! Stay excited! Stay motivated! You know what you want and what you need to do to achieve it. ■

And the Two Shall Become One

It's no longer the norm for women to remain at home until they marry (or after, for that matter). More couples have to make special plans to bring together two separate and complete households, which includes furniture, appliances, pets — and, often times, debt.

Careful preparation and communication can help a recently married couple avoid some of the financial pitfalls accompanying marriage. Here are a few things you can do to make the change easier.

• Before you do anything else, if your intended has never read the *Debt-FREE & Prosperous Living™* Basic Course or listened to the accompanying tapes, have he or she do so. That way you are starting out on the same page, so to speak.

• Take time before your marriage to thoroughly review your finances. Take time to examine your combined income in comparison to your combined debt. If you're in the debt-elimination process, have a copy of your plan or printouts from your Debt-FREE software and be prepared to work out a new strategy incorporating your future spouse's information.

• Once you have set the time and collected the information you'll

need, it's important you stick to it until you have both a budget and a debt-repayment plan completed.

• Determine your household income. Things may change, depending on whether you'll both be maintaining the same jobs, hours, and income streams as before the marriage.

Another variable may be the amount each partner intends to put into the household pot. If either — or both of you — intend to withhold a specific amount of your income for personal reasons, this must be taken into consideration. Once you've determined the income for your household, you'll be able to establish a budget.

• The next step in preparing your new budget will be determining your fixed expenses. These will include your rent or mortgage, church donations, utilities, groceries, etc. These are your everyday living expenses and will vary depending on where you choose to live.

• After you've established your fixed expenses, you'll need to set budget limits for clothing, entertainment, savings, and medical expenses. (This may require an understanding of the changes in your medical insurance coverage once you're married. The same goes for your automobile insurance.)

• Record all the debts both of you have. You'll need to know the remaining balance on each, as well as the minimum monthly payment.

You may have to add your wedding expenses to your calculations, or perhaps you will find

you are able to use money received as wedding gifts to pay off some of your debt.

Whatever your situation, you should now be able to establish a new debt-repayment schedule that will include the debts of both husband and wife. You may also be able to come up with a larger *Accelerator Margin* to pay off your combined debts even faster than you would have been able to individually.

• Once you have determined your budget and your debt-repayment plan, you both must be willing to commit yourself to sticking with them.

• It will also be helpful to appoint one of you responsible for paying the bills in a timely manner and keeping track of your financial status. If either of you finds your budget to be unrealistic in certain areas, take the time to sit down and adjust it before things get out of hand.

• I would suggest discussing now how you will handle financial decisions and who, if only one person, will have the final say in financial matters. Understand ahead of time how finances will be dealt with, so when these times come up in your marriage you'll have already won half the battle. And by discussing them now you'll gain an understanding of how you both deal with money and will find it easier to trust one another in the future.

Financial stress is one of the primary reasons for marital problems and divorce in this country. By following these tips and taking the time to plan ahead financially, you'll find your married life much easier and happier. ■

Check Your Check- book

In order to devise, maintain, or revamp your debt-elimination plan, it will be necessary to have all your financial facts at your fingertips. If you've organized those records well, your task should not be a difficult one.

Your records might include tax statements, income receipts, previous budgets, etc. But if you want a clear picture of how you spend your money, nothing will tell the story like a well-maintained checkbook.

Here are some tips from organizing expert Ronni Eisenberg, author of Organize Yourself. These should help you establish a more organized and accurate system for your checkbook.

• **Get the right type of checkbook.** Ms. Eisenberg recommends using the larger desk-style checkbooks because they provide more room for explaining each check. In order to write checks while away from home, order a small number of checks in the portable checkbook format. This smaller checkbook can be used when on the go. Be sure to record the date, check number, to whom it was written and the amount of these checks in your main checkbook.

• **Have checks imprinted with your name and address only.** Some places require your driver's license, phone number, or social security number, but it's better not to give this information out unnecessarily and indiscriminately.

• **Buy yourself a separate Canceled Check Folder for each bank account you maintain.** These are divided by months and you should label each with the current year, account number, type of account, and the name(s) in which it is held.

• **Be sure to note every check you write in your main checkbook.** Record the number of the check, the date, to whom it was written, and the reason for the expenditure. You may also wish to include the account number to which the check is being paid, which may help when compiling information or backtracking a payment. The records you make now may help substantiate tax deductions as well as clarify budget expenses.

• **Deposits should also be carefully noted.** Jot down the source of income on your deposit slip. Not only will the Internal Revenue Service be interested, should you ever be audited, but it helps prevent confusion if you have several sources of income.

• **Balance your main checkbook after each entry so you have an accurate view of your bank balance.** This is the only sure way to prevent accidental overdrafts and the resulting steep fees. You may find hidden amounts for your *Accelerator Margin* by avoiding these extra fees.

• **Keep all of your deposit and withdrawal slips in one section of the Canceled Checks Folder until you need them to balance your checkbook.** This keeps them from getting misplaced in purses, pockets, and car floors. When your statement arrives, compare your slips against the bank's record, and, after each is verified, put the slips in with the appropriate bank statements.

• **Balance your checkbook as soon as you get the statement.** The longer you wait, the more difficult it will become. Make check marks next to checks and deposits that are verified, and make a circle by those that have not yet appeared on a statement. These should be checked off eventually, or you may need to backtrack the check.

• **At the end of the year, the Canceled Checks Folder(s) should be stored where it will be easily accessible yet out of the way.** It is generally recommended to keep such files for at least six years. Business records may need to be kept longer.

Remember, your checkbook is probably your most important budget planning tool. Taking control of your checkbook is easy and the rewards are great.

So, check your checkbook! You'll be glad you did. ■

Laws for Success

There exist certain laws of nature which — like it or not — govern the outcome of any given situation. The law of gravity, for example. This law states, *"What goes up, must come down."* If a ball is thrown into the air, it must fall to the earth. No matter how many times the ball is thrown, it will never stay up on its own.

Such laws are undeniable and unchangeable and can be utilized in ways beneficial or harmful. The choice is ours. We can make these laws work for us or allow them to work against us.

USING THESE NATURAL LAWS FOR OUR BENEFIT

We can often use these laws to achieve our goals and make a job much easier. If I want a bushel of apples, I can either climb all the way up the tree and go from branch to branch picking apples; or I can let gravity help me by shaking the tree and letting the apples fall to the ground, where I can easily pick them up.

Let me show you some laws for success that can help you as you work toward your goal of getting and remaining debt-free.

5 LAWS FOR ACHIEVING DEBT FREEDOM

1. The Law of Belief says whatever we believe with our hearts will become reality. If we wish to change our reality, we must change our beliefs about our-selves. In reference to our financial condition, we need to believe that we CAN function on a cash basis and delay self-gratification. We do have self-control and we will use it.

2. The Law of Expectations says whatever we expect to happen will happen. We can either expect to succeed or we can expect to fail. We should expect the best from ourselves, our plans, and our relationships. These expectations tend to generate a self-fulfilling energy that literally attracts the desired result to us.

3. The Law of Concentration says if you want something to develop in your life, you must concentrate intently upon it until it becomes a habit and a reality. You will be unable to stick to your debt-elimination plan unless you concentrate on it until you have accomplished your goal. The moment your concentration fal-ters you will begin pulling out the plastic money, because it's easier and faster. Or you will unneces-sarily spend money that should be used to pay off a debt. Don't wander from your debt-elimina-tion goal.

4. The Law of Repetition says we must practice new habits over and over again until they become natural and automatic, and replace old habits. Credit, for many people, is an addiction. It is an immediate reaction to pull out their credit card, even when they have the cash in their wallet to cover the expense.

They run to the phone the moment they see a commercial promising credit to anyone who can dial an 800 number. These habits didn't occur in a day. They developed over a period of time and began with deliberate action. Only time and intentional, repeated action can break a habit.

By the way, researchers have determined if you repeat an action for a period of about 21 days, it will become a habit. Three weeks — that's not so long to develop a new way of using money.

5. The Law of Control says we feel good about ourselves to the degree to which we feel in control of our lives. It's important to keep in mind the positive emotional benefits of having control of your finances. As you work toward your goal of being "un-vulnera-ble," you will feel more and more in control of your life, and more positive about yourself.

LIFE IS ABOUT CHANGE

Change is inevitable. No one stays exactly the same for any long period of time. Why not choose to change in a positive way? Keep a clear picture in your mind of your goals and the life you CHOOSE to live. Let go of the past and begin to develop new and better habits. Become a law abiding citizen, living a life consistent with the person you would like to be.

And then, as Isaac Newton might have found, achieving your goal will be as simple as an apple drop-ping on your head. ■

Ten Procrast- ination Traps to Avoid

When you first heard about the Debt-FREE & Prosperous Living™ plan, you were all excited and ready to go, right? You made up your mind that now was the time to get out of debt and onto the right financial track. But something caused you to put it off.

So here we are...it's months later and you still haven't started paying off any debts. What happened to all those great plans?

To put it bluntly, you procrastinated and lost the emotional momentum you used to have. People don't fail because they intend to fail; they fail because they don't DO what they intend to DO. But, you can change that. You can do it now. Don't wait for some better time. If you truly want to succeed, make RIGHT NOW a better time.

Here are some foot-dragging traps to avoid.

1. Floundering — the failure to focus attention and efforts in a single direction. The cause is lack of clear-cut goals. This trap can be avoided by crystallizing your goals. Try writing them down on paper. Make them as specific as possible — and GIVE THEM ACCOMPLISHMENT DATES.

2. Wheel-spinning — trying to do something so you'll feel busy but accomplishing little or nothing. This usually happens when we let ourselves get behind in our work and try to assuage our guilty feelings by doing everything at once. You won't solve the problem by frantic activity. Survey your debt-elimination list and make a schedule to accomplish everything in a realistic time frame.

3. Fire-fighting — living in a state of perpetual crisis. We often end up like this due to a lack of planning and goals. It's important to include in your schedule planning time. Take the time to sit down and review your schedule and your goals on a daily or weekly basis.

4. Vacillation — indecision. This happens when we fail to weigh the alternatives or consider the possibilities. Get tough with yourself. Weigh the pros and cons, write down all the possibilities, and make a decision. Trying to do something and failing is better than trying to do nothing and succeeding. Of course, the alternative to paying off your bills is HAVING BILLS TILL THE DAY YOU DIE.

5. Dawdling — drifting, daydreaming, dilly-dallying. This is a failure to keep your goals clearly in mind and make them a priority. Give yourself a deadline and stick to it. Promise yourself a reward when you've done it. It will slow your payoff plan a little, but, if you need extra motivation the month after you pay off a bill, let yourself blow what would have been its monthly payment. Then get back on track.

6. Spraying — diverting your efforts to many tasks instead of one; spreading yourself too thin. This is also the result of failure to focus on your goals. After you've written down your goals, focus all your energy on accomplishing them one at a time. This is why the Debt-FREE & Prosperous Living™ plan pays off ONE debt at a time.

7. Switching — starting one project and getting diverted to another one half-way through. Again, you've lost focus of your goals and plan. Don't let yourself be satisfied until the job is done.

8. Acquiescing — the inability to say no. This can be caused by the desire to please other people, guilt, timidity, lack of self-confidence, or lack of self-discipline. You must learn that you don't have to please everyone. When someone makes a request of you that delays or interferes with your plans, politely but firmly refuse. And this includes yourself. Don't give in to self-indulgence.

9. Rehashing — dwelling on past accomplishments, problems, or failures. Here you have an unwillingness to deal with the present. Let the past go. Concentrate on what is and what can be. You do not live in the past. You live in the present. And the future will become the present faster than you want to admit, so start today to make the future debt-free.

10. Perfectionism — unwillingness to compromise; unrealistic expectations. When we set our goals too high, we run the risk of becoming intimidated by our own goals. Learn to strive for excellence, not perfection. You want to be sure to set realistic, not idealistic, goals. ■

In Every Life Some Rain Must Fall

The problem in most households today is just about the time you think you can make ends meet, someone or something moves the ends. These contingencies require finances that may not be part of a monthly budget, but you need not let them upset or derail you. Here are some tips to help you stay on track when troubles come along.

• **First, don't panic.** You may be thinking, because the DF&PL Financial Freedom Strategy discourages saving until you've paid off your debt, you're in trouble when an unexpected expense arises. This isn't so. Remember, you are in control of your finances. You've exercised self-discipline and have chosen to make thoughtful and careful decisions about how and when you'll spend your money. Therefore, you're able to redistribute your funds whenever and wherever they're needed.

• **Temporarily go back to paying the minimum monthly payment on each of your debts.** Be sure to pay at least the minimum payment to avoid extra charges and debt collection agencies. Reducing monthly payments frees both your *Accelerator Margin* and whatever money you have rolled over from paying off previous debts.

• **Use the money you now have free to pay for the emergency situation.** One month may be all it takes to pay off the unexpected expenditure. If there's any money left over after handling the problem, use it to pay the next item on your debt-repayment schedule.

• **If the expense is more than you can handle in one month, you may want to include this new debt in your debt-repayment schedule.** If so, revise your schedule to include the new debt. On the other hand, you may choose to continue to use your additional money until you've completely paid it off, then return to your original debt-repayment schedule. In either case, continue to make regular payments on your other debts.

• **It may be helpful to tighten your financial belt a notch where possible so you can pay off this new expense quickly.** Cutting out phone calls, turning the heat down a little lower, cutting back on unnecessary traveling...whatever you think may help provide a little extra cash temporarily. These cutbacks need not be severe or permanent, but you may find they are not difficult, and you will discover you can come up with a larger *Accelerator Margin* when you get back to your debt-repayment schedule.

• **Avoid using credit cards or running up more debt in order to handle the situation.** Remember, you're not only trying to get out of debt, you're trying to change debt-forming habits. Turning to credit every time things get a little tough is a hard habit to break, but it's a must if you're ever going to move ahead financially.

• **Don't hesitate to try and work out some kind of repayment plan with your creditor rather than resorting to your credit card.** Unlike credit companies, many hospitals, dentists, appliance stores, etc., are willing to work out an interest-free repayment schedule.

• **Keep your goals in sight.** Remember what you want to achieve: financial independence. Setbacks and obstacles are all a part of learning a new way of life. They can't stop you from achieving your goals unless you let them. And challenges will definitely make you wiser in the end.

• **As soon as the problem is taken care of, get right back on your plan.** Don't let anything derail you. The closer you get to being completely debt-free, the less unexpected expenses will affect you. Once you're completely out of debt, you'll be able to begin saving and investing your money so there will be no such thing as an unexpected expense. You'll be able to plan and save for every eventuality.

The key is YOU are in control of your finances. Whether the circumstance is expected or unexpected, you should be able to make intelligent and comprehensive decisions with the money you have. You're no longer a slave to those you owe.

It's been said life is a voyage in which we choose neither the vessel nor the weather. Perhaps, but much can be done in managing the sails and guiding the helm. You are your own captain now. Don't give up the ship because of a little rain. ■

Living the Good Life in Tight Times

Staying motivated toward any goal requiring self-discipline is a constant battle. As time goes by, you feel deprived and restricted. It's important to incorporate small rewards into your plan to keep you motivated. For instance, when dieting, you can eat foods low in calories and fat. By allowing yourself to eat generous portions of these, you feel fuller. You might also eat smaller meals more often, which will combat the feeling of deprivation. By using these simple methods, you're more apt to stay faithful to your diet.

The same techniques can be adapted to your debt repayment schedule. By avoiding the feelings of deprivation and restriction, you're far less likely to slip into bad spending habits and undermine your financial goals.

Here are some tips to help you enjoy life while remaining faithful to the limitations of the debt-elimination plan you've worked out.

• Grocery budgets can be very tight during this period of your life, and eating at a high-class restaurant seems out of reach. But that doesn't mean you can't enjoy fancy meals. Try making them yourself at home. Thanks to the health and nutrition industries, there are scores of delicious, healthy, and inexpensive recipes

available. Most of these recipes use less of the high-fat, and high-priced ingredients like meat and cheese, thus cutting your costs significantly. Serve them on an elegant table, put on some good music, and *bon appetit!*

• And while we're talking food, don't give up entertaining because of your budget. Try having an impromptu party. Ask the guests to bring a favorite game to play and a snack to go around. This is an enjoyable way to relax and have fun without anyone bearing the burden of the expense. This can also be a great way to get together during the football season to watch the game. You'll feel much less restricted by your budget if you're able to entertain in your home periodically.

• Missing the pampered feeling you used to get by spending money? Try getting some friends together and having a home demonstrator do facials and manicures. This is a wonderful way to pamper yourself without the cost. You'll also get the added benefit of being able to purchase some cosmetics with the credit earned from any other sales made at your party. There are many different types of party plans which allow you to earn credit toward your own purchases, and they can be very entertaining.

• Were you a big moviegoer? You can compensate for not going to the shows for little or nothing. Just check out your local library. Most libraries carry an assortment of videotapes that can be taken out for free with your library card. Supply your own popcorn and drinks and enjoy yourself in the comfort of your own home.

No VCR? That's no problem either. Many libraries show movies on a regular basis right at the library, or check out your park district or community center. They, too, often offer this service to the public.

• Not enough can be said about a good public library! I highly recommend you check into it as one of the best-kept secrets available to anyone on a limited budget. You'll find a multitude of resources at your fingertips. If you enjoy classes and seminars to keep you active, the library often offers them free of charge on a variety of topics. If museums, zoos, and parks are your activity of choice, many library systems in larger cities offer free passes to these attractions in your area.

If you wish you could spend a little money fixing up your home, try checking out some works of art from your local library to add a little class. All of these services and more are yours free with the aid of your library card.

• Don't forget our national and state park systems. Have you been longing for a vacation to some beautiful spot, but it's just not in the budget? For many of us, the sights right near home have never really been explored. Take this opportunity to see what your own state has to offer. Write or call your state tourism office and they'll send you free information on all the activities and destinations available in your state. Many of them are free or cost very little. You'll be amazed at the beauty and interests right under your nose.

Live the good life now without sabotaging your future. ■

Living Where It's Cheap:

Doin' The Maine Thing

Tucked in the upper right-hand corner of the United States, Maine is a land of lighthouses and lobsters. As big as the five other New England states combined, Maine boasts 6,000 lakes and ponds, 32,000 miles of rivers and streams, 17 million acres of forest land, and 3,478 miles of rugged and beautiful coastline.

A QUICK TOUR

Maine's gateway is the southern coast. For over 300 years — even before there was a United States — folks have been enjoying the charms and coastal scenery of the south coast. Portland, Maine's largest city, is located here. Moving north to the mid-coast, the world-famous beaches and sparkling white sands continue, while highways meander through picturesque villages and towns, including the thriving coastal community of Brunswick. The scenic wonderland of islands, harbors, and headlands of the Acadia area is next on the coastal tour, followed by the sunrise coast, so named because it pokes out into the Atlantic and is the first of our shores to be touched by the morning sun.

Moving north is the huge county of Aroostook, which some call the last frontier of the east. Its four million forested acres and the Allagash Wilderness Waterway are wild playgrounds for residents and vacationers who enjoy camping, canoeing, hiking, and fishing.

The center of the state, the Kennebec and Moose River Valleys and the Katahdin/Moosehead area, have hundreds of lakes, ponds, streams, and rivers flowing in and around rolling hills and fertile farmlands. This area includes Augusta, the state capital. Most of the Katahdin/Moosehead area is owned by paper companies but is accessible to the public.

LIVING POSSIBILITIES IN MAINE

The 100 Best Small Towns in America counts two Maine towns as best in small-town living. Bath, which builds the U.S. Navy's fleet, is a popular retirement spot on the Kennebec River, about one-third the way up the coast. A three-bedroom house in the population 9,799 town goes for about $85,000 to $95,000.

At the mouth of Penobscot Bay on a well-protected harbor is the town of Rockland, population 7,972. Rockland is a popular tourist destination because of the abundance of natural beauty and recreational opportunities in the area. A three-bedroom house averages $100,000 in this neck of the Maine woods.

A MAINE RATING

Three metro areas in Maine were listed in the Places Rated Almanac, which rates 343 metro areas in the U.S. The best Maine showing was Bangor, about three-quarters of the way up the coast. Bangor scored 159 out of 343 with its most impressive ranking in the area of crime (39). Its worst rating came in climate (275), a subjective category.

Lewiston-Auburn was listed at a low 325 — near the bottom of the ratings. Once again, crime was a very good 45, but this metro area scored poorly in the areas of transportation, housing, and recreation.

Portland fared better, with a middle-of-the road composite rating of 185. Cost-of-living is high in Portland, however, and therefore wouldn't fit well within the Debt-FREE & Prosperous Living™ plan.

Maine sales tax is six percent, while state and local taxes would consume about $3,102 of an average family's household income. Housing costs are generally on the high side. In Bangor, for instance, the average price of a house is $76,200, while a one-bedroom apartment rents for $520 a month.

If you like severe winters with heavy snowfalls extending well into springtime, Maine's climate will sit well with you. On the bright side, the summers are extremely pleasant and the falls are spectacularly colorful and famous the world over. ∎

Virginia is for Lovers — of Debt-FREE Living

For 25 years Virginia has been saying Virginia is for lovers. What they mean, of course, is Virginia is for lovers of history. The first permanent English settlement was located in the Commonwealth, eight U.S. presidents were born here, and numerous Revolutionary and Civil War battlefields are located on Virginia soil.

Virginia is also for lovers of nature. The longest stretch of the Appalachian Trail runs along the western bend of Virginia, and the Shenandoah Valley and Blue Ridge Parkway cradle gorgeous vistas and mysterious underground caverns. If you're a lover of the beach, Virginia's eastern shore is hundreds of miles of delightful, warm sand and some of the coast's best saltwater fishing.

But Virginia is also home to lovers of debt-free living, because the state offers some interesting and inexpensive living alternatives.

WHAT OTHERS SAY

The 100 Best Small Towns in America suggests two Virginia locales as the best in small-town living. Bedford, Virginia, is just a half-hour drive from both Roanoke and Lynchburg, and has become popular as a retirement haven because of its proximity to these two metro areas. Bedford has a population of just over 6,000, and a three-bedroom home sells for about $90,000.

The gently rolling hills of Culpeper, Virginia, just 75 miles southwest of Washington, D.C. is the second small town of note. Culpeper has seen an astounding 23 percent growth rate since 1980, and a three-bedroom home sells for about $105,000.

50 Fabulous Places to Raise Your Family speaks highly of two Virginia towns. Reston, just 20 minutes from Washington, D.C., is like a city in the country. This planned community earns recognition because of its beautiful town center, excellent schools, attractive park settings, and vast historical and cultural offerings. However, I can't recommend this popular suburb because of its inflated real estate prices. The median housing price in Reston is $183,000.

Family-oriented Richmond is the other Virginia city mentioned in 50 Fabulous Places. Richmond is a fast-growing metro area with booming business, great recreation, diverse housing, and award-winning schools. Median housing prices are still on the high side, though, at $112,657.

AND THE RATINGS ARE...

Of the six Virginia metropolitan areas listed in the Places Rated Almanac, five rated in the top 100 in the composite ratings of 343 metro areas. Richmond fared best, coming in at 78, with Charlottesville, Lynchburg, Roanoke, and Norfolk following close behind.

Looking just at the cost-of-living category, Lynchburg rated the best of the five, coming in at number 79. The median price for a home in Lynchburg is $62,000, and an apartment rents for about $490 a month.

The climate in Virginia varies from east to west. Richmond residents, for example, in the southeast, can expect warm, humid summers and generally mild winters. The mountains to the west often act as a barrier to keep much of the cold, continental air masses out. The open waters of both the Atlantic Ocean and the Chesapeake Bay contribute to the mild winters and humid summers.

THE TAX HIT

State and local taxes in Lynchburg, Virginia, would consume an average of $2,202 in a year's time, while sales tax is 4.5 percent statewide. If you plan on moving your business to Virginia, the corporate income tax rate is 6 percent.

If you have savings set aside for use when you approach retirement, be careful. If you relocate, some states will track you down and levy taxes on your retirement distributions. In Virginia, for example, the state will tax nonresidents on income earned within the state boundaries and will tax lump-sum distributions. These taxes exclude Social Security benefits and the first $12,000 of income if you are 65 or older. ■

Moving South to North Carolina

During the winter months, any state with the word North in its name sounds awfully chilly. But this north is located in the south. Not the deep south. But close enough to the equator to take some of the nip out of the air. North Carolina would make a good choice for those seeking a small town to call their own, a place in which to renew their subscription to life.

THE MOUNTAINS
Mount Mitchell, the highest peak in the east, makes its presence known within the mighty Appalachian range, along with 42 other mountain peaks. Among these scenic mountains, and the breathtaking valleys that divide them, lie some of America's greatest little hometowns.

Among the many hidden gems are three towns which The 100 Best Small Towns In America says are among the nation's finest for small town living.

Boone has been called "The Second Garden of Eden." Hendersonville has been growing so fast since it was first listed as a desirable place to live and retire over 10 years ago, it seems everyone wants in. If the city fathers can manage the growth, it would make a nifty place to call home.

And Mount Airy, believe it or not, is the hometown of the actor Andy Griffith. There really is a Floyd's Barber Shop on Main Street in this quaint little town that is capitalizing on its pseudo-Mayberry fame.

The small towns and mountain parkways of the north eventually lead to wide open and wild places in the southwestern corner of the state. Remote wilderness areas, national forests, and plenty of recreational opportunities are available in this enchanting region of North Carolina.

THE FOOTHILLS
As you move eastward, the dramatic mountain scenery makes way for the foothills, where you'll find the largest natural habitat zoo anywhere, plus Civil War and Revolutionary War battlefields. The Foothills offer history, museums, natural wonders, and plenty of reasons to celebrate. North Carolina holds hundreds of festivals each year celebrating the many wonders of the state.

The town of Greensboro, in the northern foothills, is listed in 50 Fabulous Places to Raise Your Family. Among its attributes are great schooling, transportation, business opportunities, and reasonable real estate. Because of all the controlled growth the area has seen in the last decade, home buyers can afford to be choosy. And the climate of the Greensboro area is nearly ideal, with January highs averaging 49 degrees and lows just a tad below 32.

THE HEARTLAND
In the heart of North Carolina the soil is rich and perfect for growing cotton, peanuts, and peaches.

There are also parks, forests, lakes, and plenty of places to relax. The heartland is also home to more PhDs per capita than anywhere else in the U.S. Raleigh houses three major universities, two world-renowned teaching hospitals, and a famous research park. A very smart place to live.

The area has seen phenomenal growth because of outstanding medical care, endless recreation, low crime, great schools, and affordable real estate. 50 Fabulous Places to Raise Your Family says Raleigh is like living in a beloved Christmas carol.

THE COAST
If you like the beach but would rather come across wild ponies than wild parties, North Carolina's Atlantic coast might interest you. These enchanted shores, with their mountain-sized sand dunes, are where the brothers Wright first spread their wings. You could do worse than to spread your wings over the many villages of North Carolina's Grand Strand, where time seems to stand still.

If you enjoy fishing, boating, and beaching, the North Carolina coast will certainly fill the bill. And if you like to play a round, you'll find that golf is king in North Carolina, with over 400 golf courses to slice around in. One charming yet progressive city along the southern coast is Wilmington, also listed in 50 Fabulous Places to Raise Your Family. People choose this population 123,000 town because of its waterfront lifestyle, affordable housing and living, and fabulous recreation. ■

Is Your Dream Home a Reality?

If yours is an average American family and you follow the Debt-FREE & Prosperous Living™ plan, you can wipe out ALL your debts (including your mortgage), rid yourself of $105,408 in total interest payments and build up $1,278,260 in savings...all in the same amount of time it would normally take you just to pay off your home. And you can do it ALL WITH THE SAME MONEY YOU NOW MAKE at your job!

However, if you're like most of our subscribers, you're also marketing the Debt-FREE & Prosperous Living™ program as one of our ICs. So, there's a good chance the monthly income generated by your home-based, easily relocated business has hastened the process of debt elimination. Perhaps you are now enjoying a comfortable lifestyle that is supported by your residual income (without debt, you need less income to live comfortably).

The financial stability afforded you by your hard work and wise decisions has left you in a position you may have thought previously unattainable. You may now be able to purchase the dream house you've always wanted, and

do so without adversely affecting the lifestyle you have created and enjoy. In fact, finding the dream house that fits within your budget may be easier than you think. Take a look at these:

ISN'T THIS EVEN MORE THAN YOU'VE DREAMED POSSIBLE?
Eclectic Queen Anne, circa 1913. Beautiful brick home with four bedrooms, each with a servant buzzer, one with a fireplace. Original marble shower, turret, beveled and stained glass, tile roof, central vacuum system. Curved porch with hand-laid inlaid tiles, and 24 Greek Revival flare columns. Foyer with curved alcove and open oak staircase with oak woodwork and trim throughout. Just blocks away from the Ohio River in quaint Anna, Illinois. *"How much?"* you ask. A half million maybe? A quarter million? How about just $135,000!

HAS THIS ONE HAUNTED YOUR NIGHTS?
2,400 square-foot home has been completely remodeled and used as a bed-and-breakfast. Four bedrooms, 2-1/2 baths, full basement, large front porch with swings. Fireplace, refinished woodwork, and doors with transoms on main floor. In popular lake area tourist town, Lincoln, Missouri. It will cost you only $89,900.

COULD THIS BE YOUR DREAM HOME?
Live in a local landmark. This home once served as the first law library in town. Historic 3,770-square-foot two-story home has

12 rooms — five bedrooms, 3-1/2 baths. Covered patio, swimming pool, and five fireplaces. Elba, Alabama. A gift at just $75,000.

EVER DREAM OF BUYING A PRICELESS PIECE OF HISTORY ON A BUDGET?
Circa 1880 Victorian home, completely restored. High ceilings, two fireplaces, five bedrooms, two baths, front and back porches, garage, all on a beautifully landscaped acre in Bainbridge, Georgia. A mere $80,000.

IMAGINE YOUR FAMILY HAVING SWEET DREAMS IN THIS BEAUTY:
Old oaks, pecans, and tropical plants adorn this lovely circa 1905 home set on a rock-fenced yard in a peaceful town. Dramatic entry hall with French doors, 10-foot ceilings, hardwood floors, three bedrooms — a fireplace in one of them. Huge screened porch, three-car garage. Located in Wildwood, Florida. Yours for $79,900.

Even though they sound too good to be true, these and other affordable dream homes really exist. If you're not quite to the point where you can afford one, use the descriptions as an extra incentive to keep systematically eliminating your debts. Soon you will be able to live where YOU want to instead of where your job and your creditors keep you. And if you find the property you've been dreaming about, you can live like the debt-free king or queen you are. ■

A New Life of Options: Now What?

Part of the magic of the Debt-FREE & Prosperous Living™ strategy is the freedom you gain once you've eliminated debt from your life. John Cummuta calls it finally having options, meaning you have the option to work or not to work, the option to move or not to move, and the option to buy something now or wait until it goes on sale.

Once you're free from the shackles of debt and the days of living your life at the beck and call of creditors are behind you, life slows down to a more sane and relaxed pace. Many folks begin to think about where they want to spend their retirement years although that term means different things to different people.

Having a new world of choices opens up the possibility of living where it's cheaper — maybe even living somewhere you've always wanted to live, or in the house of your dreams. Once you're free from debt, you don't have to continue living in what I believe to be the ultimate Catch-22: You have a high-paying job, which you need because you live in an area where the cost-of-living is high; and you live in an expensive area because you need a big city job to pay all your bills that

result from living in a high-cost-of-living area.

Now you have options, and within those options some choices need to be made. It's helpful to make a list of lifestyle and living goals before searching for your ideal relocation alternative. On a clean sheet of paper write, *"We want to relocate because..."* across the top. Then write the following categories (and any others you can think of) along the left-hand side of the paper:

- We want to live where it's less crowded/congested
- We want to live where it's warmer year round
- We want to live near family
- We want to live in the country
- We want to live near a large metro area
- We want to live in a bigger house
- We want to live near a lake or ocean
- We want to live near lots of recreational options
- We want to live where there's lots of culture
- We want to live where the schools are good
- We want to live where the jobs are plentiful
- We want to live where the salaries are high
- We want to live near good health care facilities
- We want to live where the cost of living is minimal
- We want to live where taxes are low

Next to each of these relocation goals, make four boxes and label the boxes Not Important, Important, Very Important, and Absolutely Necessary. Checking the appropriate box will give you a better idea of what's important

to your family and aid in relocation.

Here are some other factors to consider before beginning your life in a less expensive area.

FAMILY

Cost of living, climate, crime, or overcrowded conditions notwithstanding, one of the biggest considerations may be family. Are you prepared to move away from family, friends, and your church or school community? How important is your social life as it relates to these various groups? Maybe your dream home is an easy two- or three-hour drive from your current home and is, therefore, convenient for family and friends to visit. Is there reasonable transportation near the place you're considering? This could make it easy for you to visit others and for family to see you.

BUSINESS

Will you require employment at your new destination or do you own a mobile, home-based business? If you own your own business, or if you plan on living off your investment income, you'll find many more options open to you.

COST OF LIVING

As suggested above, one of the benefits of being free from debt is you will no longer depend on big-city salaries. So why not take the opportunity to live where it's cheaper?

Although necessities like groceries, health care, and utilities are relatively universal, the two biggest factors to consider when moving are housing and the local tax structure. Refer to previous "Living Where Its Cheap" columns for specific information about various living options. If you're curious about the states covered in previous columns, back issues of *Debt-FREE & Prosperous Living™* newsletters are available on cassette in handsome and convenient storage albums.

CLIMATE

Climate comes down to a simple matter of personal likes and dislikes. Although it's undeniable that the sunbelt states have seen plenty of growth in the last few decades as sun-seekers flock south, others seem to enjoy the experience of all four seasons. One man's International Falls, Minnesota is another man's Tampa, Florida. Using the check-list above, determine what priority climate plays in your relocation decisions.

TAXES AND PENSIONS

Each state and some municipalities vary widely on sales taxes, property taxes, income taxes, and the method in which retirement savings and pensions are taxed. These cost centers can ultimately affect your living standards. Before making any relocation decisions, study the area carefully to determine if the tax structure will affect your lifestyle.

CRIME

There's no arguing this one. I don't know anyone who wants to live in a high crime area, where personal safety is often threatened. Although high crime rates are typically associated with larger cities, this isn't always the case. Once again, check the community carefully before making a move.

RECREATION AND LIFESTYLE

Finally, determine what types of lifestyle and recreation options you're looking for. Are you active and always on the go, searching for new outdoor adventures? Or are you a hobbyist who prefers spending time in the workshop building birdhouses? Do you want lots of property so you can be a wildlife watcher, or do you prefer museums, the opera, and a wild life? ■

Southern Florida: Still a Retirement Mecca

Not violent crime. Not rampant drug trafficking. Not even hurricane-force winds can keep sun worshippers from seeking refuge and retirement happiness in southern Florida. The biggest draw, of course, is southern Florida's semitropical temperatures and plentiful sunshine.

Florida's climate is influenced by the state's latitude and its proximity to the Atlantic Ocean and the Gulf of Mexico. No place in Florida is more than 70 miles from open water. Winds that blow over the ocean current of the Gulf Stream moderate the climate.

The Florida Keys, in the southernmost part of the state, have a tropical climate, with average temperatures ranging from 71 degrees Fahrenheit in January to 84 degrees in midsummer. The southeastern coast receives an average of 64 inches of precipitation each year. Thunderstorms occur frequently, especially in central Florida; hurricanes often develop in the Caribbean and the Atlantic in late summer and early fall, and can be a cause of great concern for Florida residents. More than 20 major hurricanes have hit Florida since the beginning of this century, mostly in the southern and panhandle areas of the state.

WHAT OTHERS SAY

According to 50 Fabulous Places to Raise Your Family, three southern Florida cities would make reasonable living options: Tampa, Fort Myers, and Coral Springs.

Tampa was cited by 50 Fabulous Places, because of its semitropical climate, fabulous recreation, low living costs, no state income tax, good schools and health care, and affordable housing. Likewise for Fort Myers, which also boasts one of the hottest job markets in the country and real estate in all price ranges. Coral Springs, just 10 miles from Fort Lauderdale, is one of the most successfully planned communities in the U.S., featuring fabulous neighborhoods, award-winning parks, endless family recreation and events, and the best public schools in the country.

Arcadia (population 6,488) is located just 49 miles southeast of Sarasota. According to the author of 100 Best Small Towns in America, Arcadia represents the best in small-town living. Arcadia has had an eight percent growth rate since the early eighties, yet a three-bedroom, two-bath home can still be found for about $70,000 — although mobile homes are popular in Arcadia.

According to *Entrepreneur* magazine, Sarasota/Bradenton is one of the top mid-sized cities in which to start a business. Buoyed by no personal income tax, relatively low corporate tax, low labor costs, and minimal licensing fees, small business in Sarasota is booming. Places Rated Almanac ranks Sarasota/ Bradenton at 240 overall out of 343 metro areas, with a ranking of 235 out of 343 for cost of living and 287 out of 343 for crime.

Home Office Computing magazine calls St. Petersburg one of the top 10 places to start and operate a home-based business. Economic opportunity abounds in the fields of health care, financial services, real estate, marine science, and tourism. Places Rated Almanac ranks the St. Petersburg and Tampa area at an impressive standing of 62 overall among 343 metro areas, with a reasonable 181 ranking among 343 for cost of living. Crime, however, is still considered high.

THE COST OF FLORIDA LIVING
Using the Tampa/Clearwater/ St. Petersburg area as an example, let's look at the cost of living in this Gulf Coast playground. The typical household income in

Tampa is $47,695, with state and local taxes consuming only $856 of that amount. The average price for a small home in Tampa is $87,900, while a one-bedroom apartment rents for $565 a month. Sales tax in Florida is six percent and there is no state income tax in the sunshine state.

If you're planning on moving your retirement nest egg to Florida, you'll be glad to hear that the state does not tax Social Security benefits or pensions. Florida does, however, levy an intangibles tax on money market funds, stocks, bonds, and non-Florida municipal bonds. And taxable amounts are doubled for couples. ∎

Cost of Living — The Best and Worst of the U.S.

Since the name of this column is "Living Where It's Cheap," I thought I would take the opportunity to highlight some of the cheapest places to live in the United States. As a contrast, I'll also let you in on some of the most expensive places to live in America.

Why do you live where you live? Before looking at our cheapest (and most expensive) list, ask yourself why you currently live where you live. Is it where you

grew up? Did you relocate because of a job offer or promotion? Do you live where you live because you want to be around family? Or is it because it's just plain cheap to live there?

Right now you may be living in a major metro area because that's where the jobs are. And for the living expenses you pay, you need a high-paying job. But what if you didn't have those expenses? Once you're free of the shackles of debt, you'll have more options open to you. Then what? Is your plan to move where it's cheaper to live? Your income might not be as great, but cheap land and no taxes might make up for a smaller paycheck.

Are you happy right where you are? How important is quality of life to you? Is climate a big factor? How about crime rates, transportation, or recreation? Everyone has different priorities and you'll undoubtedly weigh relocation on

a variety of criteria. But for the purpose of this column, let's just look at cost of living.

THE COSTS OF LIVING
Places Rated Almanac studied 343 metro areas and rated them for cost of living (among other things). The Almanac created indexes to which six costs were applied: housing, utilities, property taxes, groceries, health care, and transportation. These indexes were then weighted by their importance based on consumer surveys in various cities.

The biggest cost factor is housing, where mortgage payments consume an average of 30 percent of household income. Next in the indexes came transportation, taking about 17 percent. Cars, gasoline, tires, and repairs are all lumped into this category. Groceries are the next-largest family expenditure at 16 percent. It's interesting to note that groceries are pretty much equal over much of the country except for New York, Anchorage, and Honolulu, where even a tomato has to be trucked in.

Health care comes in at seven percent of the annual budget, accounting for everything from a box of Alka Seltzer Plus cold medicine to an overnight stay at the hospital. Utilities also claim around seven percent. Property taxes round out the list of indexes, taking about four percent of the household's budget.

THE TWO BIGGEST COST CENTERS

What you pay for a haircut, a pound of hamburger, or a gallon of gas might be important to you today. But over the long haul, cost of living comes down to basically two things: housing and taxes. No matter where you live in the U.S., you won't escape federal income and Social Security taxes. But state and local taxes can vary tremendously, as can the costs of housing.

THE CHEAPEST 10

According to the Places Rated Almanac, here are the cheapest (not necessarily the best) metro areas in which to live:
1. Joplin, MO
2. Enid, OK
3. Gadsden, AL
4. St. Joseph, MO
5. McAllen, TX
6. Anniston, AL
7. Texarkana, TX/AR
8. Pine Bluff, AR
9. Florence, AL
10. Terre Haute, IN

In Joplin, for instance, the typical household income is $40,606, with state and local taxes consuming about $2,457. The median price of a house in Joplin is just $39,500.

THE MOST EXPENSIVE 10

According to the Places Rated Almanac, here are the most expensive metro areas in which to live:
1. San Francisco, CA
2. New York, NY
3. San Jose, CA
4. Honolulu, HI
5. Orange County, CA
6. Santa Cruz, CA
7. Santa Barbara, CA
8. Ventura, CA
9. Long Island, NY
10. Los Angeles, CA

In San Francisco, the typical household income is $80,087, with state and local taxes taking a $4,793 bite. The median price of a house is $329,800.

The ratio between family income and house prices between the cheapest place to live and the most expensive place tells the story. In San Francisco, the average family income is just twice that of a family in Joplin, but San Franciscans pay ALMOST 10 TIMES AS MUCH for a house. Whoa!

Of course, as I mentioned above, there are other factors to consider. If your roots were in San Francisco, for instance, and you had family there, you might want to stick around, regardless of the astronomical cost of living. Just understand that it will take you much longer than average to reach your debt-freedom date. It's also interesting to note that San Francisco was rated number one for climate out of 343 metro areas listed in the Places Rated Almanac.

No matter where you currently live, you can start now on your debt elimination plan. Follow the simple steps in the Basic Course, and use this newsletter as your monthly guidepost to saving money and adding dollars to your *Accelerator Margin*. Then, if you want to move on to the next step in living debt-free and prosperously, consider relocating someplace where it's cheaper to live. ∎

A Grand Life in the Grand Canyon State

Arizona is one of the fastest-growing states in the U.S. Sunbelt, with a population rapidly on the rise and an ever-diversifying economy. Our sixth-largest state in terms of area, Arizona is bordered by Utah on the north, Colorado on the northeast, New Mexico on the east, Mexico on the south, and California and Nevada on the west.

A QUICK TOUR

Arizona is made up of two distinct geographic regions. The northern section is known as the Colorado Plateau, while the south and west is known as the Basin and Range Region. The Colorado Plateau area, about two-fifths of the state, comprises a series of generally level plateaus separated by steep-sided chasms. One of America's most famous landmarks lies here — the one-mile deep Grand Canyon of the Colorado River. Other well-known scenic areas in northern Arizona are the

Canyon de Chelly, with its sheer red cliffs; the Painted Desert; the Petrified Forest; and Monument Valley, which you've probably seen countless times in TV and silver screen westerns.

The Range Region comprises several mountain ranges, close together in central Arizona, but separated by wide valleys in the southern part of the state. The scenic Sonora Desert is in the southwest.

Arizona has a varied climate pattern. The Colorado Plateau region has cool to cold winters and warm summers. In Flagstaff, the mean January temperature is 28 degrees and the average July temperature 66 degrees, while the Basin and Range Region has mild winters and hot summers.

WHERE TO LIVE

The number one city in *Money* magazine's annual rating of the 20 best places to retire is Prescott, Arizona. As the county seat, Prescott has many conveniences for retirees — health care, government services offices, etc. But the big draw is the near-perfect weather, making it the ideal spot for active, sun-loving folks who want to spend every minute possible playing tennis, golfing, hiking in the foothills, and reveling in the 45 percent humidity. According to *Money*, the laid-back lifestyle in Prescott draws more than 600 relocators a year to the mountain town. But this bountiful living comes at a price. Studies show that settling in Prescott requires three times more income than the national median.

The 100 Best Small Towns in America included a northern Arizona town, Page, and a southern town, Bisbee, among its picks. Page, just south of the Utah state line, is a population 6,600 town which has seen 26 percent growth since 1980. This frontier town is near Lake Powell, attracting water-lovers of all ages. The sun shines 88 percent of the days in Page, and a 3-bedroom house can be had for as little as $70,000.

Bisbee, a former copper mining town, is only four miles from the Mexican border in the dry and sunny Mule Mountains. If this kind of living appeals to you, you'll be glad to know that a three-bedroom home in this unique and funky town goes for as little as $30,000.

Tucson and Fountain Hills are both listed in 50 Fabulous Places to Raise Your Family. Fountain Hills is a draw because, while it is very close to three major metro areas (Phoenix, Scottsdale, and Mesa), it lies just over the McDowell Mountain range, making it a secluded retreat in the beautiful Sonora Desert. Because of its proximity to the core of Arizona life, however, housing prices are steep, with the average home in upwards of $115,000.

According to 50 Fabulous Places, Tucson is breathtaking mountain scenery, dry, sunny climate, and one of the fastest-growing job markets in the U.S. A diversified housing market, great schools, and excellent health care are more reasons to consider Tucson. The median house price in this southeastern Arizona city is $80,000.

RATING ARIZONA
Home Office Computing magazine rated Phoenix number two in its rating of best home-based havens. It cites low start-up costs, accessibility to business information, and an abundance of free start-up and support services as reasons to consider Phoenix for a home-based business.

Entrepreneur magazine also named Phoenix one of its 25 best cities in which to own a business. According to *Entrepreneur*, the weather is hot in Phoenix, small business is hotter. A highly-skilled labor force, entrepreneurial resources, and a strong local economy make the move to Phoenix a good choice.

Tucson made Places Rated Almanac's Top 35 list, coming in at number 28 out of 343 metro areas in the U.S. Phoenix came in at a still impressive 38 (although the areas of cost of living and crime didn't fare well in the ratings), while Yuma scored a poor 297 out of 343, being dragged to the lower part of the list by its dismal education and health care, rampant crime, and lack of the arts.

In Tucson, the typical household income is $42,988, with state and local taxes consuming about $1,766 of that amount. Housing is on the high side, with an average home running about $92,400. Phoenix fares even worse — an average home costs about $101,200. Sales tax in Arizona is five percent. ■

Rocky Mountain High

Colorado is a landlocked, rectangular state located in the Rocky Mountains. It's bordered by six states: Wyoming and Nebraska on the north, Utah on the west, New Mexico and Oklahoma on the south, and Kansas on the east. Since World War II, Colorado has been one of the U.S.'s fastest-growing states. Three main regions dominate the topography of Colorado — the Great Plains, the Rocky Mountains, and the Colorado Plateau.

SMALL-TOWN LIVING
Aurora, Colorado, a suburb of Denver, made the list of 50 Fabulous Places to Raise Your Family. Aurora, where the median price of a house is $85,932, was cited because of 300 days of sunshine, a bright economic outlook, phenomenal recreation and family fun, the top-rated Cherry Creek school district, excellent medical care, and great neighborhoods.

Three Colorado small towns made the list of The 100 Best Small Towns in America: Glenwood Springs, about 160 miles west of Denver; Montrose, located on the western slope of the Continental Divide; and Durango.

WHAT OTHERS ARE SAYING
The state of Colorado showed up in the highly visible *Money* magazine's "20 Best Places to Retire." Durango was *Money's* city of choice. This population 13,000 town is five to 10 percent above the national cost of living average, and a two-bedroom home will cost you between $80,000 and $110,000, but 300 sunny days a year and spectacular views of the snow-capped San Juan Mountains attract many retirees. *Home Office Computing* magazine recently rated Boulder number six in its compilation of "Home-Based Havens." Although Boulder can be an expensive place to live and raise a family, the city boasts the fastest-growing economy in the state. More than 300 technology-based businesses are located in Boulder, as well as the University of Colorado. The average unemployment rate is a mere 3.7 percent.

RATING COLORADO
Six Colorado metro areas were large enough to be rated by the respected Places Rated Almanac. The highest-rated Colorado city was Denver, which came in at 32 out of 343 metro areas. Although cost-of-living and housing are high in Denver, the surrounding suburbs, recreation, education, health care, and transportation all rated high enough to give Denver its impressive composite rating.

Pueblo rated best in the areas of cost of living and housing (29 and 35 out of 343, respectively), but was in the basement in the area of crime (a high 316). The other Colorado cities rated were Boulder, Colorado Springs, Greely, and Fort Collins. All were unspectacular in the ratings, especially in the areas of cost-of-living and housing. Fort Collins was the best in the category of crime, with a fairly low 89 out of 343, but high housing costs forced this town into 183rd place out of 343 metro areas. All Colorado areas scored well in the area of recreation, for obvious reasons.

SPENDING IN COLORADO
Using Fort Collins as an example, the typical household income is $49,546, with state and local taxes consuming about $2,676 of that amount. The median price for a home is $84,000, while a one-bedroom apartment rents for about $510 a month.

Sales tax is a low three percent in Colorado, with no sales tax on groceries. Colorado also imposes a three percent flat rate on state individual income tax. Colorado will tax your retirement nest egg by making your lump-sum distributions (which are deductible for federal tax purposes) non-deductible for state tax purposes. Pension income is excluded. ■

Wake Up To Missouri

Missouri is often an overlooked state because it's, well, average. It sits smack in the middle of the country. It has a population that's not too big, not too small. And its terrain and recreation opportunities are so diverse, one single attribute doesn't stand out. But Missouri is quietly making its way to the top as a vacation, business, and relocation destination.

THE FIFTY CENT TOUR

The northern regions of Missouri are known for their historical significance and extensive outdoor recreational opportunities.

Missouri's center is made up of the Kansas City area, the Osage Lakes, Lake of the Ozarks, and the St. Louis area. Kansas City is considered an All-American city with a distinctly European character, while the lakes regions mean water — and plenty of it. It's also packed with scenic countryside and friendly towns.

Southern Missouri is the Ozark Mountains and the River Heritage Region. The Ozarks are everything the name conjures up — forested hills, blue lakes, and a colorful lifestyle. The southeastern corner

of the state abutting the Mississippi River contains some of Missouri's oldest towns and the river delta and lowland terrain.

SOME SMALL TOWNS TO WAKE UP TO

50 Fabulous Places to Raise Your Family lists Columbia as one of its fabulous spots to call home because of its highly educated population, award-winning schools, affordable housing, abundant green space, and a booming job market. The median price of a house in Columbia is $80,900 (15 percent below the national average), with overall living costs 10 percent below the average.

The 100 Best Small Towns in America lists three Missouri towns among its best: Boliver, Rolla, and West Plains, all in the southern part of the state.

RATING MISSOURI

Home Office Computing magazine ranked Kansas City, Missouri number seven in its recent feature on "Home-Based Havens: The Hottest Cities for Running Your Business."

Entrepreneur magazine listed four Missouri cities in its compilation of the best 25 cities to own a business: Kansas City, St. Louis, Springfield, and Columbia all rated well in the *Entrepreneur* study.

The respected Places Rated Almanac lists two Missouri cities

in its Top 35 metro areas: Kansas City at number 35 and St. Louis at number 22. Other Missouri metro area ratings (out of 343 areas rated) were Columbia (148), Joplin (200), St. Joseph (263), and Springfield (80).

It's interesting to note, however, St. Louis earned a low composite score because of great ratings in the areas of transportation, health care, education, and the arts. If cost-of-living and low crime are more important to you than the number of ballets and art museums, St. Louis' score is less impressive. Joplin rated NUMBER ONE (out of 343) for low cost of living with a low 75 on the crime rating scale, while St. Joseph also rated well in cost of living, at number four.

In Joplin, Missouri the average price of a house is just $47,300. The state and local taxes in Joplin will consume about $2,457 of your annual wage (Missouri has one of the lowest income tax rates in the U.S.). Sales tax is 6.5 percent.

The climate in Missouri is seasonal. Winters can vary widely, with frigid temps one day and semi-balmy thermometer readings of 50 or 60 degrees the next. Summers can be hot and somewhat humid, while most of the rain falls in the spring. Falls are comfortably warm and delight residents with lush, colorful foliage. ■

Discov-ering Ohio: The Heart of it All

If any state in the lower 48 can be described as typically all-American, it would have to be Ohio. Ohio is a test marketing hotbed for new products because manufacturers know the residents of the Buckeye State are as average as can be and offer a representational cross-section of America.

Ohio borders the sandy shores of Lake Erie to the north, where the cities of Toledo and Cleveland are located. Moving toward the center of the state you'll find Columbus, the state capital. As we move to Ohio's southern border, we find the city of Cincinnati, as well as the rolling bluffs and hills overlooking the Ohio River, where more than a century ago adventurous pioneers loaded their belongings onto flat-boats and began their journeys west.

OHIO'S SMALL TOWNS
The book 50 Fabulous Places to Raise Your Family claims Blue Ash, a suburb of Cincinnati, is a great choice in which to settle down. Accomplished city government, great parks and recreation, outstanding schools, exceptional low-cost health care, endless diversions, and a booming business environment. These are just some of the features cited by 50 Fabulous Places. Blue Ash is 1.4 percent below the national average for annual living costs, although housing — because of

its desirability — can be relatively high.

The 100 Best Small Towns In America selected three Ohio towns for distinction. The gently rolling farmlands of Wilmington, about 50 miles outside of Cincinnati, has grown by seven percent since 1980. Wilmington is popular with residents because the urban amenities of not one but three cities (Columbus, Dayton, and Cincinnati) are within easy reach. Wilmington also serves as the hub for Airborne Express, which has virtually guaranteed the town a prosperous future.

Moving to the northwestern part of the state, The 100 Best Small Towns lists Celina as another popular choice. Celina sits on the shores of Grand Lake St. Marys, the largest man-made lake in the eastern U.S. In this population 9,650 town, you can buy a three-bedroom, two-bath home for between $50,000 and $80,000.

Sixty miles southwest of Toledo, in the flat farmlands of Ohio, is the small town of Bryan. Bryan is the home of Ohio Arts, who produce the popular toy Etch-A-Sketch. A three-bedroom, two-bath home in Bryan goes for between $50,000 and $60,000.

BUSINESS PROSPECTS IN OHIO
Two Ohio cities showed up in Entrepreneur magazine's rating of the 25 best cities to own a business. Columbus' mix of service businesses and wholesale manufacturing has helped keep the Central Ohio economy stable, reports Entrepreneur. Columbus' proximity to the rest of America may be another factor in its desirability. Seventy-five percent of the

U.S. population resides within a one-hour flight of the city.

Canton, home of the Professional Football Hall of Fame, is also listed in Entrepreneur's top 25. Canton's small-business scene is peppered with manufacturing firms and service corporations.

RATING OHIO
Ohio boasts the NUMBER ONE metro area in America as rated by the respected Places Rated Almanac. Out of 343 metro areas rated, Cincinnati came out on top. Categories where Cincinnati rated well: jobs (34 out of 343); transportation (46), education (43), the arts (56), and recreation (64). Even crime was a relatively low 131 out of 343, respectable for a large city. The median price of a house in Cincinnati is $69,700, while the average price is $86,200.

The Cleveland-Lorain-Elyria area was also in the top 35 metro areas in the Places Rated Almanac, coming in at 14, with education, transportation, health care, and the arts making consistently good scores.

Columbus, Ohio also rated well, coming in at 46 out of 343 metro areas, with jobs and education making the best showings.

Sales tax in Ohio is five percent, while state income tax rates are between 0.74 and 7.5 percent, with the lowest amount for incomes under $5,000 and the highest amount for incomes over $100,000.

The climate in Ohio varies from north to south. Cleveland, in the north, gets a lot of lake-effect snow courtesy of cold Canadian air masses passing over Lake Erie. Spring is a brief transition period, while fall is the most desirable season, with lots of sunny days.

In the southern part of the state, around Cincinnati, residents still experience a continental climate (all four seasons) but in a milder version. Fall is pleasant while

summers can get hot. Roughly once every three years residents along the Ohio River experience some flooding. ■

Living in the Land of 10,000 Lakes

If you're looking for a place to escape the hustle, bustle, and high costs of city life, Minnesota is a good place to begin your search. Minnesota is dotted with well-mannered small towns, and those of you who consider the virtues of small town living to be important will feel right at home.

Minnesota is known for long, cold winters. But from those winters are born a lively spring, temperate summer, and colorful autumn. If you appreciate the passage of the seasons, you'll experience all four very distinctly in Minnesota. But be forewarned: subzero temperatures can last from November through March, and the summer humidity and mosquitoes demand an extra dose of tolerance. Despite the extremes, 75 percent of Minnesota's residents never move out of the state. Maybe they know something we don't...

Here is a quick tour of the state's three main areas:

SOUTHERN MINNESOTA
Southern Minnesota stretches from quaint Mississippi and

Minnesota river towns, past charming lakeside resort villages, to the old western towns of the plains. Southern Minnesota is a land of contrasts. You'll discover lively cities with culture and entertainment, and quiet townships with more horses than cars. You'll find state parks with modern facilities, and woodlands and river bottoms familiar since the days of the pioneer.

Southern Minnesota is also known for its friendly and sincere population. The 100 Best Small Towns in America lists two southern Minnesota towns as great places to live. Marshall, population 12,023, has grown at a rate of nine percent since 1986. Red Wing, where a new four-bedroom house can be had for roughly $85,000, is a strong and stable community of 15,134.

The outskirts of the Twin Cities hide a few small town gems. Eden Prairie is listed in 50 Fabulous Places to Raise Your Family. Just ten miles southwest of Minneapolis, this burgeoning small town combines the benefits of a stable, big city economy with a variety of recreational and outdoor experiences, all within a backdrop of shimmering lakes and rolling hills.

NORTHCENTRAL/WEST MINNESOTA
If boating and fishing are your things, take a look at Northcentral/West Minnesota. Although known as the land of

10,000 lakes, Minnesota has closer to 15,000, and this part of the state harbors more than all other regions.

The dazzling beauty of the lakes is surpassed only by the abundance of friendly communities and recreational opportunities Northcentral/West Minnesota offers.

The 100 Best Small Towns in America boast of Bimidji, whose name means "a lake with water flowing through." Appropriate, because six million acres of lakes and forest lands surround the area. A three-bedroom house in Bimidji goes for just over $60,000.

NORTHEASTERN MINNESOTA
The North Land is clear air, pure water, majestic woods, and a night sky filled with millions of stars. This pristine land consists of some of the world's most famous remote wilderness areas. But Northeastern Minnesota is not all hiking boots and granola bars. Several cosmopolitan areas and plenty of small, peaceful towns are also located within this part of the state.

If you're not adverse to the ever-present whine of snowmobiles, The 100 Best Small Towns in America recommends Grand Rapids for small town living. In this 8,000 person town you can purchase a three-bedroom home for as little as $40,000. ■

Living Prosper- ously in the Heart of Dixie

Despite an image of violent racial unrest, Alabama has come a long way since the dark days of the mid- to late sixties. The state is now known for its lush gardens, access to the Gulf shores, some of the best golf courses in the country, friendly residents, a low average cost-of-living, and community spirit.

Alabama is bordered by Tennessee on the north, Georgia on the east, the Florida panhandle on the south (Alabama has a short coastline along the Gulf of Mexico), and Mississippi on the west. About two-thirds of Alabama is low-lying coastal plain, which merges toward the northeast into regions of medium-altitude hills and mountains. The state has a population of 4,040,587, giving Alabama an average population density of 79.6 persons per square mile. In the last 10 years, Alabama has seen a 4.3 percent rate of growth.

A MONEY TOP 20
Surprise! Money magazine rated Fairhope, Alabama, near Mobile Bay, number two in its annual feature, "20 Best Places for Retirement." Money calls Fairhope, where novelist Fannie Flagg wrote the best-selling Fried Green Tomatoes at the Whistle Stop

Café, a congenial and lively community in a splendid setting. Crime is practically nonexistent, and a two-bedroom bungalow goes for about $80,000.

SMALL-TOWN LIVING
50 Fabulous Places to Raise Your Family calls Vestavia Hills, a suburb of Birmingham, a great place to live because of its lush, green streetscapes, outstanding public schools, access to a fast-growing job market, very low crime and pollution, great recreation and culture, and tremendous community spirit. The median housing price in Vestavia Hills, however, is a somewhat steep $105,000.

The 100 Best Small Towns in America lists three Alabama towns as good relocation opportunities: Fort Payne, a town of 11,900 folks located about 100 miles northeast of Birmingham, where a three-bedroom home goes for between $50,000 and $85,000; Hartselle, just south of the Tennessee border, which has seen a 10 percent growth rate in the last 10 years; and Brewton, about 60 miles north of Pensacola, Florida. Brewton, with a population of just under 6,000, boasts inexpensive housing prices from the high $40s to the high $50s.

RATING ALABAMA
The trusted Places Rated Almanac, which rates 343 metropolitan areas in the U.S. and Canada, shows several Alabama metro areas scoring well in the cost-of-living category. Gadsden, in the northeastern part of the state, came in number three out of 343, while Anniston, just south of Gadsden, ended up in the number six position. Florence, at number nine, was right behind.

But since cost of living isn't the only factor you should consider before making a big move, you should also know Anniston and Gadsden didn't fair too well in the composite ratings, being dragged down by poor job prospects, excessive crime, substandard education, and other factors. Florence, however, remained fairly strong across the board, finishing with an overall rank of 185 out of 343.

Birmingham had the most impressive metro showing, with a composite rating of 53. Excellent health care, good transportation, and a reasonable cost-of-living helped boost Birmingham into the top one-sixth of all cities rated.

The winters in Birmingham are mostly mild, although the city does receive its share of freezing temperatures. It can get humid and hot in the summer, and the annual rainfall of 53 inches is somewhat high. Although a safe distance from the tropical storms of the Gulf of Mexico, Birmingham does receive heavy rains as a result of these systems.

TAXING ISSUES
In Birmingham the typical household income is $49,945, with state and local taxes consuming $2,702 of that amount. State income tax rates range from two to five percent, with sales tax running at four percent. Alabama also taxes nonresidents on income earned within its state borders and generally requires retirement income to be included in your gross income and, therefore, subject to tax (with exceptions allowed for specific categories of retirement income). ■

Bad Boys... What You Gonna Do?

One of the reasons I enjoy living in rural Wisconsin was made crystal clear when I read the Police Report in my town's newspaper. The lead story was about a stolen tricycle that had disappeared from the front yard of a resident's home. A few days later the trike turned up at a neighbor's house a few doors down. It hadn't been stolen; it had rolled, innocently enough, down the sidewalk. This was the big crime news in town.

But that's the way I like it. I grew up in suburban Chicago, and today gangs and drugs proliferate my old neighborhood. For four years I raised my kids in Memphis, where crime is rated an appalling 307 out of 343 metro areas in North America. So it's a relief to be able to allow my children to walk to their friend's houses or ride their bikes to Wal-Mart without the fear that they'll be abducted. I'm not an alarmist. I just want my kids to enjoy their childhood, as I did in simpler days.

If a relocation decision is in your future, you may be like me and determine that, in addition to cost of living, cost of housing, and quality of education, crime (or the lack of crime) is a major consideration.

SOME BACKGROUND

Cities with poor crime ratings might have received that rating because of excessive crime in one part of town or even one neighborhood. Statistically, you might be perfectly safe in another part of town. But you're also a victim of crime if you have to spend extra money on motion detectors outside your home, or a car alarm for your vehicle, or if you're afraid to run to the grocery store after dark.

Although it is not true in every case, the population of a city is often tied to the crime rate. For example, cities like Los Angeles, New York, Chicago, and their associated metro areas all rate high in crime, while smaller towns and cities rate low almost without exception. Some cities defy the norm. Places Rated Almanac points out Toronto's crime rate is as low as that of Great Falls, MT. Tallahassee's crime rate is as high as New York's.

HOW CRIME IS MEASURED

Each year the FBI releases statistics on crime in the U.S. An index is created by looking at the incidences of eight types of crimes, four violent and four nonviolent. The violent crimes are murder, rape, robbery, and assault. The non-violent, or property, crimes are burglary, larceny, theft, and auto theft. These are the starting points Places Rated Almanac used to develop its rating of 343 metro areas in the U.S. and Canada. Places Rated took the violent crime rate and the property crime rate (divided by 10 because it's less serious) and added the two together. The sum was the metro area's score. The higher the score, the more dangerous it is to live in that area.

Places Rated Almanac only deals with the 343 metro areas with populations greater that 50,000. So you won't be seeing small towns like Boscobel, WI, or Mount Airey, NC, in the ratings.

The 10 safest places to live in North America are:
1. Johnstown, PA
2. Wheeling, WV
3. Parkersburg, WV
4. Williamsport, PA
5. Altoona, PA
6. Scranton, PA
7. Sharon, PA
8. Danville, VA
9. Lancaster, PA
10. Danbury, CT

So are Johnstownians free from crime? Not completely. If you lived in Johnstown, the odds of your becoming a victim of crime after residing there for one year is about 60 to one.

But, the odds increase to about eight to one for residents of Miami, FL.

The 10 most dangerous places to live in North America are:
1. Miami, FL
2. New York, NY
3. Tallahassee, FL
4. Baton Rouge, LA
5. Jacksonville, FL
6. Dallas, TX
7. Los Angeles, CA
8. Gainesville, FL
9. W. Palm Bch, FL
10. New Orleans, LA

SETTING THE TRENDS

If a metro area has seen a 25 percent or more improvement in its crime index since 1987, it is considered an area that's getting safer to live in. If a metro area has experienced a 25 percent decline since 1987, you can bet it's getting more dangerous to live there.

Crime is getting better In:
- Bloomington, IN
- Tuscaloosa, AL
- Fort Pierce, FL
- Vallejo, CA
- Hagerstown, MD
- Worcester, MA
- Janesville, WI
- Yuba City, CA
- Redding, CA

Crime is getting worse In:
- Athens, GA
- Montgomery, AL

- Clarksville, TN
- Pittsfield, MA
- Dothan, AL
- Steubenville, OH
- Kokomo, IN

Finally, it's interesting to note that the most dangerous places are hot most of the year. Climate does influence crime rates, so it's not surprising to find that large southern cities are often the most violent in America.

For a professional criminal, the pickings are easier in Florida resort towns than in colder, industrialized parts of the country like Cedar Rapids or Bismarck. So if you're considering making the move to Las Vegas, Tampa, or El Paso, be prepared to protect yourself.

The odds may be against you. ■

Living in a State of Confusion

Let's look at how to gather and sort out all the information on your prospective new home.

START WITH THE CHAMBER
The best place to begin gathering information is the chamber of commerce of the city to which you're considering moving. You can get in touch with them by calling the directory assistance in that area or by visiting the library to see the World Chamber of Commerce Directory. Either write or phone the chamber and ask for a newcomer's package.

If you need any more specific information, like a list of the areas largest employers, be sure to ask. Usually the chamber will send you this packet free of charge, although some may charge you a nominal fee to cover administrative and postage expenses. The best part about inquiring with the chamber is

you'll suddenly begin receiving mail from local real estate agents, insurance companies, and other businesses who want your money. But that's OK — it's all part of the information gathering process.

NEXT STOP: THE CVB
Although smaller towns can't support a full-time convention and visitors bureau, most medium-sized and large cities will have one. If the city or town you're considering doesn't have a CVB, contact the state bureau.

The convention and visitors bureau will send you information on recreation, cultural sites, special events, and things to do in the entire state, region, or city about which you inquire. This can be a gold mine of useful information and can help cement your relocation decision.

GET THE LOCAL PAPER
Subscribing for a month or two to the local paper will be of great value to your investigation. The Sunday paper, if they have one, is usually best because it will give you real estate information, list job and business opportunities, recap the week's happenings, and give you a flavor for the commu-

nity. You can get the phone number and address of the paper from the chamber.

CONTACT A RELO SPECIALIST
Through the chamber or ads in the local paper, find out the names of several real estate agents who specialize in relocations. You'll usually see the initials "CRS" after their name in their ad or on their business card. This stands for Certified Relocation Specialist and signifies the agent has been trained to work with out-of-town buyers.

Begin a dialogue with the agents who impress you the most. Discuss the type of property you're looking for, the price range you're interested in, and an estimate of your move date.

If you're not yet ready to commit to a real estate agent but you're interested in property and housing costs in the area, ask a local contact or the chamber for a current *Homes for Sale* real estate magazine. These are great for browsing and will provide you with an idea of what's out there. You can also subscribe to *United Country*, a quarterly catalog of country real estate for sale published by United National Real Estate. You can call them at 800/999-1020 to subscribe, or check out your local newsstand or magazine store, where you might find a copy hiding among the home and lifestyle magazines.

KIDS? CALL THE SCHOOL DISTRICT OFFICE
Another prime consideration is the quality of the area schools. Your new real estate agent can provide you with the number of the area's school district office. Ask for specific information about curriculum, special programs, facilities, test scores, gifted programs, and anything else of concern. This information is usually free for the asking.

GO ON-LINE
If you're connected to an on-line service like CompuServe or America Online, or you have access to the Internet, this can be a great place to gather information about prospective relocation options. Since there's so much out there, it's difficult to offer specific addresses and key words, so just start your search the way you would when you're just out surfing. Type in some obvious key word, like the name of the city you're considering, or go to a search engine and begin your investigation there. When you find a likely site, make a note of it and download any information which might be useful in helping you make your decision.

MAKING SENSE OF IT ALL
Now that you gathered all this stuff, what's next? You should've determined by now exactly what you're looking for in your new home and you already know the needs of your family. So write the names of the cities you're considering across the top of a sheet of paper and the features you're looking for along the left side. Now go through all your materials and check off under each city or town its benefits. This simple process will help you narrow your choices or define a clear winner if it's a toss-up — and end your state of confusion. ■

Appendix D

Operating 100% on Cash Newsletter Articles

Dollars and Sense
Buying and Maintaining Your Automobile
Buying, Maintaining, and Selling Your Home

APPENDIX D

Selected Debt-FREE & Prosperous Living™ Newsletter Articles Dealing With Living on Cash

The following articles have been organized according to the column under which they appear in the *Debt-FREE & Prosperous Living™* Newsletter, making access to a specific topic more convenient for the reader. To subscribe to the *Debt-FREE & Prosperous Living™* Newsletter, call 1-888-DEBTFREE.

Dollars and Sense:

"Financial Dollars and Sense" gives you the knowledge required to maximize the value of the business dollar in a wide variety of ways. Entrepreneurs and home-based business owners might take special note of this column. Authors Scott Talbot and Barrett Bryant caution against wasteful spending that stems from an ignorance of tax laws, choosing the wrong financial services representatives, and purchasing insurance far too costly to satisfy need.

Buying and Maintaining Your Automobile:

A great majority of people rely on their automobiles to transport them safely to and from work during the week and to whisk them away from it all for a weekend excursion. Nothing interrupts the best-laid plans as effectively as a car that refuses to run properly, and a malfunctioning vehicle is not only expensive to repair but also a danger to the car's passengers and other motorists. Jim Gaston, author of <u>When</u> <u>There's</u> <u>No</u> <u>Mechanic</u> and host of the weekly radio show "Car Keys," offers his expertise on how to keep any car running safely and efficiently in his column, "Buying and Maintaining Your Automobile." Gaston shares maintenance tips that will help prevent major breakdowns (and expensive repairs), exercises designed to improve driving skills, and methods that discourage auto theft – everything you need to know to save money when you're behind the wheel.

Buying, Maintaining, and Selling Your Home:

The most expensive purchase of a consumer's lifetime is a home, and a little research (coupled with a little hard work) goes a long way toward insuring your home will be an asset, not your greatest liability. "Buying, Maintaining, and Selling Your Home" addresses the questions you want to ask when looking to buy or sell a home, and solutions to the problems that inevitably arise during ownership. Tom Passaro, Realtor,® and Caren Bugay, a real estate appraiser and freelance author, both write about strategies to guarantee your family a fair price, whether you are trying to buy or sell. Jack Miklasz, our Building and Facilities Manager and resident home maintenance expert, tells you about the most cost-effective ways to keep your home looking new, as well as the right time to upgrade a home's major appliances.

Financial Dollars & Sense:

Choosing a Financial Services Representative

If you need financial advice, or you would like to buy insurance or invest money, you probably need the help of a financial services representative. This person may be an insurance agent, a registered representative, or someone specializing in another field of financial services. To whom do you turn?

Naturally, you would want someone who is a professional — someone who can make the right recommendations while providing you with sound advice. It's important that you find someone with skill, objectivity, and integrity.

SKILL
If you needed brain surgery, would you settle for a doctor who had just started practicing? Hardly! By the same token, you probably wouldn't want to trust your finances to an inexperienced and unskilled financial planner. But you may unknowingly be doing just that!

According to LIMRA (the Life Insurance Marketing and Research Association), more than 95 percent of those who enter the finan-cial services business drop out within the first five years. This means less than five percent of financial planners have five or more years experience in their field.

The financial planning industry requires no degree or formal training. One need only obtain the appropriate licenses or registrations. To do so involves passing a test in order to insure the applicant is familiar with certain basic principles. Simply passing a test does not guarantee a high level of skill.

Certain conscientious individuals in the business strive to sharpen their skills by taking voluntary courses. In addition, more and more states are requiring continuing education courses and routine compliance meetings in an effort to maintain and promote acceptable skill levels.

I recommend you seek help from someone who's had at least five or 10 years of full-time experience in the business. A CLU, ChFC, or CFP designation is a big plus. Also, membership and participation in various trade associations is an indication the individual takes his or her work seriously.

OBJECTIVITY
One might assume a financial services representative is completely objective and unbiased in giving advice and making recommendations. This is not always the case.

For example, let's assume you want to buy a 20-year-level term life insurance policy with a $250,000 death benefit. The agent may recommend a plan under-written by the Sinking Sands Life Insurance Company of Iowa. But is this the best plan for you? Maybe not.

Several factors may limit the agent's options (and therefore your options), or may influence him or her to offer one plan over another. The agent may be captive. This means he or she can offer only one company's product. Or, if the agent is not captive, he or she may be licensed with only a handful of companies, each with certain quotas or incentives.

It's best to choose someone who is independent — someone whose hands are not tied by a company or an agency requiring he or she to sell their products in exchange for office space or marketing assistance. An independent agent, or a broker, has the freedom to shop around for you and provide you with more options.

INTEGRITY
Perhaps the most important quality to look for in a financial services representative is integrity. Your rep may have a great degree of knowledge, skill, and experience. And being independent, he or she may have the ability to make an objective analysis of your needs and of the best manner in which to satisfy those needs. But without integrity, these qualities are worthless.

Integrity, honesty, character, trustworthiness, and morality should be evident in professionals in all fields. And yet this trait may not always be easy to measure. There are realities which could tempt the representative to violate his or her integrity.

If the representative works on commission, for example, his or her paycheck is on the line. This can lead to a conflict between what's best for the rep (commissions) and what's best for you

(intelligent and objective advice).

There may be individuals in the business whom you already know. If you don't know anyone in the business whom you would feel comfortable working with, start asking around. Talk to people you know and respect, and ask them whom they've worked with. Ask

them how they feel about the service provided to them and whether or not they would recommend this individual.

Finally, when you do find someone who you feel may be qualified to help you, get referrals. ■

It's Time to Evaluate Your Medical Insurance

America's health care system is the envy of the world, but the privilege of using it is very costly. An appointment at the doctor's office followed by a short stay at the hospital with surgery can cost thousands of dollars. Treatment for a prolonged illness can escalate into the millions.

Therefore it makes sense to secure quality medical insurance to protect yourself from the financial devastation of an unforeseen illness or injury. Let's consider a few practical guidelines that will help you make a wise choice.

BUY QUALITY FIRST
Since finding a reliable policy can be complicated, it's wise to seek out the counsel of a reputable agent who is independent and,

therefore, has the ability to research what's available and make solid recommendations.

Make sure you understand the policy completely. Scrutinize the clauses in fine print before you are ill. All of the information will be in the company literature and the policy. Ask how emergency and outpatient care, prescriptions, and diagnostic testing are covered, as well as major medical. Determine if there are deductibles or co-payments. Note the maximum amount the insurance company will pay for each insured person during their lifetime. While $1 million is common, many now offer $2 million dollars or more of lifetime coverage with very little difference in price.

Insist on dealing only with insurance companies that have a high rating from A.M. Best, an independent rating firm. They should have an A or A+. This makes it more likely that they will be capable and cooperative when you make a claim.

CONSIDER DEDUCTIBLES AND CO-PAYMENTS
A deductible is the flat-rate amount you must pay in a calendar year before your insurance covers any of your claims. A co-payment is a percentage of each covered claim you must pay in a

calendar year, up to a certain limit called a stop loss. As you might expect, you must pay a higher premium to obtain a policy with low deductibles and low co-payments. Let's suppose, for example, that you have a policy with a $500 deductible, a 20 percent co-payment, and a stop loss of $5,000. If your medical bills exceeded $5,500 for a year, then you would have out-of-pocket expenses of $1,500. Many companies offer substantial savings if you pay 50 percent of the next $2,000 after your deductible. Others will pay all of your major medical expenses if your hospital stay is fewer than 48 hours. Shop around, ask questions, and compare notes. Then do the math.

In order to determine the best plan for you, look at your family's medical history realistically. If your medical expenses averaged less than your premiums for each of the last five calendar years, then you may want to consider simply planning medical expenses into the budget. Even so, you should still have a catastrophic-loss policy with a high deductible and a high overall benefit cap. Such policies are very inexpensive and, while they typically provide no coverage for the first $5,000 or $10,000 of expenses, after that they will cover several million dollars in claims and save you from bankruptcy.

MINIMIZE COVERAGE OPTIONS

Some policies provide coverage of no value to your situation. Coverage for dental and eye care, for example, is very expensive. It may be more cost-effective to plan these expenses into your budget.

Examine your policy in regards to maternity. If you are carefully avoiding pregnancy or your child-bearing years are behind you, you may be able to save money by excluding maternity coverage. If you think there is a chance you may become pregnant, be certain you are adequately protected. The cost for optional maternity coverage varies between $5 and $20 per month (depending on the woman's age), while the expense of medical complications can be staggering.

EVALUATE CURRENT AND FUTURE COSTS

When choosing insurance, consider potential increases in premiums as well as the current rate. Ask your agent for the projected average cost of the premiums based on age and health-related factors.

Ask for a history of the company's rates during the last five years. Note the size and frequency of increases they made to keep pace with rising medical costs. Research their cancellation rate. With this information, you will be able to anticipate what you will be paying in the years to come and whether it is likely to pay off if disaster strikes.

In general, you should look for a solid company that specializes in medical insurance, has a long-term reputation of affordability and fine service, and is designed to deal with all the uncertainties inherent in medical insurance. ∎

Should You Invest in an IRA This Year?

Taxes may be due only once a year, but there is never a bad time to consider the advantages of investing in an IRA (Individual Retirement Account). It is sensible to maximize your allowable deductions and decrease your tax bill or increase your tax refund, and people consider investing in an IRA for the tax benefits it will provide. Should you invest in an IRA this year? Let's look at some of the pros and cons.

ADVANTAGES OF AN IRA

Advantage #1: Tax Deductibility. One of the advantages of an IRA is you can usually deduct your contributions on your tax return. If you are in the 28 percent tax bracket you will save 28 cents in taxes for every tax-deductible dollar you invest into your IRA. Or, to look at it another way, you can invest 72 cents ($1 minus the 28-cent tax credit) to have $1 in your account, an immediate return of over 38 percent!

Advantage #2: Tax Deferral. Taxes on an IRA's earnings are deferred (delayed) while they are accumulating in your account. Compare this with a taxable investment, with which you receive a 1099 form at the end of the year to report your taxable earnings.

Let's assume that you earned $1,000 in interest last year. You will need to pay the IRS $280 of that $1,000. So in reality, you netted only $720. If you earned the same $1,000 in an IRA, you could keep that $280. You now have almost 40 percent more in your IRA because you aren't required to pay taxes on your earnings this year. In fact, that additional $280 you are allowed to keep will continue to earn interest for you year after year. Its earning potential would have been forever lost in a taxable investment.

DISADVANTAGES OF AN IRA

Disadvantage #1: Taxable Income. Lest you become too giddy about Uncle Sam's apparent generosity, bear in mind these tax benefits are only temporary. Yes, you can deduct your contributions to receive a tax credit, and you can defer the taxes on the annual growth in your account. But, sooner or later, Uncle Sam will want to be paid. This tax bill comes due when you withdraw your money. Any income you pull from your IRA will be 100 percent taxable when withdrawn. So it's a trade-off — you save money on your taxes now, but you must pay it back later.

But it's not such a bad deal, particularly if one is wise in the way he or she uses an IRA's tax deferral. Look at it this way. Suppose the IRS told you that you could wait about 20 or 30 years to pay your taxes. In the meantime, you could invest the money that would have been paid in taxes in an investment account. Later, you would pay the taxes (your principal) but keep your earnings (interest), less any taxes you owe on those earnings. You still come out ahead.

Disadvantage #2: Limited Access. Any funds devoted to an IRA cannot be touched until retirement age (59-1/2). If you make an early withdrawal, you are required to pay taxes on the amount of the withdrawal, plus a 10 percent penalty. This penalty cuts so deeply that many choose not to make the withdrawal, even if it is desperately needed.

Before investing in an IRA, be sure you are financially able to support both the retirement account and a separate, liquid account that can be accessed in emergency situations.

Disadvantage #3: IRS Guidelines. If you want the benefits an IRA offers, you must be willing to abide by the guidelines laid out by the IRS, which can be somewhat restrictive.

An IRA holder cannot withdraw prior to age 59-1/2 without penalty, and withdrawals must begin by age 70-1/2. Contributions are limited to $2000 or less per year. There are limitations regarding how much of your contribution you can deduct for tax purposes if you're eligible for a Qualified Retirement Plan through work. And there are limitations regarding the types of investments that

can be used to fund your IRA.

ANALYSIS
There is no such thing as the perfect investment or the perfect tax strategy. There are always trade-offs. To gain certain advantages, you must be willing to pay the required price or play by the rules. This is true with IRAs. But, considering taxes are one of the great enemies of saving and investing money, it makes sense to take advantage of every legitimate opportunity we have to minimize your tax liability.

A few final words of advice. First, be sure you have adequate reserves in savings that are readily available before tying up money in long-term vehicles such as IRAs. And second, consult with your accountant before making a final determination regarding what's best for you. ∎

Annuities: One of the Few Remaining Tax Shelters

The minimization of tax liability is the key to successful saving and investing. On a taxable investment, 15 to 39 percent of earnings are lost to taxes. With a six percent return, you would net 3.7 percent to five percent after taxes,

depending on your tax bracket. When you factor in a four percent rate of inflation, you will net only about one percent, or possibly even lose ground to inflation. Therefore, minimizing taxes is absolutely essential for generating a reasonable net return on your investments.

Options for investing money on a tax-sheltered basis are somewhat limited. The following is a brief explanation of the few in existence.

QUALIFIED RETIREMENT PLANS
QRPs are those plans which qualify for tax-deferred and possibly even tax-deductible status. These include individual retirement accounts (IRAs) and certain employer-sponsored pension and

profit sharing plans. Numerous investment vehicles are available for funding these plans, but the IRS limits the flexibility of these accounts by imposing strict requirements and early withdrawal penalties. Furthermore, your company may not offer such a plan.

TAX-FREE MUNICIPAL BONDS
A tax-free municipal bond is similar to a U.S. savings bond or a corporate bond. The investor, in essence, is loaning money in order to generate a return. Municipal bonds are tax-free because the money is used to fund local government projects such as parks, zoos, and parking garages. Muni-bonds are safe but typically provide only a four to six percent return. Such a low return may not even outpace

inflation, meaning investing in municipal bonds may cost you purchasing power.

CASH VALUE LIFE INSURANCE

Cash value life insurance is another vehicle in which the investor can accumulate money on a tax-sheltered basis. However, it's not a very profitable investment and does not meet the guidelines of the Debt-FREE & Prosperous Living™ principles.

ANNUITIES

An annuity is an investment account offered through an insurance company that allows for tax-deferred accumulation, as well as tax-deferral during the period of withdrawal. The concept is similar to investing in a secure fixed account like a CD or mutual fund with a tax umbrella that allows for the deferral (postponement) of taxes.

WHAT ARE THE DISADVANTAGES?

First, unless the annuity is used to fund a qualified retirement plan (like an IRA), contributions are not tax-deductible. Also, insurance companies impose early withdrawal penalties (they usually start at 10 percent and decrease to

zero percent over 10 years). The IRS also imposes a 10 percent penalty for withdrawals prior to age 59-1/2, unless the withdrawals are spread out in equal lifetime installments, as they are with qualified retirement plans. Clearly, an annuity would be best used as a long-term savings vehicle.

WHAT ARE THE ADVANTAGES?

Annuities offer competitive returns. Fixed annuities lock in the rate for usually a year at a time, and these rates have generally paid about two percent more than those of CDs over the last 10 years. Also, annuities generally offer a guaranteed minimum return of three to five percent. The more aggressive investor may be interested in a variable annuity, which presents a choice of several sub-accounts that invest into underlying mutual funds, providing the kind of returns you could expect on a mutual fund, but with the tax umbrella of the annuity.

Unlike qualified retirement plans, there are no maximum contribution limits, nor are there stiff IRS restrictions regarding participation requirements among

employee groups. So an annuity could be an ideal way to supplement your IRA or company retirement plan.

Annuities also allow for beneficiary designation, which, upon your passing, forwards the earnings from your account directly to the person you have named as beneficiary, thereby avoiding probate and other hassles of estate settlement.

An annuity offers tax-deferred growth while your money is growing, and offers further tax deferral of your tax liability during the period when you are drawing an income. The longer you can defer your tax payment, the longer you have the ability to earn interest on those moneys.

Annuities are flexible. Many annuities allow for limited withdrawals — up to 10 percent of your account's value — in any given year. Regarding investment options, most variable annuities allow you to switch accounts and reallocate your funds several times a year, if desired. And when you decide to withdraw, the payout options offered by annuities are plentiful and diverse. ■

Join Your Local Credit Union

Imagine what it would be like to own your own bank. Banks are

businesses and therefore must make a profit. Banks build profit margins through fees and established rates of interest on savings and loan accounts. As the owner of your own bank, you could avoid many of those fees and realize higher savings rates and lower loan rates.

Sound too good to be true? It's not, if you're a member of a credit union.

A MEMBER-OWNED BANK

A credit union is a financial institution owned by its members. Credit unions have no built-in profit margin and profits are not distributed solely to an elite group of shareholders. Instead, all revenues generated by the credit union are used to cover basic administrative expenses, and the remainder is distributed back to the members in the form of reduced fees, higher savings rates, and lower loan rates.

By definition, a credit union is a financial cooperative, a group of individuals who have banded together to create their own bank for the mutual benefit of everyone in the group.

The credit union movement in the United States began around the turn of the century, forming partnerships intent on helping the employees of various businesses or organizations save money through the convenience of payroll deduction.

The employees of these businesses decided it made more sense managing their own money by forming their own bank than it did investing money in the bank down the street. Employees who needed to borrow money could borrow from the savings pool at low interest rates. The interest paid on these loans created adequate revenues to pay interest (dividends) on the savings accounts at rates typically higher than those being paid by the banks.

Over time, many of these credit unions evolved into full-service financial institutions and offered all of the services generally available through a bank. Today, many credit unions offer checking accounts, debit cards, IRAs, ATM cards, automated bank-by-phone systems, Christmas Clubs, mortgages, and much more. Funds are federally insured through the NCUA (National Credit Union Administration), offering more security than the FDIC. Perhaps the most noticeable difference between banks and credit unions today is found in the fees and rates. Without a doubt, it's much more cost effective to bank at a credit union.

NOT EVERYONE CAN JOIN

Credit union membership is governed by certain eligibility requirements. To join a credit union, you must be employed by or related to an employee of a company that has either formed their own credit union or has become a charter member of another company's credit union.

If you're not currently a member of a credit union, there are two ways you can join. The first way is to inquire among various family members as to whether or not they are members — or are eligible for membership — in a credit union. Most credit unions grant membership to the immediate family of existing members, such as a spouse, child, parent, grandchild, or grandparent. If someone in your family is already a member, that family member would likely be able to sponsor you for membership as well.

The second way you could join a credit union is to secure eligibility through your employer. Talk to the owner of your company or the individual in charge of employee benefits, and ask if credit union membership is provided for their employees. Most employers are open to this idea because it enables them to provide an additional benefit to the employees at virtually no direct cost to the company.

If management resists, offer to do the necessary legwork yourself. This process is not difficult. The Yellow Pages of your phone book will provide a listing of local credit unions. By making a phone call to each one, you'll find someone who's willing and eager to provide you with an abundance of information and the assistance necessary to implement the credit union at your place of business.

Keep in mind that not all credit unions are created equal, so you may want to shop around. Compare the services offered, the current rates and fees, and the location of branch offices. As a rule, larger and more established credit unions offer a greater array of services on a more consistent basis.

Perhaps the greatest benefit is knowing, as a member of a credit union, you are one of the owners! ■

Home-owners Insur-ance: What You Really Need

Homeowners insurance is required by mortgage lenders. Often, however, people don't know how adequate their coverage is — or isn't — until disaster strikes. Now would be a good time to determine whether your policy provides coverage that is too little, too much, or just right.

WHAT IS HOMEOWNERS INSURANCE?

Homeowners insurance provides coverage for the structure of the house, the contents of the house, and legal liability in case you or your family damage someone else's property or injure someone at any location.

Before purchasing a policy, you need to find out the replacement value of your house. This is different from its market value. Replacement value is what it would cost to rebuild your house; market value is its selling price. Also, it's a smart idea to do an inventory of everything in your house, and keep this information somewhere other than in your home, such as in a safe deposit box. It's much easier to get reimbursed for a claim when you have documentation, such as receipts, canceled checks, or a videotape to prove ownership.

You should insure your house for at least 80 percent of the total replacement cost, although many experts now recommend coverage at 100 percent. The small increase in the premium may be worth it if you need to rebuild.

GUARANTEED REPLACEMENT COST

Guaranteed replacement cost in a policy will add approximately 10 percent to your premium, but insurance will pay to rebuild your house at today's prices. There may be a cap on the total amount or other conditions with guaranteed replacement. Also, you may want to keep an eye on the amount the annual premium increases.

The contents of your home — your belongings — are generally covered by your homeowners policy for up to 50 percent of the coverage on your house. If the structure of your house is insured for $100,000, your belongings are insured for $50,000.

Guaranteed replacement value for your belongings will add 10 to 15 percent to your premiums. However, this feature may be well worth the money if, for example, your 1985 television set is stolen.

Standard coverage probably won't adequately cover items such as jewelry, silverware, artwork, antiques, or other valuables. Look into additional coverage for these possessions; ask about the differences between a floater and an endorsement for these items, to see which will better fit your needs.

Consider umbrella coverage if your property or investments are worth more than the liability limits of your homeowners policy. Umbrella coverage provides extra liability, and also covers libel, slander, defamation of character, and invasion of privacy.

WHERE YOU CAN FIND SAVINGS

Lowering the deductible is a quick and easy way to lower your insurance payments. The standard deductible is $250. If you raise it to $500, your premium should decrease five to 10 percent. At $1,000, your premium should be about 15 percent lower. Decide on an affordable deductible, keeping in mind the way it affects your payments.

There are other ways to lower your insurance costs. Many companies will slice up to 15 percent off your premium if you have another policy, such as auto insurance, with them. Some companies offer discounts for smoke detectors, burglar alarms, deadbolt locks, or proximity to a fire hydrant. Others offer discounts for non-smokers, for people who are at least 55 years old and retired, or for long-term policyholders. Ask your agent and get quotes in writing.

Homeowners insurance is an important element in your overall financial picture. You want to make sure that your coverage is adequate, both for your house and your belongings. ■

Don't Get Caught in the Money P.I.T.!

Let's assume you're on your way toward eliminating your debts, and soon you'll need to start thinking about saving and investing some money for your future. Before you take action, you need to beware of the Money P.I.T.!

The Money P.I.T. is characterized by the three greatest hurdles you will face when saving money for your future: procrastination, inflation, and taxes.

PROCRASTINATION
Perhaps the greatest hurdle you'll face regarding saving and investing money is getting started. There are a million reasons why you can't do it today, but as long as you tell yourself that you will get started someday — maybe tomorrow, next week, or next month — you'll take comfort in thinking that you've addressed the need.

But tomorrow never comes. If now seems like a difficult time to get started, it only gets harder if you wait.

Saving money begins with paying off your debts, and if you haven't started on your debt-elimination plan yet, start TODAY.

If you were planning a trip from New York City to Los Angeles, would you wait until all the traffic lights were green to leave? Of course not. So don't wait for the perfect time to start your financial engine on your journey to debt freedom and prosperity. Starting NOW will allow you to overcome perhaps your greatest stumbling block to success — procrastination!

INFLATION
You've overcome the first hurdle. You're paying off your debts and you want to begin looking for a good place to invest your money. In order to win the money game, one major battle you must win is the rate-of-return battle.

It's easy to believe getting a good return is optional rather than necessary. If you understand that one of your greatest opponents in the money game, inflation, could rob you of a significant amount of your investment return, then you'll realize you MUST find an investment with a higher return rate and a reasonable amount of safety.

Over the last 70 years, inflation has averaged 3.1 percent. While at times it has been as high as 24.8 percent (1980), it has hovered around four to six percent in the last 10 years. In order to maintain your dollar's buying power, your investment must grow at least at the rate of inflation. Your only real gain in terms of buying power is what you earn over and above the rate of inflation.

For example, if you earn five percent on a bank certificate of deposit, and inflation rose four percent, you actually gained only one percent in terms of buying power. If you earn 2.5 percent on a bank savings account with the same four percent rate of inflation, you've lost 1.5 percent. So you can see why it's so important to invest your money where you have the best opportunity to outpace inflation.

And where might that be? The only investments which have significantly outperformed inflation over the last 70 years are stocks and stock mutual funds. In fact, if you were to combine the rates of return on ALL mutual funds since 1924, they would average just a little better than 12 percent. Banks, on the other hand, have averaged about 3.7 percent over that same 70-year period.

TAXES
In reference to taxes, there are only three ways money grows — taxed, tax-deferred, or tax-free. Let's look at an example of each, using a mutual fund for illustration.

Let's say your $10,000 mutual fund earned 10 percent, or $1,000. Assuming you pay federal tax of 28 percent, and state tax of 7 percent, this would total 35 percent in taxes. You made $1,000, but you have to pay $350 in taxes. You really gained $650. This is a net return of 6.5 percent. Subtract four percent for inflation, and you've netted only 2.5 percent. Taxes can eat you alive!

TAX-DEFERRED is a much better option. An IRA, a 401(k), or a SEP (what the IRS calls a qualified plan) grows tax-deferred. You could also use a non-qualified variable annuity. What you're doing is choosing a good mutual fund and putting a tax-deferred umbrella over it, like an IRA or annuity.

The benefit is that you don't pay the $350 a year in taxes to Uncle

Sam. It stays in your mutual fund and grows tax-deferred. However, there are a few negatives.

The instant you take your money out of a tax-deferred account, you're taxed. You're not eliminating the taxes; you're just deferring, or postponing them until the time of withdrawal. You still come out ahead, however, because you can still earn interest and dividends on the money that would have otherwise been paid in taxes. It's like an interest-free loan from the IRS, in which you invest the tax money, pay it back later, and keep the interest you earned!

Another negative — generally you cannot withdraw your money until you're 59-1/2 years old without paying a hefty 10 percent penalty. So you should earmark for tax-deferred savings only the money you can afford to live without until you reach age 59-1/2 or older.

TAX-FREE would work like this: Your money grows tax-deferred. But you can also take it out tax-free. (And you don't have to wait until age 59-1/2.)

One way you can invest money tax-free is through municipal bonds, which are a form of tax-

exempt bond. The good news is they grow tax-free. The bad news? The interest rate is generally quite low — about four to six percent. So you win the tax battle, but you may lose the battle with inflation.

One of the best ways, therefore, to avoid the tax hurdle, is to invest in a good mutual fund using a tax-deferred umbrella (for example, an IRA or a variable annuity). But be careful to do so only with money you will not need to access prior to age 59-1/2.

If you keep these rules in mind, you will be much less likely to fall into the Money P.I.T.! ■

Shopping for Term Life Insurance

When dealing with clients interested in life insurance, I'm often confronted by those who are shopping for the best price. As responsible consumers, it's wise to shop around. As with any other purchase, you want to make sure you're getting the best bang for your buck. However, the process of shopping for term life insurance is often an overwhelming and confusing task, even for the insurance agent, and one in which cost isn't the sole consideration.

Here are some guidelines to make sure you get the life insurance plan that's best for you.

WHAT'S TERM LIFE?
It's important to first understand term life insurance and how it works. Term insurance is what I like to call plain vanilla insurance. There's no cash value and no equity to withdraw or borrow. It's just insurance protection. You pay the premium, and if you die during the term, your family collects the insurance.

There are three basic elements in a term life insurance policy which are factored to determine the total cost. All three elements are combined, and the cost of the policy (premium) and the death benefit (insurance amount) results. These three elements are: 1) mortality costs 2) administrative costs, and 3) marketing costs.

MORTALITY COSTS
Mortality cost is the amount the insurance company must charge to cover their risk. In other words, it's the amount of money they must collect from you in order to have enough money to pay out

when someone dies.

Determining the mortality cost is actually a precise science of statistics handled by mathematical experts called actuaries. Their job is to determine the exact cost of the risk the company takes when they provide you with insurance.

Sound complicated? Let me try to simplify. Let's assume that you're a 30-year-old female and you want $100,000 of life insurance. To determine your mortality cost, the actuaries must determine the odds of you dying during the coming year. Let's assume that, according to statistics, one 30-year-old female out of 1,000 dies every year. If the insurance company is on the hook for $100,000, they must collect enough money from those 1,000 policyholders to generate that $100,000 of insurance money. If you divide $100,000 by 1,000 policyholders, the mortality cost comes to $100 per person. In other words, assuming those statistics, it would cost $100 for a 30-year-old female to purchase $100,000 of life insurance for one year.

ADMINISTRATIVE COSTS

Another cost that must be considered when providing insurance is the administrative costs of doing business. There's the cost of buildings, utilities, office furniture, postage, supplies, employees, etc.

Like any other business, an insurance company must include in the cost of their product or service the amount necessary to operate the business. So if the company's annual operating budget is $2.5 million, and there are 100,000 policyholders, an additional cost of $25 per policyholder per year would be needed to cover overhead.

MARKETING COSTS

A third cost the company must cover is marketing. This is the cost required to get the product into the hands of the buying public, or the cost of finding customers.

What is the source of these costs? The salaries and commissions paid to the insurance agents, company advertising, or both.

The job of an insurance agent is not typically one of prestige. Some of us would rather watch three hours of Merv Griffin reruns than invite an insurance agent over to the house.

But salespeople are necessary. No business could survive without someone doing the selling.

THERE'S ONLY 100 CENTS IN A DOLLAR

When these costs are taken into consideration — mortality cost, administrative cost, and marketing cost — it becomes evident that the total cost for any company to provide insurance is going to be roughly the same as it would be for another company.

The mortality cost doesn't vary among companies. Your chances of dying are the same regardless of the insurance company you choose. The per-person administrative costs are going to be roughly the same. A large company may require a larger operating budget to service their clients, but they have more clients to spread out the costs.

So when Company A says that they can offer you $100,000 of annual renewable term life insurance for $17 a month, and Company B offers it to you for $12, what is the logical conclusion? Company A must have something Company B doesn't. Otherwise Company B would take all the business.

The expression, "You get what you pay for," often holds true with insurance. There's no such thing as a free lunch. If Company B's insurance is drastically cheaper, it's probably not an apples to apples comparison.

Company B may not have a guarantee to renew the insurance past a certain age. They may not have a decent renewal rate, or they may have stringent qualifications (such as a physical exam) to renew the policy each year. Whatever it is, the difference in price usually means a difference in value.

Here are a few guidelines for making your decision: 1) Decide how much insurance you need. 2) Decide how much you can afford to pay. 3) Decide what features are important to you and your family in a life insurance policy. 4) Decide how long you plan to keep the insurance.

With these points in mind, my final word of advice is to find an experienced and trustworthy agent who will do the shopping for you. Work with that agent to find a plan with the right company. Then you'll be able to sleep at night knowing you have the best plan your money can buy. ■

Buying and Maintaining Your Automobile:

The Green Machine

During the 1980s, you may have noticed new cars had an additional warning light called the CHECK ENGINE light. The engine computer could actually monitor several emission control systems and turn the CHECK ENGINE light on if it detected a problem.

Since 1996, a more stringent version of emission controls, called On-Board-Diagnostic II (OBD-2), is required on all new cars.

EMISSION MISSION

The goal of the emission program is building and maintaining cars with better gas mileage while at the same time reducing harmful pollution. In order to achieve these goals, cars are produced with an increasingly complex and expensive technology. Each step towards simplification seems to take us further down a complex road. There are, however, several things you can do to make your car less polluting.

CHECK THE TIRES

Under-inflated tires create more rolling resistance and cause your car to use more gasoline. They will also cause faster tire wear and maybe even a blowout at highway speeds. Purchase an accurate tire gauge and check the pressure at least once a month when the tires are cold. Add more air, if necessary, but never over-inflate the tires.

GET AN ANNUAL TUNE-UP

New spark plugs, air and fuel filters, and PCV valves are inexpensive items and easy to install on most cars. A fouled spark plug can reduce the fuel efficiency as much as 30 percent on many of today's cars. Many newer cars do not have a distributor, but if your car has one, replace the distributor cap and rotor. Check the spark plug wires and replace them if they are several years old or are damaged.

DO-IT-YOURSELFERS

If you do some of your own auto maintenance, dispose of used parts and fluid correctly and safely. Used oil and coolant/antifreeze can be recycled. Old tires and batteries can also be recycled. Each year more than 10 times the amount of oil spilled by the Exxon Valdez is dumped into the environment by do-it-yourselfers. Call your local recycling center for a location near you and help prevent this environmental disaster.

SLOW DOWN

Fuel mileage decreases sharply when you drive over 55 mph. Of course, I am NOT suggesting that you drive 45 mph when the speed limit is 65, but driving a little slower could save gas, save money, and reduce pollution. Ask your insurance agent what will happen to your auto insurance rate if you get a few speeding tickets. The answer you receive should be an additional incentive to slow down. Driving is not a race. In fact, fast drivers usually lose.

DRIVE STEADY

Avoid jackrabbit starts and jerky stop-and-go situations when possible. Use cruise control on open highways, where it can maintain your car at a steady speed. Try to schedule your driving trips when traffic is light. Avoid excessive errands with careful planning. If possible, join a car pool with neighbors or coworkers to save both time and fuel.

LOSE WEIGHT

Remove any unnecessary heavy items from your car. An additional 100 pounds of weight in your car can reduce the fuel mileage by one mile per gallon. Avoid the use of car top carriers, which can increase wind resistance and decrease fuel economy. If you do use a car top carrier, be sure it is properly and safely fastened to the car.

A GREEN MACHINE?

Any car on the road today can endanger lives, cost too much money, and cause pollution. How you drive and maintain your car will, in many ways, determine the safety of your car. A well-maintained car can last up to 50 percent longer and will preserve its original value longer.

Drive safely and drive a green machine. ■

How to Buy A Good Used Car

Perhaps your next new car should be a used car. With new car prices soaring and many quality used cars on the market, you should definitely consider the possibility of owning a used car. Buying a car is a big decision and making a poor choice can be very costly. The following tips just might save you a bundle of money down the road.

FIRST THINGS FIRST
Take your time and do some research. Consider your budget and driving requirements in order to find the best car for you. A two year-old car with 20,000 miles will usually be the best buy. You might want to consider buying at an auction; however, this is not recommended for novices. Good negotiating skills will come in handy regardless of where you buy, so be prepared.

INSPECTING THE CAR
Once you find a car you like, get it inspected by professional technicians and have a report written on both the current condition and upcoming maintenance needs of the car. You'll need to pay for such an inspection, but it's your best protection against buying a "lemon." Also, before you take the car for a professional inspection, perform your own routine inspection.

INSIDE THE CAR
Check the inside of the car for comfort and operation. Sit in every seat and look for unusual signs of wear. Check every button and switch on the dashboard to be sure they operate properly. Look under the seats and floor mats for signs of rust.

Start the engine and take a test drive while you check for unusual noises or vibrations. If possible, take a test drive in both daylight and nighttime conditions. Pay close attention to how smoothly the car idles, shifts gears, and stops. NOTE: Turn the radio off so you can listen for unusual noises while you drive.

OUTSIDE THE CAR
Check the outside of the car for signs of damage from major collisions, not normal scratches or dings. Look underneath the car for signs of rust or unusual damage. Check the doors, hood, and trunk for proper alignment. Carefully inspect each tire (including the spare) for signs of wear or damage.

Beware of a car with new tires; this could be hiding an alignment problem. Bounce the car at each corner to check the suspension system. Make sure the car sits level and does not lean or sag. Look inside the exhaust pipe for black powder, which could indicate poor engine operation. Check for dark smoke or steam when the engine is running.

UNDER THE HOOD
Look for leaks from the engine. Check the different fluids under the hood for both quantity and condition. Radiator fluid should be light green, not brown. It should not have any oil floating underneath the radiator cap.

Brake fluid should be light brown, not dark or milky. Automatic transmission fluid should be light pink with a sweet smell. If it is dark and smells like burnt coffee, you can expect transmission trouble soon. The engine oil may be black, but it should not be thick or smell like gasoline. Check the engine belt(s) and hoses for signs of age or damage.

SPECIAL ALERTS
Although some owners will pay to have a car professionally cleaned (or detailed) to improve the appearance, this might be a warning sign. A real clean engine could indicate the engine has been replaced recently. Check the odometer (or dashboard) for signs of tampering. Be wary of an old car with low mileage. Also, watch out for a car that may have experienced flood damage or other extensive repairs. Some really nice looking used cars have actually been "rebuilt" after being declared a total loss by insurance companies. You would not want one of these cars.

THE PROFESSIONAL INSPECTION
If the car passes your inspection, it is still a good idea to have a professional do a complete inspection and give you a written report. Doing your own inspection first will save you money by eliminating those cars that might look great at first glance, but, upon closer examination, are potential problems. ∎

Cold Weather Driving Tips

Driving in cold weather, especially at night, requires some extra precautions. You want to be sure that your car is in good shape and you are prepared for unexpected situations. The following cold weather driving tips just might come in handy during the winter season.

RADIATOR FLUID

You are aware radiator fluid keeps the engine from overheating in the summer heat, but did you know it also keeps the engine from freezing in cold weather? Radiator fluid is a mixture of plain water and antifreeze (coolant). The proper mixture for most cars is 50:50 or equal parts of water and coolant. You should check both the concentration of the radiator fluid and also the amount of fluid in the overflow reservoir when the engine is cold. Never open the radiator cap on a hot engine; beneath it lurks steam under great pressure that could shoot out from the radiator and burn you.

BATTERY

The battery has a very hard time in cold weather. First off, the battery loses power in cold weather. A fully charged battery has only about 50 percent of normal power at freezing temperatures. Secondly, the engine requires additional power to start because engine oil is thicker and gasoline

less able to mix with air when it's cold. These two factors contribute to the death of many car batteries each winter season. Make sure the battery terminals are clean (no corrosion) and tight. If the battery is three or four years old, have it tested and replace it, if necessary. If the battery is five years old, it is time to get a new battery.

WINDOWS

You can't drive very safely if you can't see out the windows. Clean all the windows inside and out. This will help reduce fogging on the inside of the windows. Running the air conditioner and defroster together will help remove fog from the windshield. The AC removes moisture from the air. Check the windshield wipers and replace them, if necessary. Many wipers come with several adapters for different cars, so read the directions carefully or ask the auto parts technician for help. Finally, check the window washer fluid. Plain water can freeze in the reservoir and cause damage to the pump. Purchase some premixed washer fluid at an auto parts store and fill the reservoir as needed.

TIRES

Cold weather will cause tire pressure to drop. Using an accurate gauge, check tire pressure when the tires are cold (before driving more than five miles). The correct tire pressure can be found in the owner's manual or on the side of the tire. Do not over-inflate the tires, and remember to check the pressure in the spare tire, too. Many compact spare tires need a much higher pressure than the regular tires. Driving on over-inflated or under-inflated tires can be dangerous and cause rapid tire wear.

FUEL

Cold weather also causes some unique fuel problems. Fuel contaminated with water can cause the fuel system to freeze, which in turn can cause the engine to stop or run poorly. If the fuel tank is almost empty, water can condense from the air inside the tank and run down into the fuel. To prevent this from happening, keep the tank over one-half full during the cold weather. Additives are available to remove water from the fuel, but these additives can damage rubber and plastic parts of the fuel system. Don't use fuel additives too often or in stronger-than-recommended concentrations. If you drive an older car that has a carburetor on the engine (not fuel injected), ice can form inside the carburetor and cause engine problems when the air is damp and temperatures are around freezing. The carburetor should have some type of heating device to prevent icing in cold weather.

CLEAN CAR

You probably can think of many things you would rather do than wash your car in cold weather, but a trip to the car wash is a necessary and beneficial act. Salt that has been dumped on the highways can get splashed up onto your car and cause serious damage to the paint and metal parts. A quick jaunt to the car wash once a week might help prevent damage down the road. If you remembered to polish your car in the fall with a good coat of wax, the paint should survive the cold winter. You might want to check the floor mats in your car and replace them if the old ones are about worn out. Good floor mats will help protect the carpet from snow and ice. ∎

Getting Started

Many years ago, people struggled with a crank handle inserted into the front of the car to start the engine. Today, you simply turn the ignition key to bring the engine to life. If the engine doesn't start, you may need a jump start or other repairs to get the engine going again.

THE BATTERY

The large, 12-volt battery underneath the hood of your car supplies the power needed to get the engine started. Most new batteries are maintenance free, which means they do not need more water added under normal conditions. If the battery has removable caps, you should check the water level and add more distilled water as needed. Most batteries will last three to five years. Replace the battery before it dies and leaves you stranded. When replacing a battery, make sure it has the same amperage, or more Cold Cranking Amps (CCA).

CONNECTIONS

The battery has two large cable connections: a positive (+) and a negative or ground (-). These cables must be attached tightly to the battery to ensure a good electrical transfer between the engine and the battery. Install anti-corrosion washers on the battery terminals to prevent corrosion. If corrosion has already occurred, clean the terminals and cables before installing the washers. Also, check the other ends of the battery cables to be sure they are securely fastened and clean. The positive cable is attached to the starter; the negative cable is attached to the engine or frame of the car to provide a ground.

THE STARTER

The starter is a strong, 12-volt electric motor. When you turn the ignition key to the start position, the starter turns parts inside the engine so the fuel-air mixture will start burning. Release the ignition key as soon as the engine starts and never turn the ignition key to start if the engine is already running. If the engine does not start after 10 seconds, wait several minutes before trying again. If the engine does not start after three tries, stop and look for another problem. Continued cranking could damage the battery and the starter.

THE ALTERNATOR

Once the engine is started, the alternator produces the electrical power needed to recharge the battery and operate the engine and accessories. Older cars use a generator that's not very efficient at slow engine speeds. Today's cars need much more electrical power to run the more powerful sound systems and lights, so our modern cars use alternators instead of generators. The absolute worst thing you can do to an alternator is disconnect the battery cable while the engine is running. If you do this, the alternator is immediately damaged (another good reason to check the security of the battery cables).

VOLTAGE REGULATOR

On some older cars, the voltage regulator was a small metal box outside the alternator. On most newer cars, the voltage regulator is inside the alternator. If the voltage regulator goes bad, you may notice the lights becoming very bright at high engine speeds or dim when the engine idles. You might also notice a buzzing noise on the radio if the engine is running.

The alternator should last at least six years or 100,000 miles, but it depends on the quality of the product. If you buy a replacement alternator, insist on a reputable product and warranty. There are many cheap alternators on the market that will not last very long and are a waste of money.

A GOOD BELT

The alternator is turned by the engine belt. Some cars may have several belts; most new cars have a single, long belt. This belt must be tight enough to turn the alternator without slipping, but not so tight as to damage the alternator. The engine belt should last about four years or 60,000 miles. It's wise to change the belt before it breaks and leaves you stranded or damages other parts of the engine.

START WITH CONFIDENCE

Thank goodness you no longer have to start your car by turning a manual crank. Not only was this hard work, but it was potentially dangerous. Today, starting your car is as easy as turning the key provided you've maintained your cars electrical system properly. ■

Ready, Set, Stop

Good brakes are not a luxury you can do without.

EASY TEST

You can easily test your car's brakes by pressing the pedal three times and holding it down. It should feel firm, not soft or spongy. The pedal should not sink slowly to the floor. Continue pressing the pedal while you slide your left foot underneath the pedal. If you cannot get your left foot under the pedal, it may be too close to the floor and in need of adjustment.

While you drive, watch out for important warning signs of brake problems and get a brake inspection immediately if any of these signs appear.

WARNING SIGNS

There are several important warning signs indicating a brake problem. A low sinking brake pedal can indicate either a leak in the brake system or a low amount of brake fluid. A soft pedal usually indicates air in the brake system. A pulsating pedal can be caused by a warped or damaged brake disc, which often happens when you apply the brakes very hard and often.

NOTE: If you slam on the brakes very hard, the pedal might vibrate (if you have anti-lock brakes). If your car pulls to one side during braking, it indicates some of the brakes are not operating properly. Any vibrations or unusual noises during braking are signs you should have the brakes checked.

EVERY SIX MONTHS

Have a brake inspection every six months or 6,000 miles, even if no problems appear. Many repair shops offer a free inspection, or you can ask the mechanics to inspect the brakes when they rotate and balance the tires. If you wait until there is a problem, such as noise, vibrations, or a soft pedal, the car may already be unsafe to drive, or you can seriously damage the more expensive parts of the car. Keep your car in safe operating condition with good preventative maintenance.

BRAKE PAD THICKNESS

New brake pads are 1/4 to 3/8 inch thick. Every time you press the brake pedal, some of the brake pad is worn off. The harder you press, the more material is worn off. When any part of the pad wears down to 1/16 of an inch, it is time to replace all the pads on that axle. For example, you must replace all front pads (or all rear pads) at the same time.

When replacing the pads, install new hardware clips and springs, too. And be sure to purchase the proper replacement pads for your car, because improper pads may make noise, wear out very fast, or even damage the disc or drum.

DRUMS AND ROTORS

There are two types of brakes on most cars today: Disc and Drum. The second part of a brake inspection is to check the disc or drum for damage. If these parts are warped, cracked, or otherwise damaged, they should be repaired or replaced. NOTE: Very small circular grooves are normal.

The most common repair is called turning. Turning a disc or drum is when the mechanic spins it and removes some metal to provide a very smooth and symmetrical braking surface. The key to proper turning is to carefully remove only the minimum amount of metal to achieve a smooth surface.

WATCH FOR LEAKS

Another part of the brake inspection is looking for leaks and checking the brake fluid reservoir under the hood. The fluid level may slowly drop as the brake pads wear, but any sudden drop indicates a leak in the system. Also check the flexible rubber brake hoses and calipers or cylinders at each wheel for signs of leaking brake fluid.

You can avoid leaks in the brake system and the need to replace expensive brake parts, such as a master cylinder, calipers, or wheel cylinders, by changing the brake fluid every two years. Old fluid becomes contaminated with dirt and water and causes leaks in the system.

KEEPING COSTS DOWN

Drive at a steady speed. Constantly speeding up then applying the brakes will wear down the brake pads quickly, and it wastes fuel, too. Avoid sudden stops and do not tailgate other cars. When you brake suddenly, the brake pads heat up and wear faster and can damage the disc or drum.

Set the parking brake firmly each time you park your car. A firm parking brake holds the car safely and prevents driving with a partially engaged brake. Most importantly, never drive with your foot touching the brake pedal, called "riding the brakes." This will quickly wear the pads out. ■

To Buy or to Lease?

If it appreciates, buy it. If it depreciates, lease it. This old rule of financing may have made sense for some purchases, but it does not apply to buying versus leasing a car. Of course, the Debt-FREE & Prosperous Living™ philosophy teaches us to NEVER buy a new car and, if you can at all avoid it, never finance a car purchase, regardless of the auto's age.

But, because leasing has been touted as such a great bargain — and many people are unfortunately believing this propaganda — we'll discuss how leasing works in this article. Here are the chief claims of leasing companies and their true explanations.

LOWER UP-FRONT COST

Most leases do not require a down payment. However, when you add the first month's and sometimes last month's advance payment plus the security deposit, you still have a sizable amount due when you sign a lease contract. And, because this deposit is not calculated as a down payment, it does not reduce the lease balance...UPON WHICH YOU ARE PAYING INTEREST.

LOWER MONTHLY PAYMENTS

If you lease a car, the monthly payments will be lower, sometimes much lower, than if you purchase the car. The important thing to remember, however, is that you will own NOTHING at the end of the lease. You give thousands of dollars of your money to the leasing company over the course of the lease — and you end up with NOTHING!

DRIVE MORE CAR FOR YOUR MONEY

This feature is really based on one of the greatest deceptions of the credit-based lifestyle. Credit's big attraction is that it lets you live an apparently higher lifestyle than you actually deserve at any given point in your financial growth curve. But the hidden cost of this charade is great — and it all comes out of your long-term wealth.

If you lease a car, you can APPEAR to drive more car for your money. Many leased cars, however, come equipped with high-profit, over-priced options such as power seats, CD stereo player, sunroof, security system, custom paint, and a turbocharger. You might get more car with a lease, but you're paying MORE than a reasonable price for all the extras.

NO RESALE/TRADE-IN HASSLES

This is their pitch, but there are mileage limits in the lease. In most cases, if you drive more than 15,000 miles a year, you will pay 10 cents per mile over that amount. Driving an extra 5,000 miles will cost you an additional $500. There is also a charge for any excessive wear and tear. Unfortunately, this is an extremely subjective determination. You might also be assessed charges if the car does not run properly, even if you had it serviced according to the owner's manual.

TAX ADVANTAGES

There are some tax advantages which apply to lease contracts, especially for business use, but the salesman will often exaggerate or even lie about these advantages. If you hear him or her say, lease payments are 100 percent tax deductible, don't be misled. The payments will only be deductible to the extent that you use the vehicle for business — and even then they are only fully deductible if the fair market value of the vehicle is no more than $14,000.

If you use the car 25 percent of the time for personal travel, you'll lose 25 percent of the lease payment deductibility. And if the car is worth more than $14,000, you will have to add an amount to your taxable income — based on the car's value — that will increase your taxes enough to compensate for the higher lease payment deduction. So no matter how big the payment deduction appears to be on your Schedule C, it will be effectively reduced back down to the deduction for a $14,000 car.

THE COST OF CHANGING YOUR MIND

There are, by the way, major penalties and fees for terminating a lease prematurely. If you buy a car, you can trade it or sell it any-time you wish, for maximum value. But it could cost you thousands of dollars to turn in a leased car before the lease term is fulfilled — the earlier you do it, the worse the penalties.

DRIVE SMART

Leasing sounds like a good deal, until you take a second look at the numbers and read the fine print. For most people, leasing is the dumb way to drive. You're paying too much, for an over-priced car...which you never end up owning. Just buy a good car with cash, drive it safely, maintain it properly and keep it running great for a long time. ■

Protect Your Car and Avoid Theft

If your car was stolen several years ago, chances were very good it would be recovered with only minimal damage. Today, amid the $8 billion global stolen car market, the chances have fallen to under 25 percent. In other words, only one in four stolen cars is recovered, and those that are recovered most likely have severe damage. What can you do to protect your car?

PARKING
Park your car in a safe place and always lock it. Never leave your keys in the car, even for a minute. Check your car keys to be sure that the key code has been removed. Of course, you should record this code in a secure place at home (in case you need to have extra keys made). Never park in secluded spots or dark areas. Never leave valuables in your car where a thief might see them. You should also reconsider installing expensive stereo systems in your car, or if you do, install them out of sight.

ANTI-THEFT SYSTEMS
There are two basic types of anti-theft systems: active and passive. An active system is one you must install each time you lock your car and include steering wheel locks, brake locks, wheel locks, and steering column locks. These systems are relatively cheap and easy to install, but you must remember to install them each time you park your car. Most active systems will slow down and discourage a thief, but they can be removed in minutes by a professional. Passive systems activate automatically each time you park your car. These systems usually involve electronic disabling of the starting system, fuel system, or ignition system. These systems are more expensive, but can qualify you for insurance discounts of up to 20 percent.

ACTIVE SYSTEMS
Many of the steering wheel locks, brake pedal locks, and tire locks on the market are either easily disabled or are so much trouble that most of us forget to install them. One exception is the device marketed as the Electronic Nightstick, which combines the steering wheel lock with an audible alarm. This device attaches to the top of the steering wheel and prevents the steering wheel from turning. It also incorporates audible alarms and flashing lights that activate if anyone tries to break into your car. This active device sells for about $100 and comes with a $1,000 auto theft protection guarantee.

PASSIVE SYSTEMS
There are a wide range of passive systems on the market today. Many new cars come from the factory with a passive anti-theft system. A good system will deactivate the ignition or fuel system, and utilize motion sensors, alarms, and flashing lights. The newest addition to anti-theft devices emits smoke if a thief tries to steal your car. If you buy an after market system, remember that the installation of the system is very important. Poor installation can produce false alarms and unusual problems while driving.

Tracking devices utilizing silent transmitters allow police to locate a stolen car and are probably the most effective and most expensive anti-theft systems on the market today. This service is not available in all areas of the country, but if you live in a high-crime area and drive an expensive car, it might be a good investment.

CHEAP ALARMS
A simple electronic active system is the ignition kill switch. For a few dollars you can buy a small switch and connect one terminal to the negative (-) side of the ignition coil and the other terminal to a ground (metal frame). When you turn the switch on, the engine will crank, but it won't start. You can also install a fuel system kill switch on the electronic fuel pump. Install the switch in line with the power going to the fuel pump. If the switch is off, the engine will not start.

Many of the best electronic alarms on the market utilize a small red blinking light on the dashboard to indicate the alarm is set. You can purchase a similar light and install it in your car and the thief might think your car is protected. You can even purchase warning labels and stick them on the windows even if you don't own an alarm.

BATTERY CHECK
If you have any type of electronic alarm system, check the condition of the car's battery. Dirty terminal connections and low battery charge are two primary reasons for false alarms.

Hopefully with these ideas about car protection you will avoid having your car stolen and enjoy many years of safe driving. ■

Safety, Warranties and Recalls

Most people believe they are safe drivers driving a safe car. Unfortunately, some cars on the road today are dangerous and in serious need of repairs. But what can you do when something breaks?

First, try to find out what caused the problem with your car. Why did it break? Was it the wrong part? Did the mechanic install it improperly? Are other cars having similar problems? Perhaps something was past due for replacement and simply broke. There are many reasons why a car might break down, and asking the right questions can save you money.

WARRANTIES

Every new car comes with at least four warranties: the basic warranty, a powertrain warranty, an emission control warranty and a corrosion warranty. Some of these warranties may still be in effect if you buy a car only two or three years old.

Other parts of the car, such as the battery, tires, and radio, may have additional warranties of their own. Some newer cars have a bumper-to-bumper warranty, meaning all parts of the car are covered for a limited time or mileage. However, some individual parts may have warranties which last much longer.

When you buy a car (new or used), or a part for your car (tires, battery, muffler), find out what type of warranty it has and how to activate the warranty. Often you must send in a registration card, have a qualified technician install the part, or just keep certain records. Read the fine print and ask questions. Don't wait until there is a problem, only to find out the warranty is voided because you didn't understand the rules.

Most used cars, especially those sold by the owner, may be offered as is, meaning no warranty of any kind. Your best protection in these cases is to have an independent mechanic of your choice inspect the car BEFORE YOU COMMIT.

EXTENDED WARRANTIES

In addition to the standard warranties, you may also have an option to purchase an extended warranty for up to seven years or 100,000 miles. Your best bet is to ignore extended warranties, because you usually never get back in service what you paid for them in the first place.

Some manufacturers allow independent agents to provide their extended warranty service. Unfortunately, by the time you need a repair, the independent agent could be out of business. Also, there is frequently a clause excluding normal wear and tear, which usually eliminates coverage for most of the things that are likely to go wrong. I have never purchased extended warranties for my cars.

TECHNICAL SERVICE BULLETINS

When an unusual problem is dis-covered with a car, the manufacturer may issue a technical service bulletin to their regional offices or dealerships. Most customers are not informed about these bulletins, which are often referred to as secret warranties.

Normally, the dealership will offer to make needed repairs listed in these bulletins for free, but only if you ask about it or bring the car in for repairs. When you have an unusual problem with your car, ask about any technical service bulletins which may apply to your problem.

RECALLS

In 1993, Saturn recalled every car it made before April 14 (over 380,000 cars) because of a wiring problem in the engine. Although only about 30 cars actually had problems, and no injuries were reported, Saturn spent over 3 million dollars to fix every car.

Recalls differ from regular warranties because the owners are notified and repairs are done for free, with no time limit or mileage limitations. If you are the second (or third) owner of a car, it pays to check about recalls, because only the original owner may have been notified. Certainly, if you are considering buying a used car, check about recalls and be sure any problems have been repaired before you buy the car.

REPORT SAFETY PROBLEMS

If you have a safety problem with your car, check with the dealer to find out what steps are being taken to correct the problem. You want your car fixed, of course, but you can help make the highways safer by making other car owners aware of possible problems. ■

The Three-Legged Stool

Owning an economical and reliable car is like sitting on a stool with three legs. If all three legs are in good shape, you can sit comfortably. If one or more of the legs is broken, you can fall down and get hurt. Some people tend to concentrate on one or two legs of their car stool while neglecting the third leg. Recognizing each of the three legs as equally important can save you time and money.

LEG 1: A GOOD CAR
The type of car you own is the primary leg. While there is no perfect car, some cars require less maintenance and repairs than others. When you shop for a car, remember to check maintenance reports from *Consumer Reports* on similar models. When possible, choose a car with fewer expensive options, such as four-wheel drive, electric windows, sunroof, and automatic seats. Of course, these options are fancy and may impress your friends, but when they break, they can be extremely expensive to repair.

AVOID NEW DESIGNS.
Advertisements try to convince us the new products are just great and wonderful. Unfortunately, in the auto industry these new advancements are often followed by new problems and recalls. Even if the repair is covered under warranty, having your car in the repair shop is not a pleasant experience. Proven designs, especially in major systems such as engine, transmission, air-conditioning, and brakes, will prove more reliable and save you money in the long run.

LEG 2: GOOD DRIVING HABITS
Good, safe driving habits will extend the life of your car. Chances are you have at least one bad or dangerous driving habit that could potentially damage your car, such as driving too fast, excessive lane changing, following too close, or daydreaming while driving.

Over the years you can develop these bad habits and then convince yourself that other drivers are the real problem. Think about this: you have little or no control over other drivers, road conditions, or the weather, but you have almost total control over your own actions while driving. Which should you try to change? Changing bad habits takes hard work. Unfortunately, it's much easier to complain about other drivers, road conditions, or the weather.

Organize driver education classes. Why not sponsor a safe-driving class for your community or church group? This would be particularly appropriate for young, inexperienced drivers or drivers over age 70 — the two groups of drivers at the highest risk of being involved in an accident. Contact the National Safety Council or local driver education instructor and request a class. Learning about the dangers on the highways may not be much fun, but it could save a life and protect your car.

LEG 3: PREVENTATIVE MAINTENANCE
Preventative maintenance helps keep your car running reliably. The key to maintenance is spending enough money on the right items to prevent unwanted breakdowns. The best guide is the owner's manual. However, you should adjust the time/mileage recommendations to account for your driving conditions. Maintenance usually requires some small part (filters, for instance) or fluid to be replaced. Avoid paying for too many checks, which are either not performed or are so easy you could do them yourself.

Before you buy a used car, have your mechanic inspect it and get a written report of both the current condition and any upcoming maintenance needs. Most mechanics will usually remind you of needed maintenance items when you have your car serviced. The goal of maintenance is to keep the car reliable and reduce cost by replacing a few items to avoid damaging the more expensive items or systems.

Remember the three-legged stool of car ownership and you should have a long and happy relationship with your car. ■

Are Your Tires Tired?

Are your tires under-inflated, out-of-balance, or worn around the edges? If so, you could be driving dangerously. The following maintenance tips can help your tires last longer and save you money.

CHECK TIRE PRESSURE — EACH WEEK

Proper inflation of each tire is very important. Underinflated tires can overheat and blowout. They are also more prone to hydroplane or loose traction on wet roads. The recommended maximum tire pressure is printed on each tire. Inflate to that pressure, but do not over-inflate. Tires heat up as the car is driven, so you must check the tire pressure when the tires are cold, or before driving very far. Buy a quality air pressure gauge and keep it in your car.

Have you ever heard of changing the air in the tires? Some people believe it makes the tires last longer. This is not true, but it would insure the pressure is being checked and maintained at the proper range. You do not have to change the air, but you should check the pressure in each tire, including the spare tire.

ROTATE TIRES — EVERY SIX MONTHS

One of my students asked, *"Don't all the tires rotate?"* Of course they do, but rotate means moving the front tires to the back and the back tires to the front. This allows the tires to wear evenly and extends their life. If you do not rotate the tires, they can develop flat spots or wear out quickly. Many repair shops offer free tire rotation. When you rotate the tires, check the brakes, too.

BALANCING — ONCE A YEAR

Tires must be balanced so they spin smoothly and don't vibrate, especially at speeds over 50 MPH. Older methods of balancing tires left much to be desired, but, new computer-controlled balancing equipment does a wonderful job. Mud or tar should be removed from the tire or rim before it is balanced. Small lead weights are attached to the wheel rim to balance each tire. As the tire tread wears down, the size and position of these weights may need to be changed to maintain a balanced condition.

Some tires come with free balance and rotation every 5,000 miles. This is highly recommended and should not be overlooked. If you have to pay for balancing each tire, then once a year or 12,000 miles is a good investment.

WHEEL ALIGNMENT — EVERY TWO YEARS

Alignment refers to the actual position of each tire. Some cars need all four wheels aligned, other cars need only a front wheel alignment. The front wheels are harder to align because they move up/down and also side to side (while steering). Wheel alignment involves precise measurements of angles such as toe-in, caster, and camber. A good wheel alignment requires precision equipment and a patient technician.

Some auto shops offer lifetime wheel alignments every six months for about twice the normal charge. This is a good investment if you have a newer car and plan to keep it a long time. If you already have over 100,000 miles on your car, think twice. Alignment may also be needed when replacing the struts, after an accident, or when you hit the curb too hard.

TREAD WEAR INDICATORS

How can you tell if your car needs new tires? Check the tire tread. When the tread wears down to about 1/16 inch deep, a bar will appear across the tread. If you do not know where to look, ask a tire salesperson to show you. You can also use a penny to measure the tire tread depth. Place the penny into the tread. If you see the top of Lincoln's head, it is time for new tires.

Always buy tires in pairs for the same axle. In fact, it is best to buy four new tires at the same time. Using different size tires or one new tire with one old tire on the same axle can damage the transmission. (This is why the owner's manual warns you not to drive over 45 MPH or more than 50 miles with the little compact spare tire installed.)

100,000 MILE TIRES

Tires are expensive, so you want them to last a long time. If you take care of them, they can last a very long time, possibly over 100,000 miles. If you abuse them, they might need replacing after only 20,000 miles. New tires can make your car ride smoother and handle much better. Good care of your tires (and your car) will help keep your car running great and give you more miles of safe and happy driving fun. ■

Buying, Maintaining, and Selling Your Home:

When Your House Won't Sell

When your home has been for sale for months and hasn't sold, it's time to re-evaluate the situation.

Step 1. Have any houses sold? During the time you've had your home for sale, how many homes in your general area have sold? Are they similar in price, condition, and amenities? If nothing has sold, there may be very little you can do to make the market for your home any better.

Step 2. Check the competition. With how many homes are you competing? If there are 50 homes for sale in your area and price range, research the number of similar homes sold last year. You can probably expect a similar number of homes to sell this year. This means if 10 sold last year and 50 are on the market now, you have one chance in five of selling, because only 20 percent of the homes can be absorbed by the available buyers.

Step 3. Make your home one of the five that sell. How can you make sure you're in the 20 percent? Your home must be the best priced, the best-marketed, be in the best condition, and offer the best terms among your

competition.

A. Take an objective look at your home and the others available in your market. A Realtor is of great benefit because he or she can actually look at your competition and make the comparisons for you.

B. Get a fee appraisal done on your home. For $200 to $300 you can hire a member of the Appraisal Institute to do a market appraisal of your home. This differs from a Realtors opinion in two ways.
1. The appraiser is licensed to do appraisals, which qualifies him or her to appraise homes for Federally Insured Lenders. Most Realtors are not.
2. The appraiser is doing work for a fee, not for the opportunity to list your home for sale, so he or she won't be tempted to just give you a price you want to hear. He or she will give you an accurate price based on good market data. If your home is in an area where FHA- and VA-insured financing is common, have it done to government standards so it will be ready for your prospective buyer's lender. You'll save the time usually needed to perform the appraisal, and since the buyer normally pays for the appraisal, you'll be able to offer this pre-paid incentive to prospects looking at your home.

C. Offer incentives
1. Pay some of the buyer's expenses (the appraisal, for instance). Most buyers are struggling to gather a down payment, and covering some of their costs can give you an edge.
2. Offer a home protection war-

ranty. This covers the buyer for a year on most of the mechanical systems in the home (there is a modest deductible).
3. Offer to buy or leave appliances that are not usually included with the sale.

D. Make improvements to the home.
1. Paint areas in need.
2. Replace worn out or outdated carpeting or flooring.
3. Buy larger light fixtures to improve brightness.

E. Make the place sparkle.
1. Wash windows.
2. Polish floors.
3. Clean, clean, clean. Pay particular attention to the kitchen and bathrooms.
4. Outside: Trim it, edge it, cut it, plant it, fertilize it, and water it.

BEING MORE FLEXIBLE PAYS
To be the first home sold, you have to be the best value. Value is in the eye of the beholder and is based on how your house looks compared to the other choices available to the buyer. In a tough market you have to be prepared to be in better condition, more flexible, and more accommodating.

This may mean giving better terms than your competition, such as offering to carry a second mortgage. If things are tough, lenders are more conservative with higher loans-to-value ratios. You can make up the difference by helping with the financing, in effect allowing the buyer to purchase your home. ■

When You Have to Rent

Renting a house or an apartment instead of buying may be necessary for a number of reasons:

• You're saving for a down-payment.
• You're waiting for an increase in income to qualify for a bigger house.
• You're considering a job opportunity in another location.
• You know you will be relocating in two years or less.
• You want to study the area to determine whether or not to buy.

Regardless of your reasons, you'll want to choose your rental residence with the same care and criteria you would implement if you were purchasing a house.

TIPS FOR RENTING SUCCESSFULLY
How much can you pay? This depends on your income and what's included in the rent. A good rule of thumb is 30 percent of your gross monthly income for rent. A $2,000 per month income would support about $600 a month for rent. What's included in the rent can affect this amount. For example, many rentals include heat, electricity, or even everything but your phone.

Who pays for...
    Heat
    Hot water
    Air conditioning
    Cooking energy
    Water/sewage

    Rubbish removal
    Electricity
    Cable TV
    Lawn maintenance
    Landscaping
    Repairs and maintenance
      (outside and in)
    Repairs to heating/cooling
      /appliances
    Snow removal

If you're planning to rent a single-family house, you will most likely be asked to pay for all of the above IN ADDITION to your rent. However, with apartments and condos, some or even all could be included in the rent.

OTHER CONSIDERATIONS
Moving into any living quarters presents other single or periodic costs, and each rental comes with its privileges and restrictions. Some of these include...
    Draperies or blinds
    Washer and dryer (if not
      included, how much do the
      coin-operated machines
      cost?)
    Dishwasher
    Microwave
    Assigned parking
    Garage or car port
    Security
    Pools, health club, exercise
      equipment, tennis courts
    Planned activities

Some of these points will be unimportant to you, but use the list to help you consider all the factors influencing the quality of life in your new residence.

THE LEASE
The lease will outline the responsibilities of both the tenant (lessee) and the landlord (lessor). It should cover every eventuality and should answer such questions as how long is the lease, how much is the rent, and what happens if you get transferred or you're late with your rent?
    What if you want to sublet?
    Who else (how many) can
     live in the apartment?
    How long can visitors stay?
    Can you have pets?
    How much is the security
     deposit and what is it used
     for?
    Do you get it all back?
    Can you paint or wallpaper?
    What if my neighbor does
     something that makes my
     apartment unlivable?
    Is my furniture and personal
     property covered under the
     building's insurance?
    How much notice do I have
     to give before renewal or
     lease termination?

Get anything you feel has been promised to you verbally in the lease. Everything must be in the lease or attached to it — otherwise you are asking for later misunderstandings and conflict. Make sure you understand every word of the lease you're signing. If you don't understand it, go to an attorney and have the questionable areas explained to you. The few dollars you'll be charged for this service will be far less than what they would charge to represent you for settling it in court later.

YOU'RE STILL AFTER A HOME OF YOUR OWN
Renting may be the appropriate action for this point in your financial journey, but if you don't ever buy a home of your own, you are assured of monthly payments for the rest of your life. You can never completely pay off a rental, so make sure your strategy is always moving you toward home ownership. ■

Upgrading — Key Places to Invest in Your Home

Upgrading your single largest investment — your house — should be done as frequently as routine maintenance because it is a practical way to save money and improve the house's re-sale value when you are ready to sell.

Buyers today know what to look for when buying a home and property, and before they can secure a home loan from the bank, they must produce an appraisal of the property in which they are interested. Appraisers, as well as buyers, take careful note of such easily-upgraded appliances as the furnace, hot water heater, and water softener. Quality upgrades translate to extra money in your pocket when you decide to sell.

Let's start with your furnace Is it an energy-efficient model? What is the percentage of its efficiency? Eighty-two percent or lower requires a chimney. Eighty-five to 90 percent does not require a chimney and can be vented directly outside. If your chimney requires repair, you may

consider simply replacing your old furnace with a high-efficiency unit (unless your fireplace uses the same chimney). Then you will have handled two problems with one expense-saving money and upgrading your property at the same time.

Savings on a new efficient furnace, compared to 15 to 20 year-old models, can be 50 percent on fuel and 20 percent on electricity costs (to operate the blower). Plus, for more even heating and cooling, you can add ceiling fans to your rooms and you'll save a pile of money over a short period of time.

AIR CONDITIONING
The cost of adding air-conditioning while you are upgrading the furnace is considerably less than if you were to replace your AC at another time — about 15 to 20 percent less.

HOT WATER HEATERS
More recent models of hot water heaters also pay for themselves over time. New models require less energy to do the same job. Also, they perform more quickly and are safer to operate. Combine this with water-saving shower heads and aerators on all your faucets and you'll be able to save yourself some significant cash over the long run, plus enhance the value of your property. This will also give your real estate agents some nice low energy bills to show prospective buyers when you're ready to sell.

The new water softener models have aqua sensors, which tell the softener when it's time to flush

and recharge, instead of the old type, which forced you to guess how much water you would use by family size or age. Newer units save water, sewer, and energy. This can add up to tremendous savings. Also, if you're thinking of selling your home in the not-so-distant future, upgrading your furnace, AC, and hot water heater will give you a double pay-back — lower utility bills and a better resale value on your home. Keep track of your utility bills before and after your upgrades so your real estate agent can use this information when showing your home to prospective buyers.

CURB APPEAL
The area outside your home is the first thing a prospective buyer sees and makes an immediate, indelible impression. Is your house clean, freshly painted, and caulked as part of your general maintenance or upgrading? Consider either renting a power washer or hiring someone to clean the exterior of your house before you decide how much, if any, painting and caulking is necessary. This is not a costly procedure; it is good maintenance as well as good business.

When you're buying a car, the first thing that appeals to you is the vehicle's appearance — a clean and detailed engine compartment, a spotless interior, and even a tidy trunk. It's the same with the appearance of your home. Think of the attic or garage as the trunk. This will not only make your home more marketable and more pleasing to look at, but it will protect your investment. ■

How to Settle the Asking Price of Your Home

When it's time to sell your home, systematically determining the proper asking price can save you both time and money.

If you ask too little for your home, you'll lose some of the hard-earned capital and labor you have invested in it over the years. If you ask too much for your home, it will remain on the market longer than necessary and you'll endure unnecessary maintenance and mortgage expenses. Surveys have shown the longer a house is on the market, the greater the discount from the asking price when it does sell. In all free economies, the market ultimately sets an accurate price for everything. The goal is to anticipate the realistic market price for your house and then ask just a little more. If the buyer then tries to talk you down, you will still get a fair price for your home. If the buyer agrees to your initial asking price, so much the better.

KNOW YOUR MARKET
Comparable sales are the key to proper pricing. Nothing matters as much as completed transactions involving homes that match yours as closely as possible. You need to find recently sold homes that are similar to yours in location, square footage, style, condition, and lot configuration. The closer they are in all respects, the more likely they are to render accurate, useful information for setting the price of your home.

In addition, you should study a complete list of homes currently on the market in your area and pay particular attention to those that seem most similar to yours. Buyers will be looking at homes from that group. Consider the choices through their eyes and you may come to see your asking price in a more realistic manner.

IMPORTANT FACTORS
With your market analysis in hand, here are some additional factors to consider when zeroing in on your asking price:

URGENCY TO SELL
You should reduce your asking price in proportion to your urgency for a quick sale. If you must leave the house vacant, add up what it would cost you to carry it for three or four extra months (mortgage payments, insurance, taxes, utilities, etc.). You might be better off listing below market value rather than incurring those expenses and, in the end, selling at a lower price anyway.

COMPETITION
If your location is popular and few desirable homes are for sale there, the laws of supply and demand will allow you to mark up the price of your home. On the other hand, if there are numerous houses for sale near yours in the same range as your asking price, the flooded market may force you to reduce your demands.

SPECIAL FINANCING
If your home has an FHA or VA loan that can be assumed at a lower percentage than current mortgage rates, your mortgage may be the most valuable part of the property. The house may sell at a premium price because a buyer will accept the higher initial costs to benefit from savings in interest payments over the years ahead. You may also gain a price advantage if you are selling in a tight mortgage market and you are willing to hold the loan yourself.

THE $10,000 BARRIER
There is very little difference in buyer reaction to a house priced at $97,000, as opposed to one priced at $99,000. But there is a great deal of perceived difference between a house priced at $99,000 and another priced at $101,000. Remember this point if you are considering an increase that will elevate your asking price beyond a $10,000 breaking point. In the above example, you may be eliminating all those buyers who told their agents not to show them anything over $100,000.

LESS IMPORTANT FACTORS
Here are some items that are of lesser importance to most potential buyers. Although some of these may seem important to you, they may not be to your buyer and you must avoid overestimating their significance when determining your asking price.

ORIGINAL PURCHASE PRICE
Informed buyers may go to the courthouse and research the amount paid for your home. This figure is useful as a reference point or to help them determine

your profit margin. However, it may have little or nothing to do with the current fair market value of your home and it is unlikely that you can use it as leverage to ask a higher price.

YOUR INVESTMENT IN IMPROVEMENTS

Don't count on the value of improvements regarded as a matter of individual taste. This is particularly true if they made the total investment in your house higher than the fair market value of the houses around you. If the buyer happens to have the same style or values as yours, the improvement may actually speed the sale of your home for a higher price. However, it is far more likely that buyers will not consider it at all. Worse yet, they may even view it as a negative feature and try to subtract the estimated cost of removal from your asking price.

ASSESSED VALUE

The assessed value of your home is the value the tax assessor uses to calculate your real estate taxes. Assessed values are seldom a dependable indication of real market value.

YOUR NEEDS AND CONCERNS

A compassionate buyer may empathize with your situation, but not if it costs him or her time or money. Trying to leverage up the price of your home by calling attention to your hard luck is only likely to drive an otherwise interested buyer away in guilt or frustration. ■

Keeping the Home Fires Burning

The traditional fireplace is, by design, an inefficient device. Some heat is radiated into the room. Some heat is conducted directly outside through the fireplace walls. Unfortunately, about 90 percent of the heat is lost up the flue by convection. Modern high-efficiency fireplaces are considerably more cost effective than old-fashioned ones for several reasons.

MODERN UNITS

The new fireplaces require fewer accommodations in new building design and fewer modifications to existing structures. Traditional brick and mortar constructions typically weigh about 5,000 pounds and require support from the foundation. Newer fireplaces are prefabricated heavy-gauge sheet metal or cast iron and weigh between 200 and 1,000 pounds. Most can be supported by a standard wood construction floor.

Modern units can be installed in a very tight wall enclosure or can be installed to occupy a very small portion of the living space. They use heat-efficient materials and are tightly sealed to allow maximum control of the fire's burn rate. They also use triple-wall metal flues that are cheaper and easier to install.

Units that are freestanding (not built into the wall) radiate heat in all directions and don't lose heat by immediate contact with an outside wall. Many of them also use systems that increase the amount of heat put into the room. A flue heat exchanger is designed for that very reason. This device is a honeycomb of metal tubes. While exhaust gases pass by the outside of the pipe walls, room air is blown through the inside of the pipes. As a result, heat is recovered from the flue that would be otherwise lost.

If you are planning a new installation in a construction blueprint or existing structure, prefabricated freestanding units are, from an efficiency standpoint, the only way to go.

IMPROVING TRADITIONAL FIREPLACES

If you already have an inefficient conventional fireplace, there are a number of measures you can take to improve it (most of these are incorporated on prefabricated units). Materials will be available through your local home-improvement center.

Install a metal heat reflector in the back of the fireplace. By radiating heat forward and into the room, the reflector reduces the amount of heat lost by conduction through the outside wall.

Add glass doors to the opening of the firebox. These are heat-resistant tempered glass. They will allow you to restrict the amount of air the fire gets by using a damper and, thereby, control the rate at which the fire burns.

Have a qualified contractor

install an outside-vented cold air inlet. This tactic is a little more costly than the others I've mentioned, but it will prevent the fire from creating a vacuum that sucks the warm air out of the room and draws cold air in through every crack and crevice of your house. Instead it will draw cold air directly from the outside.

Purchase a convection grate.
This device holds the logs above the fireplace floor like a standard grate, but the convection grate is made of hollow tubes. As the tubes heat, they draw cooler air in the bottom and push warmer air out of the top and into the room. Some even have small blowers that force the air through more rapidly and warm the room more quickly.

CLEANING THE FLUE

No matter what kind of fireplace you have, you will need to inspect the flue regularly and clean it when necessary. Creosote forms when moisture is released from burning wood in the form of steam and combines with combustible gases that escape unburned up the flue. If unchecked, layers of the tarry deposits will eventually bake into a flammable shiny coating. Burning well-seasoned (dry) wood and building roaring blazes that send a lot of heat up the flue will discourage creosote accumulations, but you will still need to inspect the flue at least once per year.

Shine a flashlight into the flue from the top. Look closely at the walls of the flue for any signs of sooty buildup. If you have a small camcorder, you can wrap a rag around it for protection and then use a rope to lower it and a small flashlight into the flue to get a video record of the conditions. If your flue needs cleaning, you will need some rope, a quality steel cleaning brush that matches the shape of your flue, and some heavy weights. Seal the fireplace off from the interior of your home (to prevent dust from entering). Tie the weights and then the steel brush to the end of the rope and lower them, in that order, from the top of the flue until they reach the bottom. Work the brush up and down the full length of the flue several times until the deposits are scraped away.

You may also wish to clean any smoke or soot stains from the fireplace. A solution made of one heaping tablespoon of trisodium phosphate dissolved in a quart of warm water works well in this capacity. Make sure you're wearing rubber gloves as you apply the solution with a brush, as it is very strong. Don't let the solution get on anything but the masonry.

If you follow the simple advice offered here, you will be able to safely enjoy the beauty of a natural wood fire and warm yourself considerably on a cold evening. ∎

Home Warranties — What Good Are They?

Most people buying a new home look for a builder who will back up his work with a warranty period, during which they will fix just about anything that isn't right. But more and more home buyers, sellers, and owners are buying home warranties on used homes. Unfortunately, when something does go wrong, these policy holders often find gaping holes in their warranty coverage.

WHAT THEY DO COVER

Home warranties cost anywhere from $245 to $400 a year, plus $35 to $100 per service call. These warranties are usually annually renewable.

Warranties will generally provide coverage of your heating, plumbing, and electrical systems, and most major appliances. Some warranties cover washers, dryers, and central air-conditioning systems, but these coverages frequently cost extra.

WHAT THEY DON'T COVER

On most of these warranty policies, the exclusions and exceptions take up most of the space.

These exceptions include any defects in evidence before the sale to the current owner, plus leaky roofs or wet basements. And, because the warranty companies get reduced rates from selected tradesmen, you may have to use only those service companies your policy allows.

Other exclusions include many of the typical problems you'll run into as a homeowner: leaks in the water heater, water holding tanks, tub/shower enclosures, problems with window air conditioners, appliance problems caused by rust or corrosion, and problems with well pumps and regulators.

SHOULD YOU BUY A HOME WARRANTY?

First of all, you know our Debt-FREE & Prosperous Living™ system states you should NEVER waste money on warranties. However, there is one exception when it comes to home warranties. If you are selling your home, you should get a home warranty to add value to your offer and reduce buyer apprehension about purchasing your house.

In marketing, the game is to stand out from the competition. In marketing a home, there are generally dozens, if not hundreds, of comparable houses in your general area — and they all offer something different for the same or a similar price. But there's always that little voice in the buyer's mind asking, *"What might be wrong with this place that nobody's talking about?"*

The home warranty gives the buyer a measure of security and, according to ERA Products, which offers the Home Protection Plan

warranty, homes with a warranty sell for an average 1.1 percent higher price and 38 days faster than uncovered homes.

NOTE: If you are selling your home, it's best to get serious problems fixed before you put the house on the market, because, in an increasing number of states strict disclosure laws require that you either reveal these problems to potential buyers ahead of time, or be financially responsible for them when they later crop up for the new owner. Don't think buying a home warranty for the new owner will make up for problems you're already aware of, because most home warranties exclude conditions that pre-existed the sale date.

On the other hand, if you are a home buyer or a homeowner, don't bother with a warranty at all. The $245 to $400 a year you'll save by not buying the warranty should more than cover any expenses that would have been paid for under the policy. According to American Home Shield, which charges an average of $330 for their annual warranty premium and $35 for a service call, the average warranty holder makes two covered claims during the year at an average $140 per claim. That means they're paying

$330 for a warranty that saves them $280.

IF YOU'RE BUYING A HOME

If a home you're considering comes with a warranty, don't let that lull you to sleep. Pay for a pre-sale home inspection. That way, presuming you've put an inspection contingency into the sale contract, you can ask the seller to foot the bill or compensate you for the repair of any problems the inspection reveals. If they refuse to make the financial adjustments necessary, the contingency clause voids the contract, and you can get your deposit back and look for another house. You won't be locked into buying a home with known flaws.

If you do buy a home with a warranty, read it carefully. Then take a close look at covered structures and systems. If you have any doubts, call in a professional for an estimate. Then — if you feel you have a claim — make it.

If you have any specific questions about home warranties and what they cover, talk to your local Realtor®. Most major real estate companies offer their own warranty or they're affiliated with a company that does. ■

Appliance-Buying Tips and Tricks

Whether you're a new home buyer, renovating your current home, or updating and upgrading your number one investment, major appliances are an important consideration. Not only are major appliances typically large, up-front expense items, but they can be expensive to operate each month, as well.

When purchasing a new major appliance, it's tempting to fall for a superstore's deluxe installment payment credit plan. Avoid purchasing major appliances — or anything, for that matter — with credit, or your $1,500 refrigerator will end up costing you $3,000 when you add in all the interest payments. If you need to replace a major appliance, put your debt elimination plan on hold temporarily, save up your Accelerator Margin money for a few months, and buy the appliance with cash. Then get right back to your plan.

Also, appliance salespeople love to push extended warranties. As reasonable as they make it sound, DON'T DO IT. The retail store where you bought the appliance is always a winner in the extended warranty gamble. If you're truly worried about an unexpected breakdown after the manufacturer's warranty has expired, put a little cash aside in an emergency repair fund.

Before buying any major appliance, ask yourself these questions:

DO I REALLY NEED IT?
If a major appliance in your home rattles and smokes and is otherwise ready to expire, you obviously need a new unit. But there are other reasons why you may want to consider upgrading your current appliances to a newer model. Here are just a few...

• A high-efficiency furnace and air conditioner can save you $300 to $400 a year in energy costs, plus give you peace of mind because of newer safety features.

• The new water softeners sense hardness and only recharge the system when it's needed. Older units use a timer that recharges the system whether it needs it or not. Remember, you pay for water, salt, and electricity each time your water softener recharges.

• Many people forget to turn hot water heaters down when they go away for the weekend. The newer models are high-efficiency units that have simple and well-marked settings such as *vacation* and *unoccupied* (for commercial models). Some hot water heaters even have setback timers to automatically cut back heating during predetermined times, such as midnight to 5 a.m.

WHAT'S THE BEST TIME TO PURCHASE AN APPLIANCE?
Most buying cycles are common sense, but it's best to buy a furnace when winter is over — in the springtime. An air conditioner is best bought in the dead of winter. A lawn mower? You'll find the best deals when the grass is covered with snow. For appliances like stoves, refrigerators, and washers and dryers, fall is the best buying time.

Think, too, about how long you're planning on keeping your current home or apartment. This will help you determine the color and size of the appliance. For instance, if you're planning to move soon, don't buy an avocado-colored stove because it matches the '70s-vintage tile in your kitchen. Think about how that appliance would look in your new home.

WHAT WILL THE PAYBACK BE?
When buying a new — especially a major — appliance, you must factor payback into the purchase equation. Take a new furnace, for instance. A model that is 90 percent efficient will save you X amount of dollars over a period of time. That's the payback. Let's say that your annual savings from this new, energy-efficient furnace is $125 and the purchase price of the furnace is $1,000. You'll see your payback in just eight years. You expect the new unit will last at least 10 years, so this would be a good purchase decision because the furnace is essentially paying for itself over a period of years in the form of real energy savings (reduced heating bills).

Also, if you're planning on selling your house soon, a new dishwasher, for example, would increase the selling value of the home. This is another form of payback. ■

Pampering Your Hot Water Heater

Let's talk about your hot water heater, the second-greatest user of energy (heating and cooling being the first) in your home. Significant savings can be realized by the proper care and maintenance of this unit.

A water heater is run all year, so the type of fuel used and the size of the unit are important, as is maintenance.

LETS START WITH SIZE.
An oversized water heater wastes energy. One that's too small will not only overwork itself, but most likely run out of hot water before you're through needing it.

There are three sizes: standard, tall, and short. Tall units make the most efficient use of electricity. Standard sizes are the most efficient burners of natural gas. Short water heaters run by electricity have a 45-gallon capacity, while tall units hold 80 gallons. Gas burners hold about 30 gallons for a standard unit, and 45 gallons in the tall size.

Gas costs less to operate — about half that of electric — and has a quicker recovery time.

Both gas and electric water heaters are now available in high-efficiency models. They're priced higher, but are much more cost efficient to operate, saving you money in the long run.

A water heater's overall efficiency is listed as the energy factor, or EF. This rating describes the recovery efficiency, standby loss, and energy input. The higher the EF number, the more efficient the unit.

Check with plumbers and find out if you'll need plumbing or venting changes, especially if you're changing from electric to gas.

BEFORE PURCHASING A WATER HEATER...
Should you decide to buy a water heater, here are some questions to consider.
1. What is the units energy factor?
2. What tank size do I need?
3. How long is the warranty period, and what's covered?
4. What venting system is right for my home?
5. Is there a manufacturer or utility rebate, and is it easy to apply for?

If you don't have it in your debt-elimination plan to buy a new water heater now, here are a few ideas to lower your hot water bill with the unit you currently have.
1. To avoid scalding, you should run your heater at a temperature of no more than 115 to 120 degrees Fahrenheit. This will give you adequate hot water for most situations.
2. Insulate the heater and pipes. Kits are available at hardware and home improvement outlets.
3. If you have an older, non-energy-saving gas unit, you can add a vent damper. This prevents already-heated room air from escaping up the chimney.
4. When leaving home for more than two days, turn your heater to pilot. Some units have a vacation setting. Don't heat what you don't use.
5. Install water-saving shower heads and aerators on your faucets. You'll see a 70 percent savings with this alone.
6. Drain a pail of water each month from the bottom of the heater to reduce sediment buildup. This improves efficiency and extends the life of the unit.
7. Repair leaky faucets and pipes immediately. One drop of water per second from a leaky hot water faucet can waste up to 48 gallons a week. That's a whopping 2,496 gallons a year! You pay for this waste on your water and sewer bills, plus the cost of heating wasted water can shorten the life of the heater.
8. Since the dishwasher uses lots of hot water, make sure its full of dishes before you run it. Heres a tip I learned the hard way: When buying a dishwasher, make sure it has its own hot water heater. Most dishwashers require 140-degree temperatures to work properly. You don't want to have to set your water heater to run higher than necessary, day and night, all year just for dish-washing needs.
9. Wash clothes in warm water. Rinse in cold. Again, run a full load.
10. Clean out your kitchen garbage disposal by running a tray of ice cubes through it once a week. (The ice shatters and scours the inside of the unit.) Run until the ice is chopped and then flush with water. It's been said that there are as many germs in a disposal as in a septic tank. One cap or tablespoon full of household ammonia poured down the disposal with a morning flush will keep it germ-free. ■

Appendix E

Building Health & Wealth Newsletter Articles

Building Your Wealth
Planning for Your Retirement
Your Prosperous Health

APPENDIX E

Selected Debt-FREE & Prosperous Living™ Newsletter Articles Dealing With Building Your Wealth and Living Prosperously

The following articles have been organized according to the column under which they appear in the *Debt-FREE & Prosperous Living™* Newsletter, making access to a specific topic more convenient for the reader. To subscribe to the *Debt-FREE & Prosperous Living™* Newsletter, call 1-888-DEBTFREE.

Building Your Wealth:

Once you have rid yourself completely of all debt and broken free of creditors, you are ready to begin building your own personal financial empire to sustain you through your retirement years. But where to begin? Mutual funds, junk bonds, annuities, tax-deferred investment vehicles — the world of investment can sometimes prove too complicated to handle alone. Douglas Carpenter, C.P.A. and chief financial officer, describes the risks and rewards of several investment strategies in language that doesn't require an Ivy League MBA to understand. You simply have to apply Mr. Carpenter's advice to your particular situation.

Planning for Your Retirement:

When is the right time to invest in your retirement? No matter what your age, there is never a wrong time, and E. Raymond Pastor, author of The 401(k) Success Plan: How Not to End Up Broke and Embarrassed When You're 65, says even relatively small amounts of money, when invested wisely, can make a big difference a few years down the line. Pastor cites startling statistical data while arguing most Americans are not even marginally prepared for retirement (from an economic standpoint), and tells you why you can't depend upon Social Security to support you in your retirement years.

Your Prosperous Health:

What is the best way to fight the common cold? How can a diet rich in Vitamin E and exercise quicken the flow of blood through the bloodstream? Why is lifelong health every bit as important as financial prosperity? Most people don't understand the effects certain dietary habits have on the human body and one's state of mind. Jan Gerber, registered nurse and mother of four, and Arlen Smith, D.C., a chiropractor with ten years experience in his field, share their beliefs on how to live a healthier, more energetic life. Mrs. Gerber and Mr. Smith stress the importance of a well-balanced diet fortified with foods rich in vitamins and minerals, and share ways you can help your children break the diet soda and candy habit for sounder, healthier alternatives.

Building Your Wealth:

Choosing a Fund by Time Horizon

Time horizon, in terms of mutual fund investing, refers to the amount of time between the day moneys are invested and the point when they are withdrawn from a fund. Most people, when they invest in a fund, have no exact number of years in mind. An investor may put money into a fund, intending to keep it there for 20 years, and wind up pulling it out after just six months. For an investor, however, time horizon depends on two main factors: their age and the purpose for which they intend to one day use the money.

How does one determine the appropriate time horizon? The most important consideration is the investor's age as it pertains to his or her potential for earning income. A person who is 35 will have a much longer horizon than someone who is, say, 50 or 75. Someone who is 75 will probably not be investing for a 30-year time horizon. Consider two 35-year-olds, however, one intending to retire by age 50 and the other intending to work well into his or

her 60s. The latter will have a somewhat longer time horizon for investing than the former. The reason is the individual who retires at 50 can't be subjected to as much risk as the one who intends to keep working.

The other determinant of time horizon is the ultimate use of the money. If the investor intends to use the money to purchase a car in five years, he or she has a short time horizon. Retirement money, on the other hand, tends to have a longer time horizon (depending upon the expected time until retirement). The time horizon will help to determine how much risk the investor should assume. Longer horizons allow for more risk. Let's assume five different time horizons: ranging between 30 years and one year.

An investor with a 30-year time horizon should not avoid risk. An aggressive growth fund that invests almost exclusively in high-growth low-dividend stocks is appropriate. Over time the fluctuations found in such a fund will be outweighed by long-term gains. It's also important that, with such a long time horizon, the portfolio returns more than inflation. If it doesn't, the fund may grow, but the purchasing power of the money 30 years from now will actually be less.

A 20-year time horizon warrants aggressive funds as well, investing about 80 percent in equities and

20 percent in fixed-income securities. Such a portfolio will still have fluctuations, but a small amount of growth will also come from steady interest on the fixed-income securities. This will only slightly lower the portfolio's expected return while providing a small buffer against major market movements.

A time horizon of 10 years warrants a more conservative approach, while still allowing the portfolio to achieve substantial growth. Approximately 60 percent of the fund's assets should be in equities, while 40 percent would be in fixed-income securities. A portfolio with a five-year time horizon would generally have an asset mix of 40 percent equities and 60 percent fixed income securities. With a five-year horizon, inflation is not as significant a factor, but a rapidly changing equities market would be. The shift of assets into a majority of fixed-income securities will provide a reasonable overall return from interest, while still allowing for some growth through equities.

An investor with a time horizon that is roughly between six months and two years should not be investing in mutual funds unless the fund is a money market or the investor clearly understands the risk in doing so. ■

What's So Precious About Metals?

Gold. Just the name conjures images of wealth, riches, and security. And, indeed, owning gold has historically been a hedge against inflation and has been used as a safeguard against severe economic downturns. But gold and other precious metals are not the shining investments they once were. Even gold, whose price rose 5.7 percent in 1994, is still — over the long term — a poor investment.

Here are several reasons why gold has lost its luster:
• Gold pays no dividends. Since 1926 almost one-half of the returns from owning stocks has come from dividends, but investors in gold have no such return.

• When an investor makes an investment in a corporation through a stock purchase, the company can retain earnings and use it as fuel for future growth. Gold cannot compound investors' gains.

• While once believed to be a safe-harbor investment, gold hardly offers that promise today. True, gold spiked after the stock market crash in 1987 and after the junk bond collapse in 1990. But it quickly declined. And after Iraq invaded Kuwait, gold didn't even maintain a 10 percent price increase.

As a hedge against inflation, gold is no stellar performer, either. True, the purchasing power of an ounce of gold is the same as it was a hundred years ago, while inflation has reduced the power of the dollar by 50 percent since 1980. But the price of gold has fallen, too, from a high of $850 an ounce at the start of 1980 to a rock-bottom low of $304 early in 1985.

So, what can you do if you still see gold or other precious metals as part of a well-rounded portfolio?

First, if you're after security in time of war or disaster, consider a different, high-yielding, and secure investment, like U.S. Treasury securities. But if it's bars of bullion or nothing for you, here are a few tips on getting started in gold.

• Experts suggest any gold purchase should be modest — perhaps as little as 5 percent of a well-diversified investment portfolio.

• Owning a hard asset like a bar of gold may not be the way to go if you're ready to dabble in precious metals. Ancillary costs such as storage, insurance, and even transporting your ingots to and from dealers can easily eat away at your investment income.

• Certificates of ownership are easier than dealing in the real thing. These certificates proclaim your ownership in a specified amount of gold (or silver or platinum) stored away in a vault. Buying and selling are as simple as picking up the phone, although you will pay a one to three percent commission when

you buy and a one to two percent commission when you sell. Also, you may have to pay an annual fee for storage of the metal.

• Another option is gold coins, which can be purchased through coin shops, jewelers, or mail-order houses. South African Krugerrands were popular several years ago, but Canadian Maple Leafs, Chinese Pandas, and American Eagles are available and all are much more easily bought, sold, and transported than bars of gold. You will pay three to six percent more than their gold content would tell you these coins are worth, but their portability can make up for the loss.

• You can also invest in shares of mining companies. These investments do offer the chance at capital appreciation. Since the political situation in South Africa has stabilized, this type of investing is not as risky as it once was, but the potential for volatility still exists.

• Finally, for built-in diversification, you could try gold mutual funds. These funds acquire shares of gold-mining companies. They've often been big winners, but you better have a hide of iron, because the roller-coaster rides they typically take are not for the faint of heart.

Unless double-digit inflation is imminent, gold is not likely to be the great investment it was once considered. If you want to make gold a part of your portfolio, buy smart, get references (there are a lot of scams out there), and invest small — five percent or less. ■

Mutual Fund Annuities

A little-known option for buyers of mutual funds is the universal annuity. Technically, the investment is not a mutual fund but rather an insurance product. It offers significant tax advantages and a somewhat lower risk of loss, and does so for a slight additional cost. Yet, it features close to the same returns offered by the mutual funds an investor might normally purchase.

THE STRUCTURE

For purposes of the tax code, the universal annuity falls under the rulings related to insurance products. From the investor's standpoint it behaves more like a mutual fund. When you invest in a mutual fund annuity you purchase shares in a mutual fund through an insurance company. Your investment in the fund will produce the same results as if you had invested in the fund directly, except the insurance company will charge you a fee (typically around one percent annually) to pay for a life insurance policy tied to the mutual fund. The policy states that in the event of the

investor's death, either the current market value of the fund or the original amount of money invested in the fund, whichever is higher, is distributed into the investor's estate. Thus, in the event of the shareholder's death, the estate is protected from loss.

Example 1: Suppose an investor puts $100,000 into an insured mutual fund annuity. Assume several years later the investor dies and the fund is worth $125,000. The annuity will distribute to the estate the current value of $125,000. Suppose, instead, the value of the fund went down to $85,000. The insurance feature of the fund would determine the liquidation value and the estate would receive the original $100,000. This insurance feature is usually re-indexed every few years. In other words, the current value of the fund every five years (for example) becomes the insured amount.

Example 2: Suppose an investor placed $100,000 into the insured mutual fund annuity, and the annuity re-indexes every five years. Assume in five years (at the time of re-indexing) the value is $160,000. A year later the fund rises in value to $175,000. Three years after that the investor dies, when the value of the fund is $140,000. In this example the fund will pay $160,000 into the

estate of the investor.

THE REAL ADVANTAGE

The real advantage of a mutual fund annuity isn't the life insurance feature but rather the significant tax advantage it offers. All dividends, interest, and capital gains are taxed at the time they are withdrawn, not when they are earned within the fund. This means an investor can accumulate dividends in the annuity by reinvesting them and deferring the taxes on these amounts until withdrawn. Mutual fund annuities offer various types of funds (just as a family of funds within one mutual fund group). An investor can also switch from one fund to another within the annuity without realizing capital gains. Again, taxes are only paid when the annuity is sold, not when funds are switched.

The only extra cost of the annuity over its mutual fund counterpart is an additional fee of about one percent of the portfolio value per year, which will be paid to cover the cost of the life insurance policy. The insurance feature provides only a small added benefit. The real advantages are obtained through tax savings. This investment is similar to a nondeductible IRA investment. No tax advantages are gained initially, but all earnings are held tax-deferred until it is sold. ■

Mutual Fund Tax Considerations

Taxes affect funds in differing ways. Tax implications can range from total tax exemption to partial exemption to fully subject to taxation. Outlined in this article is a description of several ways taxes act upon certain mutual fund investments.

TAX-FREE BOND FUNDS

These funds are tax exempt. The caveat associated with these funds is, although they are federally tax exempt, they may not be state and local tax exempt. The state and local taxability depends upon the makeup of the bonds contained in the portfolio. Usually states do not tax their own bonds. If an investor, for example, resides in New York State and purchases a New York State tax-free bond fund, they would not pay any tax.

This is because all the bonds contained in the fund are state and local, as well as federally, tax exempt. If the same investor were to purchase a tax-free bond fund that did not exclusively hold New York State issued bonds, he or she would have to pay interest on the amount of non-New York State tax-free income received. At the end of the year the mutual fund company will issue a statement giving a percentage of income that must be declared on total income received for each state. For example, if a fund derived 10 percent of its income from New York State bonds, a New York resident would have to pay state and local taxes on 90 percent of the income received from the fund (the fund would still be completely tax exempt).

It is important to remember in tax-exempt bond funds, only earned interest is tax exempt. Any capital gains earned from the portfolio are subject to taxation.

OTHER FUNDS: STOCK, BOND, CONVERTIBLE, AND MIXED-ASSET FUNDS

For most other funds, dividends and capital gains, whether paid or reinvested, are fully taxable in the year earned. Many mutual funds (growth funds in particular) let their share prices rise rather than pay out dividends. The purpose of this is to help their investors avoid paying taxes on the amounts distributed. The benefit of this, however, has been minimized by requiring investors to pay taxes on capital gains within the fund regardless of whether or not it is distributed as a dividend. This can be very frustrating to an investor, as they run the possibility of receiving no income or even see a lower share value but still have to pay taxes on the investment due to the fund's internal capital gains.

It's important to consider the timing of a fund paying dividends. Many funds pay their dividends in December. Because of this, it's sometimes not advisable for an investor to purchase a fund (especially a stock fund that historically pays its dividends once a year) in December. Investors who purchase a fund just before the payment of a dividend will find themselves having to pay taxes on the dividend, even though they just invested in the fund and have realized no gain. To avoid this, an investor should check to see how often and when the fund pays its dividends. If it does so at the end of the year, they may want to wait until the day after the fund goes ex-dividend (the last day a shareholder is entitled to receive the dividend).

MUTUAL FUNDS PURCHASED AS PART OF A PENSION PLAN

The taxability of the fund itself will not matter. Taxability will be determined by the rules of the pension plan under which it is carried. If it is in a qualified 401(k) plan, SEP, IRA, etc., all income will be tax-deferred according to the rules of the plan. The taxability of the fund itself will only come into play as funds are withdrawn. Dividends earned on a stock fund would become taxable when disbursed from the pension plan, while tax-exempt interest earned by pension investments would remain tax-exempt.

If funds are transferred out of a qualified pension plan, an investor has 60 days in which to complete the transfer into another qualified pension plan. If they fail to do so, the entire amount withdrawn from the plan becomes taxable. Investors should remain mindful that all decisions they make on their investments will have tax implications. Consult a tax professional when making decisions. ■

Are Junk Bond Funds Worth the Risk?

Corporate bonds — obligations issued by companies — have varying maturities and pay varying rates of interest. The yield of a bond is dependent upon its rating. Two major rating services are Moody's and Standard & Poor's. Although both rating services use different scales, bonds rated A to AAA are considered to be of fairly high quality, while bonds rated single B, C, or D are of lower quality.

A low rating is indicative of a company that might have trouble meeting interest or principal payments on the bond or could possibly default. In order to attract investors, these bonds must pay a higher rate of interest. Bonds are called high-yield bonds or junk bonds if their rating is low.

IS INVESTMENT JUSTIFIED?

An investor must determine if the rate premium the high-yielding bond pays justifies the added risk of the bond's defaulting. Rate premium is defined as the amount of interest a bond pays over and above safer, yet lower-yielding, bonds. For example, let's assume the average A rated utility bond yields eight percent. If we assume that a low-rated junk bond yields

10 percent, the risk premium is two percent (10 percent minus eight percent).

Historically the default rate of junk bonds has been between four and 4.5 percent. Using an average maturity of 12 years, the chance of default for a high-yielding bond in any single year is about .3 percent. In pure terms, the yield premium of two percent is worth the risk of a .3 percent chance of default. This is fine, as long as you aren't the unlucky holder of one of the bonds that defaults.

So how do you take advantage of this higher yield without assuming a chance of losing all your money? The answer is simple: you need to diversify your portfolio. By purchasing dozens of these higher-yielding bonds, you increase your chance of a few defaulting, but you also ensure the entire portfolio of bonds won't default. The higher yield these bonds pay will more than make up for any losses.

A MUTUAL FUND SOLUTION

Considering most bonds are sold in $1,000 units, it's impractical, if not impossible, for most investors to purchase enough differing bonds to properly diversify. However, investors can turn to mutual funds to solve this problem. There are many mutual funds that specialize in investing in high-yield bonds exclusively. The track record of such funds is generally very good. They tend to pay higher yields and maintain consistent levels of performance. Their only blemish occurred a few years ago when higher-yielding bonds fell out of favor with the

investment public and the bonds fell in value. When this happened, a good majority of funds experienced a temporary loss of some of their value. The situation reversed itself a year or two later as investors once again began buying a greater number of junk bonds and the funds recovered. Most junk bond funds have consistently outperformed their safer but lower-yielding corporate bond counterparts.

Ultimately for the long term, for investors who are advised that some risk in their portfolio is acceptable — yet who don't want the extreme volatility stock funds exhibit — junk bond (high-yield) funds may be worth considering. To properly evaluate if such a fund is appropriate for you, assess your personal situation in terms of the amount of risk you can accept in your portfolio.

Although owning a single junk bond is a risky investment, the diversification found in a mutual fund mitigates this risk substantially. Once you've decided to invest in a junk bond fund, obtain a prospectus. Evaluate such things as past performance, fees, and service options like the ability to transfer funds by phone. Pay particular attention to portfolio diversification. This is the primary reason the fund is being purchased, as opposed to going out and buying a few individual bonds.

The addition of junk bonds to a portfolio will likely raise the yield of the portfolio and, since it's a bond fund, a greater percentage of the return will be paid out in cash. ∎

Real Estate Investment Trusts

You've heard about owning a piece of the rock? Well, how about owning a piece of the mall, the office building, the factory outlet, or other commercial property? You can, through investments in Real Estate Investment Trusts (REITs).

REAL ESTATE IS REAL ESTATE

If you were to invest in single-family homes to rent out, you would be a landlord. The return on your investment would be a combination of cash flow from your tenants (hopefully positive) and appreciation in the value of your properties. If you were to invest in a shopping mall, your return would be based on exactly the same things.

By investing in REITs, however, you won't be called in the middle of the night if a pipe breaks, and your chances for failure are minimal because you will be teaming up with knowledgeable co-investors and managers.

The disadvantages include the same disadvantages for any real estate investment. You could lose money if you can't keep tenants in your buildings. You could lose money if the value of your property declines. And you won't get breathtaking returns.

REITs ARE LIKE STOCKS

REITs trade on the New York and American Stock Exchanges, and behave similarly to closed-end mutual funds. Their prices fluctuate daily, and they generate regular shareholder reports. Much like typical industrial stocks, REITs appreciate and distribute earnings in step with economic growth. Also like stocks, REITs are sensitive to interest rate changes. They behave like an economic sector, such as pharmaceuticals or banks, rather than like a separate asset type, such as rare coins or art.

BEWARE OF THE HYPE MONSTER

When you begin exploring REITs as an investment option, you'll run into sales people who will promise you the moon. As usual, the real trajectory will be somewhat lower.

If you hear a sales person telling you that REITs offer impressive tax breaks, make a break yourself. In the '70s and '80s, unscrupulous brokers promoted first-year tax write-offs greater than the original cash investment. The government found these people and changed both their location and their wardrobe. If the offer seems too good to be true, it probably is.

If you hear a salesperson telling you commercial real estate is getting ready to take off, secure your wallet and get out of there. The real estate industry grows in steady increments, not spectacular leaps. Individual properties or investment companies will affect your returns more than the industry in general.

TWO WAYS TO LOOK AT THE MARKET

You can approach REITs as either income generators or growth investments.

If income is your primary goal, look at companies that invest in solid, blue-collar, recession-resistant properties. These usually include the common suburban shopping center, anchored by supermarkets and a large retailer like Kmart or Wal-Mart.

If you're after growth, you will be moving into a riskier area, with investments in office buildings, industrial parks and downtown malls. These types of properties are more economy-sensitive. An economic downturn keeps the shoppers at home and would-be entrepreneurs at their jobs, so the mall stores go broke and the small businesses don't populate the industrial parks. Hence, the owners of those properties suffer the consequences.

However, when the economy is strong, these properties generally outperform their less-glamorous income cousins.

USING THE MUTUAL FUND APPROACH

Like most investment securities, REITs are available via mutual funds. There are two basic categories of these funds: those that invest exclusively in U.S. properties and those that also invest globally.

When considering an investment in real estate, as always, research thoroughly the companies with whom you want to associate. Different fund companies have differing minimum investment amounts and boast varying returns. Check out the company's recent history, as well as how it has performed over the years before obligating your investment money.

LOCATION, LOCATION, LOCATION
Whether you go for individual REITs or buy via mutual funds, bear in mind real estate values are affected by the local economy. Consider investing in properties located in the immediate area of your home or business. You will be able to monitor the affecting economic realities, make wiser decisions and have more confidence in your investments. ■

Annuities — Retire with Income

An annuity is an investment purchased from an insurance company designed to provide income during the retirement years. There are essentially two ways to buy an annuity:

1. An immediate annuity is purchased in one lump sum. The buyer transfers investments into a vehicle that provides monthly retirement income.

2. A deferred annuity is exempt from current income taxes (qualified) and is usually built up with regular investments during the investor's working life. The investor converts this fund to an annuity when he or she is ready to begin receiving retirement income.

ANNUITIES ARE LONG-TERM INVESTMENTS
Only the moneys you know you will not need in the near future should be devoted to an annuity, because withdrawing from an annuity is costly. Most annuity plans impose surrender charges on early withdrawals. These charges usually decrease, say from seven percent to zero, over a half dozen years or so, but check this point out carefully. Some surrender charges don't drop off, and some last longer than six years. Most companies waive surrender charges if the annuitant dies.

If your annuity is a deferred plan, the IRS will make it unprofitable to take out any money before your retirement years (before age 59 1/2). On top of the income taxes you must pay on the money you withdraw, the IRS will charge a 10 percent early withdrawal penalty.

THE TWO DEFERRED ANNUITY STAGES
1. Accumulation Stage
During the accumulation stage of deferred annuities, the insurance company credits your annuity account with interest. Usually they will guarantee an interest rate for a given period of time (up to about 10 years). After that period, they offer a new guaranteed rate for a new period of time. Most companies will pay higher rates during these periods if the investments in which they put your money perform better than expected.

Many annuities offer a persistency bonus. This is another option designed to reward you for leaving your annuity alone and can range from five to 10 percent of your premiums. The insurance company adds this amount to your accumulation value if you stay put.

2. Payout or Withdrawal Stage
The investor receives his or her money in the payout or withdrawal stage and can choose the method of payment (monthly or one lump sum). We recommend monthly payments, because you almost always get more money than you would from any other SAFE investment in which you could place the lump sum.

IMPORTANT — which ever choice you make...it is IRREVERSIBLE and IRREVOCABLE.

When you choose to begin taking payments from your annuity, the insurance company will calculate what is called your Settlement-Option rate. This is the number of dollars they will pay you each month for every $1,000 you have accumulated in the annuity. The figure is based upon how much longer they believe you will live (and they will be paying you) and varies according to the performance of their investments.

PAYOUT OPTIONS
• **Life Annuity:** you receive payments for the rest of your life. Payments stop when you die. There is no cash balance or payouts due to any of your survivors.

• **Life Annuity With Period Certain:** you receive payments for the rest of your life, but if you die early (within the Period Certain), your heirs continue receiving your payments for the balance of the period. Period Certain can be any length of time (usually five or

10 years). The longer the period, the lower your monthly annuity payments.

• **Joint-And-Survivor Annuity:** you receive payments for the rest of your life, and if your spouse survives you, he or she receives the full payments, or a reduced rate you pre-select. Your payments are lower if you choose to have your spouse receive a high percentage of your initial monthly payments. It's basic math. The

longer the insurance company will likely have to make the payments, the lower those payments will be.

VARIABLE ANNUITIES

A variable annuity allows you to choose where your money is invested during both the accumulation and payout period. Your annuity investments are exposed to the same risks as any similar investments outside an annuity. Your capital could actually

decrease if you choose poorly.

Variable annuities are for those investors who are confident in their ability to gain maximum return from their investments. If, however, you prefer minimal involvement in your annuity and a predictable monthly income when you retire, a fixed annuity is for you. As always, it is wise to carefully consider all investment strategies before committing yourself to one or the other. ■

Municipal Bond Fund Basics

An investment into a Municipal Bond Fund is a relatively simple transaction. It's important, however, to understand the basic nature of the fund before making an investment. Municipal (Muni) bonds are issued by state and city municipalities. Muni funds refer to mutual funds that only invest in Municipal bonds. Municipal bonds, and the funds specializing in them, offer investors tax advantages. In exchange for a certain tax-exempt status, muni funds return lower yields.

Unlike stock funds, muni bond funds do not fluctuate wildly and usually returns do not vary significantly between funds. Several factors differentiate one fund from the next. These factors include the geographic region of the bonds held within the fund, the ratings

of the bonds purchased, and the management fees.

THE GEOGRAPHIC LOCATION OF THE FUND

Many funds invest only in specific states within the U.S. The reason for this is the tax-exempt nature of muni bonds. Under the tax codes, the interest paid on such bonds is not taxable by the federal government. As an added incentive to investors, usually the bonds are also state and city tax exempt. This exemption, however, only applies within the state for which it is issued. In other words, one state may, and often does, tax another state's bonds.

For the investor buying a muni fund, it's important to buy a fund that will not be taxed in their state of residence. For example, a New York State resident should purchase a New York Municipal Bond fund if he or she wants to avoid state taxation. If he or she were to buy a California state muni fund, the New York resident would not pay federal taxes, but would be subject to state (and city, if applicable) taxation.

An exception to this are bonds

issued by commonwealths, such as Puerto Rico. As a commonwealth, neither the states nor the federal government are allowed to tax the bonds Puerto Rico issues. Information concerning the specific bonds the fund can and does invest in are available in the prospectus.

A major factor that will effect yields is the ratings of the bonds the fund purchases. The higher the rating, the lower the risk of the fund and therefore the lower the yield. Many funds specify they will only invest in bonds with a specific high rating, such as AAA. Such funds are considered to be ultra-safe. As such, their yields will be lower than a fund that invests in only A-rated and below.

Management fees also will cause differences between fund yields. Every charge lowers the funds yield. Unlike stock funds, it's usually unnecessary for one muni fund to charge significantly more than a similar fund.

EVALUATING MUNICIPAL FUNDS

Decide first what tax exemptions you need. In a state such as

Florida, with no state income tax, there are many options. The state tax exemption, if your residence is in that state, is irrelevant. If you live in a high tax state such as New York, getting both federal and state tax exemption is significantly more important. Such investors would probably want to limit themselves to bonds issued by New York municipalities and tax-exempt commonwealths. Therefore, they would only want to look at New York municipal funds.

Once the geographic requirement has been determined, find a fund that offers the level of safety you desire. Muni funds by nature are conservative investments. You may not need a fund that limits its yield by investing only in high-grade muni bonds. Once you have narrowed the selection down by region and rating, then look into management fees to ensure the fund isn't producing lower yields due to high fees. ∎

Planning for Your Retirement:

Pay Yourself First!

It's been said the difference between the "haves" and the "have-nots" is the "haves" save what they earn and spend what's left, whereas the "have-nots" spend what they earn and save what's left. If you want to be among the "haves," you'd be well-advised to pay yourself first.

You should be allocating a portion of your annual earnings to a qualified retirement plan. Even if you're still in your 20s, invest those pretax dollars to the maximum amount allowed in your qualified plan. If you have additional savings left over, invest those tax dollars in other vehicles. Of course, all of this assumes you've paid off every penny of debt first.

In a qualified retirement plan, contributions are approved by the IRS and may be deducted from your taxable income. In addition, all future appreciation and dividends credited to the qualified plan will be tax-deferred until withdrawn.

Given that you're saving taxes by investing in a qualified plan, and given that you're immediately enhancing your rate of return by 28 percent, 34 percent, or as much as 40 percent by contributing pretax dollars to your retirement plan, doesn't it make sense to put away as much as you're allowed in tax deductible and tax-deferred plans?

Since you have only so many productive years and the IRS places strict limitations on how much you can put away each year on a tax deductible, tax deferred basis, isn't it a good idea to maximize your contributions into qualified retirement plans first?

DIFFERENT TYPES OF QUALIFIED RETIREMENT PLANS
It's important to understand the different types of qualified retirement plans for different occupations. First of all, 401(k) plans and 403(b) plans are not for everyone. So the first step is to clarify the differences among retirement plans and determine who qualifies for which.

For instance, if you're a self-employed professional or businessperson, and you have full-time employees on your payroll, then you would probably find a Profit Sharing Plan (Keogh) the right plan for you. You may invest up to 13 percent of your net earnings (bottom line on Schedule C) in this type of plan to a maximum each year of $22,500. However, when you have employees, you must contribute the same percentage of their compensation for them as you do for yourself.

If you're self-employed with no employees, or function primarily as an independent contractor (earnings are reported on Form 1099), then you'll find an SEP/IRA to be the ideal qualified retirement plan vehicle for you. SEP stands for Simplified Employee Pension. The maximum allowable contribution to a SEP/IRA is 13 percent of net earnings or $22,500, whichever is the lesser.

If you're an employee of a corporation that's in business for profit, you would qualify for a 401(k) plan. Your earnings are reported on Form W-2. Although it's sponsored by your employer, it's a self-directed plan in which you make biweekly contributions via a payroll deduction into a family of mutual funds.

The maximum annual contribution to a 401(k) plan by an employee currently is $9,240. However, a 401(k) plan is special — the employer may match a portion of the employees biweekly contribution. For example, the employer may contribute 50 cents on the dollar up to the first six percent the employee contributes to the plan.

It's been shown when employers are generous with their matching contributions, there's much greater employee participation in the 401(k) plan than when the employer makes little or no matching contribution at all. Of course, that makes perfectly good sense.

If you're employed by a not-for-profit institution such as a school, church, or hospital, you may qualify for a 403(b) plan. This is similar to a 401(k) plan except there is no matching contribution by the employer. The maximum annual contribution to a 403(b) plan currently is $9,500. This is also normally done on a biweekly basis and the contributions are usually invested in mutual funds.

Always remember: pay yourself first! ∎

How to Use Your 401(k) Plan to Accumulate a Nest Egg

Perhaps the greatest long-term financial risk we all face is outliving our savings. Most Americans are going to end up facing this dreadful eventuality because they're not serious about saving for their future, nor are they wisely investing money they do save.

THE UNFORTUNATE TRUTH
In a study released last year, Professor Chris Robinson and his colleagues at York University in Toronto examined investment returns, testing four million scenarios that applied to retirees in different age groups and with varying financial resources and annual living expenses. They created a wealth consumption ratio, dividing total financial resources by annual cost-of-living expenditures, to assess basic financial needs.

A 65 year-old with $560,000 in total financial assets and an annual cost of living of $40,000, for example, would have a wealth consumption ratio of 14. The study concluded an individual with total financial resources of 14 times his annual living expenses would have to invest 100 percent of his or her retirement nest egg in common stocks to avoid running out of money.

Even investing all of his or her retirement fund in common stocks does not assure a 65 year-old of a comfortable retirement. Nineteen percent of men and 28 percent of women in similar situations would still run out of money. One out of five men and one out of four women will literally outlive their savings and end up destitute before they die.

In fact, if a 65 year-old were to play it safe and put 100 percent of his or her financial resources in Treasury Bills or CDs, the risk of running out of money before he or she dies would significantly increase. So much for safe investments!

This breakthrough research study examined the risk and performance numbers through the entire life expectancy table and concluded retirees are more likely to outlive their savings with low-risk, low-return investments than lose their money on higher-risk, higher-return investment opportunities.

Armed with 37 years of data, the York University study stated only common stocks produce a sufficient rate of growth to ensure a comfortable lifestyle in the later stages of a long life for all but the very wealthy. In fact, a number of studies have designated common stocks as the best performing asset class.

It's imperative, therefore, to make compound interest work for you. Sadly, according to a survey conducted by New York Life

Insurance Company and the Gallup organization, three out of four of the participants in 401(k) plans did not even understand the concept of compounding!

The table below illustrates how a single dollar invested each year will grow through compounding.

For purposes of illustration, let's assume you were to invest $1,200 in your 401(k) plan each year for the next 30 years. In addition, we'll assume you were able to achieve an average annual return on investment of 10 percent. Locate the factor amount in the 30 years row and the 10 percent rate of return column. Multiply the factor of 180.9 times your annual investment amount.

In this example, you'd accumulate 180.9 times your per annum investment of $1,200, or $217,080. And you would have invested only $36,000. The difference of $181,080 was entirely the result of tax-deferred compounding. That's how you accumulate a nest egg. ■

$1 PER ANNUM COMPOUNDED ANNUALLY OVER TIME

YEARS	3%	5%	8%	10%	12%	15%
5	$5.47	$5.80	$6.33	$6.71	$7.11	$7.75
10	11.81	13.21	15.64	17.53	19.65	23.35
15	19.16	22.66	29.32	34.95	41.75	54.72
20	27.68	34.72	49.42	63.00	80.70	117.80
25	37.55	50.11	18.95	108.20	149.30	244.70
30	49.00	69.76	122.40	180.90	270.30	500.00
35	62.28	94.84	186.10	298.10	483.50	1013.00
40	77.66	126.80	279.80	486.80	859.10	2046.00

YOUR MONEY: WHERE TO KEEP IT ONCE YOU'VE GOT IT

Emergency or vacation savings:
Either a money-market mutual fund or a savings account in an insured bank.

College savings:
If the child you are saving for is still young, stock-owning mutual funds that invest for growth are best. If your child is starting high school, put the "freshman-year" money into a four-year CD and do the same each year.

Home down-payment money:
If you plan to purchase your new home in about two years, put it in a two-year CD. Continue to put a new savings into that CD if the bank allows, or into a bank or money market account.

Retirement savings:
If you're still relatively young, put most of your money into stock-owning mutual funds. If you're middle-aged, put at least half into stock-owning funds and the other half into bonds or bond mutual funds.

A lump-sum payment from a pension fund:
At retirement put at least 30 to 40 percent into stock-owning mutual funds for growth or leave it in your employer's diversified stock fund. Invest the rest of the payout in bonds or bond mutual funds.

The Best Retire- ment Plan in the World

Imagine being your own boss. Imagine controlling your own destiny, living where you want, enjoying tax advantages, building wealth, and building a residual income for your rapidly approaching retirement years.

There has never been a better time to be an entrepreneur. With modern information technology it is possible to build a virtual empire.

Consider the following tangible advantages of owning your own business:

• It provides protection for you and your family in the event of catastrophic medical expenses, long-term disability, or even death.

• It gives you the means to achieve financial independence that a job never will, so you and your spouse can enjoy an active and prosperous retirement. You're less likely to end up like the vast majority of retirees — broke, embarrassed, and depending on a monthly pittance from Social Security to subsist.

• It provides discretionary income you can use to systematically save and invest in qualified plans, as well as non-qualified retirement plans, to accumulate a substantial nest egg for the future.

• It provides a way to significantly reduce your annual income tax liability, because owning your own business is one of the best legal tax avoidance strategies there is.

• It's passed on to your spouse or your children through your estate.

There is no better investment of time or money than an investment in building your own business. However, there are some things to think about before you get started.

You can start your own business from scratch on a full-time or part-time basis, but be advised that the odds are three to one against your succeeding in a traditional business. On the other hand, if you can afford it, you can buy a franchise business with a successful chain or become a distributor for a network marketing (multilevel marketing) company.

Starting your own traditional business from scratch is a very difficult way to become an entrepreneur. It costs a fair chunk of money to get started and has the greatest risk of failure.

Buying a franchise, on the other hand, is the costliest way to get into business. However, that high entry price brings with it a very high probability of success, provided you are affiliated with a long-established and proven franchise company.

Finally, you have the option to become a distributor with a network marketing company. This is the least costly and potentially most lucrative endeavor for those with the requisite persistence and determination. A network marketing business has essentially none of the negative aspects of traditional business. It can be run easily as a home-based business and features no overhead, no employees, no inventory, and minimal advertising expenses.

It's ideal for anyone looking for an opportunity with unlimited potential.

One of the most attractive aspects of a network marketing business is the passive residual income it provides. A network marketer reaps a harvest each and every year from a single planting of a crop of associates and customers that continually grows and multiplies over the years.

Network marketing companies are here to stay. Network marketing is high tech and attracting hordes of white-collar professionals who have either been downsized out of corporate life or are fed up with the rat race.

Although network marketing companies have traditionally been distributors of consumable products (vitamins, detergents, personal care products, water filters), there are also many that have no products in inventory. I'm referring to service-based and information-based companies such as Financial Independence Network Limited (FINL), which produces and distributes newsletters, books, software, audio tapes, and other high-impact informational products. ■

A Simple Retire- ment Plan for Small Biz Owners

Did you know self-employed sole proprietors and incorporated small-business owners can enjoy the kind of tax savings usually associated with large corporate retirement plans, without the burdensome expenses and administrative headaches? Well, it's possible through a Simplified Employee Pension Plan.

SEP/IRAs are an ideal retirement plan for companies of any size, whether they have employees or not. Moreover, they're available to any form of business, whether they're incorporated or not. SEP/IRAs have replaced Keogh plans for self-employed professionals, as well as profit sharing plans for small incorporated businesses.

So, if you're self-employed with no employees, or function primarily as an independent contractor (earnings are reported on Form 1099), then you might find a SEP/IRA to be the perfect qualified retirement plan vehicle for you.

An added plus is that an individual who has any self-employment income from full-time or part-time work during the tax year can contribute to a SEP, even if he or she has been employed by a separate company and included them in a pension or profit sharing plan.

TAX-FREE SAVINGS
With a SEP, a self-employed individual can put aside, on a tax-deductible basis, as much as 15 percent of his or her compensation, up to a maximum of $150,000. Thus, an individual can deduct up to $22,500 (15 percent of $150,000) from his or her gross taxable income and put it into an SEP/IRA.

This amounts to 13 percent of an individual's adjusted net income on the Schedule C Form 1040 (Income or Loss From Business/ Sole Proprietorships) because you have to deduct one-half of your self-employment tax when making the calculation.

HERE'S AN ILLUSTRATION OF HOW TO CALCULATE YOUR SEP/IRA CONTRIBUTION.
Whatever percentage of gross compensation the employer contributes to the SEP/IRA for himself, he must contribute the same percentage of pay for all of his eligible employees. If you put away nine percent of your gross into a SEP/IRA, you're required to contribute nine percent of each of your eligible employees' respective gross compensation into a separate SEP/IRA for them.

However, you may exclude employees who haven't worked during at least three of the prior five calendar years, or haven't reached the age of 21, or have earned less than $400 during the year. You may also exclude part-timers who work fewer than 20 hours per week.

Once you've established a SEP/IRA, it's advisable to transfer other IRAs into it. That is, you may have other IRAs from years past scattered among various financial institutions. Those old IRAs would best serve you in one master SEP/IRA.

This way you avoid paying custodial fees at other companies and you get to put all your IRA eggs into one basket. This is also an opportunity to get your retirement money out of bank CDs, annuities, and other non-growth vehicles.

THE ADVANTAGES OF SEP/IRAS
• They're easy plans to set up, operate, and maintain.
• They have no government filings required.
• They have virtually no administrative costs.
• They're flexible — you decide each year whether to contribute and how much.
• They provide a way to make tax-deductible contributions from your business.
• They provide an easy way to accumulate a retirement nest egg via tax-sheltered mutual funds.

Simply complete the Form 5305-SEP and the SEP/IRA application in the SEP/IRA kit. Any major mutual fund company can give you one of these. Indicate which growth funds you wish to allocate your contributions to and enclose a check made payable to the custodial firm. Be sure to indicate on the check the tax year. ∎

If You Play it Safe Now, You May End Up Broke Later

Conventional wisdom says our tolerance for investment risk should be a major consideration in deciding how much of our retirement plan money we should allocate to growth mutual funds. I disagree.

Unless your tolerance for poverty during your retirement years is greater than your tolerance for the fluctuations of the stock market during your working years, challenge the conventional wisdom. Invest as if your life depended on it.

RISK TOLERANCE
Risk tolerance is given entirely too much consideration in asset allocation strategies. Overly conservative plans, which most people tend to choose, can be just as harmful as overly aggressive plans because the return on investment isn't as great as it could be. The fact is, being too conservative with your money is just as foolhardy as being too aggressive with it.

Most people end up broke at retirement, and it's not because they were aggressively investing, but because they were too conser-

vative with their investments. They either didn't invest at all, or they left their money in bank savings accounts, U.S. government savings bonds, and other no-growth safe vehicles. Upon retirement, they ended up with insufficient savings for their retirement years.

Your tolerance for risk must not be the determining factor in your investment strategy. Think of a substantial retirement nest egg as a mission. You must cultivate a burning desire to accumulate a large sum of money for your retirement years and optimize every opportunity to do so.

Most investment fear is based on misconceptions and misperceptions. Risk is good. Without it, there would be no reward.

THE SURVEY SAYS...
The June 1994 issue of *WORTH* magazine included a revealing article titled "Americans and Their Money." The article highlighted the results of a survey of 2,000 households conducted in the fall of 1993 by Roper/ Starch Worldwide market research.

When respondents were asked what two or three things caused them the most anxiety, the number one response was making the wrong choice with a major investment. This caused them more anxiety than having major surgery, being audited by the IRS, or even public speaking (formerly the greatest fear of all and feared more than death itself). Obviously, there's a very high level of fear when it comes to making a decision about making a major investment.

The survey also revealed that one-

third of the respondents described themselves as extremely unwilling to take any financial risk. At least two-thirds are willing to accept some risk to achieve better-than-guaranteed returns from so-called risk-free investments. Nonetheless, the author of this article concluded Americans are living in a decade of anxious conservatism.

It's nothing new, of course, to be told most investors are averse to risk. They prefer certainty to uncertainty. Given two investment alternatives from which to choose, most investors will almost always choose the one with lower risk.

This doesn't mean they will not take risks at all. They will, but only if they expect the payoff for taking the risk is significantly higher than the risk itself. Most people will not take on additional risk without the prospect of much higher rewards.

People can also be risk seekers when small amounts of money are at stake, such as buying lottery tickets. Even though there's very little chance of an astronomically large return and an extremely high probability of losing the entire stake — they rationalize — it's only a few bucks!

Risk is the primary consideration in developing investment strategies and structuring investment portfolios. Intelligently managing market risk, not trying to beat the market, is what virtually all money managers are paid to do.

Nonetheless, market risk is a requisite condition to be able to achieve the above-average rates of return you'll require if you're to accumulate a sizable nest egg. ■

Balanced Asset Allocation: Better Returns with Less Risk

It's unusual for a 401(k) plan or 403(b) plan to offer foreign stock funds or even small cap stock funds among its investment options. This is unfortunate, because in neglecting to establish an international stock fund and a domestic small cap stock fund, employers are denying increased, consistent returns for plan participants.

Why? Diverse portfolios provide an opportunity to moderate the volatility of stock funds, and not having that option available prevents them from achieving the requisite diversification and balanced allocation they need to improve their chances for better overall returns with less volatility and risk.

Large cap and small cap are terms used to differentiate between large and small companies based on their respective market capitalizations. These caps are determined by multiplying the number of common shares outstanding by the current price per share.

Thus, Microsoft, with 600 million shares outstanding and a current price per share of $117, has a market cap of $70 billion dollars. That is a large-cap company! Typically, small-cap companies are those with market caps of less than $1 billion. However, many small-cap fund managers focus on companies with market caps of less than $500 million.

Concentrating all of one's investment dollars in U.S. companies listed on the NYSE makes an investor much more vulnerable than one whose investments are diversified among many different companies around the world. To quote global investing pioneer John Templeton, *"No rational investor would want to have all his assets in one stock or in one industry, so why should all his assets be invested in one nation?"*

To go one better, it's my belief that over the long term, a balanced allocation of invested dollars among the three major classes of common stocks is likely to produce better results — with less volatility and variability in annual returns — than investing solely in one asset class, whichever asset class that may be.

Systematically investing in mutual funds has been proven over time to be a nearly fail-safe strategy. It's called dollar cost averaging, and when utilized with funds whose primary objective is growth, much of the risk involved in investing disappears.

For example, if you're investing $300 a month in your 401(k) or 403(b) plan, it would be advisable to allocate one-third ($100) to

Calendar Year	Big-Cap Companies	Small-Cap Companies	Foreign Companies	Balanced Allocation (1/3- 1/3 - 1/3)
1975	37.2%	52.8%	37.5%	42.5%
1976	23.8	57.4	6.0	29.1
1977	-7.2	25.4	15.6	11.3
1978	6.6	23.5	34.3	21.5
1979	18.4	43.5	12.9	24.9
1980	32.4	39.9	25.1	32.5
1981	-4.9	13.9	-2.1	2.3
1982	22.5	39.7	25.1	29.1
1983	21.4	28.8	-0.6	16.3
1984	6.3	-6.7	5.1	1.6
1985	32.2	24.7	47.2	34.7
1986	18.5	6.9	55.5	26.9
1987	5.2	-9.3	5.0	0.3
1988	16.8	22.9	17.3	19.0
1989	31.5	10.0	23.9	21.8
1990	-3.2	-21.6	12.0	-12.3
1991	30.5	44.6	11.1	28.7
1992	7.7	23.3	-14.0	15.6
1993	9.3	17.4	32.6	19.8
1994	-2.1	-4.3	8.1	0.6
1995	32.6	27.3	9.5	23.1
Average Annual Return	16.0%	21.9%	17.5%	18.5%

large-cap blue-chip growth stocks, one-third to small-cap growth stocks, and one-third to foreign stocks through an international fund. Note: Global funds include U.S. stocks.

This way, each month you're accumulating shares in three different funds that represent three different asset classes. When small-cap stocks are out of favor with the investing public and the price is depressed, you'll be accu-

mulating more shares with each incremental monthly investment. Then, when they are fashionable again, you'll see a substantial increase in the value of those shares.

The table represents 21 years of average annual rates of return for the three major growth stock asset classes. Note that the balanced allocation had only one negative return year (1990), whereas each of the major asset

classes had three or four negative return years. Moreover, the balanced allocation outperformed both the big-cap index and the small-cap index with less variability of annual returns.

Big-cap companies are represented by the S&P 500 Index, the small-cap companies by the Russell 2000 Index, and foreign companies by the EAFE index (Europe, Australia, and the Far East index compiled by Morgan Stanley & Co.). ■

The Social Security Time Bomb!

No commentary on retirement planning can ignore the issue of Social Security. Even as the working public bears the burden of payroll tax in order to fund the system, surveys reveal that two-thirds of the American people don't ever expect to receive a nickel from Social Security. Even among people who are only 15 years from their retirement, 40 percent don't expect to receive their monthly Social Security checks.

Anyone in the boomer generation with an IQ above room temperature knows the Social Security system is a time bomb waiting to explode. It's also partly to blame for the financial anxiety felt by members of the boomer genera-

tion during relatively prosperous times in our history.

A large number of Americans still believe Social Security is a big bundle of individual retirement accounts comprised of the taxes they have paid into the system. They don't want to admit the checks they are getting are funded by their kids' payroll taxes.

IT'S PAY AS YOU GO
Social Security payroll taxes are not being put aside in a trust fund. Payroll taxes are being used to pay the current beneficiaries. That is, the money your mother or grandmother receives from Social Security comes from your payroll taxes. Social Security has been on a pay-as-you-go system since 1939.

Thus, everything we receive from Social Security, even if we've been paying into it for 20, 30, or 40 years, will be expropriated via payroll taxes from the paychecks of our children and grandchildren. Most of the trillions of dollars that have been paid into Social Security over the past 60 years have been spent. The money's gone. It cannot be recovered. Therefore, the benefits

promised us can be paid only if payroll tax rates continue to increase.

The Social Security system is essentially a vast, intergenerational scheme for robbing Peter to pay Paul. Unfortunately, Peter is rapidly going broke. The success of Social Security assumes the population will steadily expand. However, as any social scientist will confirm, large numbers of people are not very predictable. Babies were conceived in unprecedented numbers immediately following World War II (thus, the term "baby boomers"), but the current birth rates of American couples amounts to only 2.2 children. Consequently, we will soon have a large retirement group supported by a relatively small work force.

THE RULES KEEP CHANGING
Legislators continually change the rules by which the Social Security game is played in an attempt to avoid bankruptcy. They frequently increase the rate of the payroll tax. When Social Security first started 60 years ago, the rate was two percent. Half was paid by the employer and half was paid by the employee. Today, it's six times

that rate. The payroll tax today is 12.4 percent with half paid by the employee and half paid by the employer.

Of course, employees are really paying the entire 15.3 percent. Employers are passing on that cost to each employee with commensurably lower wages and salaries. Everyone who works for someone else is paying the freight. Even if you're self-employed, you pay the entire 15.3 percent on the first $60,600 of taxable income plus an additional 1.5 percent for Medicare insurance.

Politicians also frequently increase the amount of earnings upon which the payroll tax is

levied. When Social Security started 60 years ago, only the first $3,000 in earnings were subject to payroll tax. The amount of taxable income is now $60,600. Since the vast majority of Americans earn less than $60,000 a year, it's clear they're feeling the full bite of payroll tax on every single dollar they earn.

If average life-spans and birth rates remain constant, the outlook for future retirees looks bleak. Many people now in the work force may not be retired long enough to collect as much as they paid into the system during their productive years. Worse yet, the system may eventually collapse if some changes are not made. By the time the youngest

baby-boomers qualify for full benefits (bear in mind that the retirement age is rising and will be 67 by then), the fund may be exhausted. There will be more Social Security recipients than ever, and the work force will be diminished. Those still working will probably be paying much higher payroll taxes by then and may also be forced into a lower standard of living.

Look at France and Italy, where Social Security taxes claim more than 50 percent of the workers pay and economic stress, as a result, is on the rise. The United States is on track to suffer the same fate because Social Security cannot exist successfully in the public realm. ■

Why Bond Funds Do Not Belong in Your Retirement Plan

Bond funds, money market funds, fixed annuities, and guaranteed investment contracts (GICs) do not belong in your retirement plan until you have accumulated all the money you and your spouse need to live on during your retirement years. When you feel you have accumulated as much capital as you need for your retirement years, then and only

then should you put your retirement plan assets in fixed-income securities.

Until you and your spouse have attained your savings goal, you are in an accumulation of capital mode. There can be no compromise. Allocate 100 percent of your retirement plan assets to common stock mutual funds, with growth of capital as the primary objective and style of investing. Stay in that mode until you achieve your financial goals. At that point, it may be appropriate to shift to a preservation of capital mode.

Neither interest-bearing investments, such as money market funds, nor fixed-income securities, such as bond funds, generate a sufficiently high return on investment to justify a place in your long-term retirement plan portfolio. Bond funds, GICs, and money market funds are income investments, not growth invest-

ments.

There is a commonly held belief that fixed-income securities, such as bond funds, are less risky (less volatile) than common stock funds. So what? When it comes to long-term investing over a 10- to 40-year horizon, the issue of short-term market volatility is irrelevant. Long-term rates of return on investment are what really matter.

Given the extraordinary difference in average annual returns, does it make sense to hold bond funds in your retirement plan account? What does it matter if in one or two calendar quarters your stock funds decline in price or don't perform as well as bond funds? It is the long-term objective and strategy that must always be foremost in our minds when it comes to our retirement plan.

Long-term bond funds and fixed

annuities are extremely vulnerable to inflation and the depreciation of purchasing power of our investment capital. Bonds constantly depreciate in real value over the long term, and here's why.

Let's imagine that you inherited a $10,000 face amount, 30-year U.S. Treasury Bond from your grandfather, which he purchased at original issue with $10,000 cash back in 1967. The bonds mature in February, 1997. Will that $10,000 you receive have the same purchasing power as the $10,000 your grandfather invested 30 years ago? Of course not. You don't have to take a course in economics to know that!

Ironically, if those bonds had been indexed to inflation these past 30 years, you would be getting not $10,000 from the U.S.

Treasury, but around $40,000! Unfortunately, the U.S. government does not index its bonds. Therefore, when they mature you will get back the original $10,000 your grandfather invested 30 years ago. Of course, you will be getting $10,000 with the purchasing power of about $2,500 since it takes four dollars to buy what one dollar could buy in 1967!

Figure out the loss of purchasing power with an average annual rate of inflation during the past 30 years of six percent steadily eroding the purchasing power of our money. It's easy to see fixed-income securities are totally inappropriate in a tax-deferred retirement plan whose sole purpose is to achieve growth of capital and accumulate funds for those retirement years.

Clearly, fixed-income securities never have and never will generate a return high enough upon which one can build a retirement account for the future. Money invested in bond funds, fixed annuities, guaranteed investment contracts (GICs), and other fixed-income securities will not grow at a great enough return over inflation to be able to accumulate enough capital for a retirement nest egg.

Thus, it is imperative investors in retirement plans persevere in an accumulation of capital mode until they have attained their goal. Accordingly, as long as your investment objective is accumulating a nest egg, investing for growth of capital is the only realistic and sensible strategy. ∎

Is Living the American Dream Possible?

Do you ever feel like you're working harder and harder, yet you have little or nothing to show for it? Does it seem like living the American Dream always takes just a little more money than you bring in?

Well, your problem may not be insufficient income. It's more likely to be unrealistic expectations,

and brain-washing!

Financial researchers have determined that, in 1991, it takes about $60,000 a year to live the American Dream. But when they interviewed people who make $60,000 a year, these folks said that they felt it would take about $75,000 to "Really" live it. And people making $75,000 thought it would take about $100,000. Of course, the people making $100,000 felt they would need around $150,000 a year to finally achieve the American Dream. And on it went up the scale.

The truth is that most of us already have enough. We just need to manage it better. We need to understand what we're trying to accomplish with the money that flows into our lives, and then craft a spending/saving/investing

plan to get us to our goals. That takes a bit of self-analysis and a lot of discipline. But it DOES NOT necessarily require a ton of self-denial. It just takes a realistic appraisal of our true needs and our reasonable wants.

And it takes a concentrated effort to take control of our minds back from TV advertisers. We are all being brain-washed every day by commercials that tell us that we won't be happy unless our car has more valves, our gym shoes have air pumps, our dog eats a scientific diet and our clothes come with a proper name on the tag. We are continually being taught to spend, spend, spend. And we obey—much more than we can afford to.

THE BIGGEST MISTAKE MADE BY MOST AMERICANS
Thinking that "Things will just

sort of work out" is the trap that catches most Americans who are running on the Madison Avenue financial treadmill. They go through life literally burning their income as fast as it comes through the door, naively leaning on the dream that something will come along to bail them out before they have to pay for their lack of control.

This is a serious problem. According to federal government statistics, 96% of Americans DO NOT achieve financial independence. And the evidence shows that the 4% who escape this fate are not just the people who finally figure out how to make more money than their family can spend. The indisputable facts show that these are simply people — from all income levels — that formulate financial goals for their lives, create workable plans to achieve those goals and then STICK TO THOSE PLANS.

THE IMPORTANCE OF GOALS AND PLANS

In 1953 the graduating class of Yale University was surveyed, and it turned out that only 3% of the graduates had formulated financial goals for their lives and written detailed plans to achieve those goals. In 1973, twenty years later, those same people were found and resurveyed. It turned out that the 3% who left college with goals, and plans to reach those goals, were worth more financially than the other 97% of their classmates COMBINED!

WHAT TO DO

1. Act Now. Just like changes in your diet can change your appearance and your health risks over the remainder of your life, changing your spending/saving/invest-

ing habits now can change the shape of your financial future.

2. Set Goals. Your family's goals should be tied to your values. Seek help from your financial planner, accountant or the professionals who write in this newsletter, if you feel you need it. Just set those financial goals.

3. Analyze Your Spending. This is the culprit. If your family is like most in America, you dribble enough money through the cracks during your lifetime to have built a very comfortable retirement. Establish the major categories of your spending and put ceilings on each. This should include EVERY area where you spend money, including those impulse trips to the pizza place and the impromptu gift for your favorite uncle (the one with the will).

4. Decide What You REALLY Need. A good measure of the worthiness of an expenditure is its "Lifetime Value." In other words, a year from now how much is it worth to you? Watch how much you're spending on "Experiences" rather than "Things." And be brutally honest about the value of both kinds of expenses.

5. Save At Least 10% Of Your Income. If you had started saving just $100 a month at age 25, at say 7% interest, by the time you reached 65 it would be worth $262,481.34. That's over a quarter million dollars! And all it took was a hundred bucks a month. Ask yourself, what's more important in the long run — a couple of dinners out each month, or a quarter million dollars at retirement?

6. Maximize Your Pretax Savings. Use IRAs, 401(k) plans and Keoughs. The effective yields are greater than table interest in other investments, and your tax calculations will be much simpler.

7. Vary Your Investments As You Age. Forty-year-olds should have 40% of their money in fixed income investments — 60% in stocks. Sixty-year-olds should reverse that distribution.

8. Dollar-Cost Average. Investing the same amount of money each month in stocks will likely more than overcome any ups and downs in the individual values of stocks in your portfolio.

9. Increase Your Savings Percentage As Often As Possible. Every time you get a raise, increase your savings/investment percentage. The 10% mentioned above is a minimum. If you want to retire early or more comfortably, it will take more. If you feel like you're depriving yourself too much, split income increases with your savings plan. Save half and allow yourself to spend the other half.

As un-fun as it might be to read this stuff, THIS IS WHAT IT TAKES TO GAIN TRUE FINANCIAL INDEPENDENCE. If you think you have a better way, please write in and share it with us all. But in the meantime, please don't fall prey to those false prophets who tell you that "Making more money is all it takes to achieve financial freedom." In your heart of hearts you know that's not enough. You have to know what to do with that additional money. ■

How to Retire Success- fully...or How Not To

Loren Dunton is the President and Founder of the National Center for Financial Education, founder of the Society for Financial Counseling, the International Association for Financial Planning, and the College for Financial Planning.

In a letter he recently sent me, he described how, over years of counseling retirees, he found a set of characteristics that defined the "Haves" and the "Havenots."

The Haves, of course, are those who retired with the means to enjoy their remaining years, through travel and other recreational activities. While the Have-nots are those who are living out lives of quiet desperation — dependent on their children, or scraping by in run-down hotels, or still working at menial jobs so they can survive on Social Security.

What surprised him the most in analyzing these two groups of people were not their dissimilarities, but rather their similarities. He had expected to find that those retiring in comfort and leisure had earned a lot more

money during their working lives, but that was not so. However, there were definite differences in the way these two groups had lived their lives.

Prominent characteristics in the track records of the HAVE-NOTS were:

- Renting instead of buying

- Being antagonistic to budgeting (we call it planned spending)

- Making impulsive expenditures

- Buying new cars more often

- Loaning money out carelessly

- Greater indulgence of their children

I would add a few additional facts to Loren's findings. The Internal Revenue Service conducts an ongoing study that indicates the most prevalent cause of financial failure in America is the inability to delay gratification. The "I have to have it NOW" syndrome.

Another chief factor in reaching retirement empty-handed is debt. In fact, I believe that this is the number one cause. You can't get ahead of the financial game in this country while carrying a load of debt. The government steals quite enough from us. If we also let Citibank and their clones siphon 20% and more out of our wealth each year, we are in fact working for them — not for ourselves and our families.

Finally, I have found that a major cause of the inability to get on financial track is the misguided concept of trying to save a little on the side, while continuing to buy on credit and service that debt. It's just plain dumb to be earning between 5% and, say, 12% on your money, while paying up to 21%. You just can't win that game.

This is where most "Conventual" financial advice — even from the priciest newsletters and financial planners — leads you astray. They all tell you to save 10% of your income, while continuing to do everything else the same way everyone around you is doing it. They concentrate on teaching all the intricate details of how to invest that 10%, but they miss the main causes of financial failure. Your chief problem is NOT that you're not putting enough money into your financial bucket — but rather that there is a huge hole in the bucket...and the government, banks and other businesses have their buckets under the hole in yours.

So this "Save a little while buying on credit and paying off debt" advice is WRONG. Need proof? Federal statistics indicate that 96% of Americans DO NOT achieve financial independence. So doing what other people are doing has a 96% chance of guaranteeing financial failure.

On the other hand, I've found that the best plan to help you make the most financial progress in the shortest period of time is another American trait — the military concept of "Massing of Forces."

The Debt-FREE & Prosperous

Living™ strategy is based on the principle of massing your financial forces on ONE THING AT A TIME. You first eliminate ALL debt. Then you being operating 100% on CASH, never to use credit again. Finally, you focus ALL your financial forces on building real wealth. Using this focus strategy, you will accomplish all three steps faster than you ever believed possible.

BACK TO LOREN'S FINDINGS
As you might expect, the "Haves" did not make the same mistakes as the "Have-nots." But more than that, they could all point to some "experience" in their lives that put them on the road to financial freedom.

In many cases it was a parent or grandparent who had taken the time to teach them the real course to having more money at retirement. Others indicated that an information source or consultant had made a strong impression on them, that financial prudence led to freedom. In your case it will be the day you subscribed to the *Debt-FREE & Prosperous Living™* newsletter.

He also noticed that the "Haves" appeared to be what he called "Fixer-uppers," meaning that they saved a lot of money by doing things themselves, and they kept older cars running rather than blowing their wealth on new ones.

The "Haves" also saw and avoided the trap of "Keeping up with the Joneses." They somehow realized the truth that the Joneses end up bankrupt.

But the number one characteristic he found in the financially successful people was that somewhere along the road they DEVELOPED A PLAN to get them to financial freedom. And that's exactly what Debt-FREE & Prosperous Living™ is all about.

Our plan is simple, and it works. Many financial newsletters and advisers will suggest plans that sound like a space shuttle mission. These may seem reasonable to people who have spent their whole lives learning the nuances of stocks, bonds and the like, but to the average citizen...they're just too complicated.

And the real truth is that many of those so-called financial experts are just restating principles they read in the other guy's newsletter. They're all saying the same things. But we're not. We are telling you the simplest way to get to complete financial freedom in the shortest time.

I hate to sound negative, because it's not my nature, but the world is changing. American industry has more world-wide competition than ever before, and the business boom cannot go on forever. That's why we can't seem to get out of this recession.

You need to start thinking a little defensively. That's why our strategy is to get you to where you are no longer financially vulnerable FIRST, and as quickly as possible. Then you can get aggressive in your investing if you want to.

I believe that if you follow our plan, you'll sleep a lot better...a lot sooner. ■

Your Prosperous Health:

Building Your Health

The importance of health as it relates to personal prosperity cannot be denied. Many Americans reach their retirement years with poor health, preventing them from enjoying their freedom. Many middle-agers don't even have the energy and stamina to enjoy their families or their work. Wealth without health is truly a worthless commodity. Vibrant health requires discipline, focus, and personal responsibility. But prosperous health makes everything else you do worthwhile. Here are some health basics to start you down the path toward prosperous health.

SUGAR
William Duffy, in his best-selling book Sugar Blues, estimates the average American consumes 120 pounds of sugar per year! Sugar contains no vitamins and no fiber, and is considered empty calories. To absorb sugar, the body has to deplete its store of vitamins and minerals. Twenty-five percent of the sugar Americans consume is in the form of soft drinks. The average American drinks between 30 and 50 gallons of soft drinks per year. You may have heard about the adverse effects of soft drinks on digestion, the teeth, and the stomach — all are real! In poor areas of the world, such as Mexico, children are drinking soft drinks rather than water and are losing their teeth before they reach their teens. And a soft drink can add one-third to the cost of your lunch. Water is a far better health and budget choice. High sugar consumption can cost you in more ways than one. You can pay for the effects of soft drinks at the dentist's office, at the doctor's office, and in loss of energy and productivity in your workday.

Keep track of what you and your family spend on soft drinks and sweets for one month and calculate what an elimination of empty calories could mean to your family budget.

FACE THE FATS
Hydrogenated fats have been artificially saturated with hydrogen atoms at high temperatures under pressure, with the use of a metal oxide. Shortening, most margarines, and the vegetable oils used in processed foods have been hydrogenated. Hydrogenated oils are dull, heavy, and lifeless, and should be avoided whenever possible.

Recent research implicates hydrogenated fats in increased plasma cholesterol levels. Hydrogenated fats do not melt at body temperature like butter. In small amounts, butter is better for you than margarine. Butter dissolves in water and has a low melting point. The elimination of shortenings, margarine and other hydrogenated fats is difficult, and those who eat fast foods and processed foods are making things tough on their bodies.

Bad fats may harden arteries, raise blood pressure, and lead to aging and disease. Avoid canola, soy, and cottonseed oils, as well as hydrogenated fats, because they are thought to combine with chlorine, fluorine, and blood waste products. Clogged arteries are the result.

Healthy fats, however, are essential to every life process. These fats act as lubricants and transducers, and are as important as amino acids, minerals, vitamins, water, and oxygen to the body. Increase your intake of flax seed oil, borage oil, olive oil, nuts, seeds, sunflowers, almonds, and fresh fish (for the benefit of the fish oils).

THE ELIMINATION OF MARGARINE, SHORTENINGS, AND FRIED FOODS WILL NOT ONLY SAVE YOU MONEY AT THE GROCERY STORE, BUT COULD SAVE YOUR LIFE!
If you're going to remain healthy into your retirement years and raise healthy and vigorous children, start today. The rewards will be worth the effort. In our fast-food, fast-paced world, eating healthy is neither easy nor simple, but it's not impossible. The care you give your body today will be reflected in the vigor with which you're able to approach your life tomorrow. ■

Overfed and Malnour- ished

Let's focus on thrifty nutrition ideas to help you identify nega- tive foods to be eliminated from your diet and replaced by healthi- er alternatives.

A GOOD START

Many Americans start their day with a diet cola or a cup of coffee. Young people are becoming addicted to soft drinks with caf- feine earlier and earlier in life. Students carry around liters of soft drinks at school. Caffeine is an addictive substance that when added to colas and diet soft drinks becomes one of the most negative foods Americans consume. Cola drinks and coffee are very acidic. The acidity of these liquids can interfere with digestion, cause food to move through the diges- tive track too quickly, and burden your kidneys by increasing their workload to bring the body into pH balance.

Early in life Americans carelessly begin to spend money on soft drinks every day. The average family of four spends $600 to $1,200 per year on soft drink con- sumption. Children can best learn spending control if they are taught to avoid recklessly spend- ing their change on pop and candy.

Besides, the aspartame (artificial sweetener) in diet soft drinks is so dangerous each can bears a warn- ing label. Aspartame is highly toxic to a number of people because of the methanol content. Methanol is converted to formic acid and formaldehyde in your body and can be toxic to the thy- mus gland. It has also been associ- ated with seizures, increased blood pressure, and headaches.

Water retention is another side effect of coffee and soft drinks. The human body retains excess water in an attempt to neutralize the acidity of these high sodium drinks. Rather than starting your day with stimulants, start with a large glass of water, deep breath- ing, and aerobic exercise. A brisk early morning walk is a great way to wake you up and get you going.

Eat a healthy breakfast to guaran- tee yourself peak performance. I prefer fruit for breakfast. My five- year-old eats eggs and cereal, while my teenagers love oatmeal and high-fiber whole-grain cere- als. Find your healthy choice and start your day right! The brain needs B vitamins and quality fatty acids such as lecithin to achieve alertness and peak performance. High-fiber, whole-grain energy bars are a great quick choice for an eat-and-run breakfast. Get in the habit of taking fresh fruit and high-fiber, low-fat snacks with you to work or school so you're not tempted to grab a mid-morn- ing soda or candy bar.

JUNK FOOD AND YOUR BUD- GET

Take time to evaluate how much your family spends on junk food, then plan a strategy to eliminate wasteful spending. Set aside the money you save every month in an account to be used for your next family vacation. If the chil- dren spend their money on pop and candy at school, keep change and money out of their pockets! lives. When you begin to drink water with meals rather than sodas, you will not only save a great deal of money, but you will be aiding the digestion of your food and not burdening your body with the need to neutralize the acidity of the soda or coffee.

SOME OTHER SUGGESTIONS

• Stay out of fast-food restaurants where it's easy to eat a high-fat, high-sugar, low-fiber snack or meal.

• Don't go grocery shopping when you're hungry. Keep snack foods and junk foods out of your basket.

• Feed children a healthy snack after school, or let them eat din- ner. Children are very hungry right after school and will eat what is quick and available. I leave a pot of chili, homemade bean dip, or sandwiches and car- rot sticks to satisfy after-school hunger.

• Praise and reward children's healthy habits. Tell them how proud you are that they care about themselves. Teach teens to cook and you might come home to a healthy meal they've prepared!

• Avoid bologna, lunch meats, and cheeses; these foods are laden with nitrites and are in some cases 90 percent fat!

• Plan a weekly menu and build a repertoire of healthy meals your family enjoys.

• When eating out, order water only. This will save your family an average of $3 per outing. ■

Vitamin E: Your Oxygen Booster

Good health and a long, vital life may lie within the kernel of a grain of wheat. Our modern American diet consists of refined and processed wheat flour with the wheat germ removed by modern, industrialized food preparation processes. Why would the food industry remove the most nutritious part of the grain? The answer is profit. The oil in the wheat germ contains valuable fatty acids that spoil quickly. The food industry prefers foodstuffs that remain on the shelves for long periods of time.

A diet of refined white flour can lead to a serious vitamin E deficiency. At the turn of the century the federal government discovered white flour leads to malnutrition and diseases. Legislation was enacted, forcing the food industry to enrich the flour with vitamin B. These products are still greatly deficient in the valuable nutrients within the kernel or wheat germ, and this deficiency may be responsible for the widespread occurrence of heart disease in Americans today.

EXERCISE AND VITAMIN E
Lack of exercise slows the bloodstream and increases the chance for deposits of cholesterol, triglycerides, and fatty acids to settle in the lining of the arteries and blood vessels. Vitamin E helps maintain blood alkalinity and reduces the accumulation of acids in the body.

Even if you take wheat germ oil or vitamin E capsules to increase your intake of vitamin E, your regimen is not complete without exercise. Exercise opens up the tiny blood vessels of the muscles and heart, increases the blood flow to the arteries, and allows the tissues to utilize vitamin E.

HOW DOES VITAMIN E WORK TO IMPROVE HEALTH?
Vitamin E increases the utilization of oxygen by the muscle tissues, improving and promoting normal circulation. Efficient circulation increases the healing time of any wound. Vitamin E may also help dilate arteries and permit a free flow of blood, thereby increasing tissue oxygenation.

Vitamin E helps keep oxygen from combining with other substances in the body so that it's readily available to the tissues.

Vitamin E may even help the mind. The human brain uses 30 percent of all the oxygen taken in by the body, so it stands to reason sufficient levels of vitamin E will even benefit mental function.

Vitamin E is currently recommended to reduce the pain from cystic breast disease and PMS, and as a preventive to heart disease. It is believed that vitamin E can increase the recovery from a heart attack and help maintain more optimal health.

SOURCES OF VITAMIN E
Wheat germ oil is the richest and most natural source of vitamin E. Wheat germ oil is unrefined vegetable oil, taken from the wheat grain, and is available in capsules or as an oil to be used in salad dressings. It's recommended that you consume between 400 and 800 units daily.

A second natural source of vitamin E is wheat germ flakes. Wheat germ flakes contain wheat germ oil, protein, vitamins, and other nutrients. Both wheat germ oil and wheat germ flakes deteriorate rapidly and require refrigeration to prevent spoilage.

Other fine sources of vitamin E are cold-pressed corn oil, cottonseed oil, peanut oil, soybean oil, sunflower seed oil, and safflower oil. You can find cold-pressed oils at your local health food store. Avoid heating the cold-pressed oils, as heating destroys the delicate fatty acid chain known as vitamin E.

Everyday foods such as whole wheat breads, avocados, eggs, soybeans, peanuts, brown rice, and even turnip greens help increase the body's supply of vitamin E. However, wheat germ oil is the highest naturally occurring plant source of vitamin E. If you want to increase your level of health, supplement your diet with vitamin E and eat foods rich in natural sources of vitamin E. ■

Minerals: The Unknown Gems

Minerals come from the ground. From the simplest point of view, minerals are really small rocks. You should not confuse vitamins and minerals. Even though you can purchase both in one supplement, they are two distinctly separate things. Plants make vitamins through the process of photosynthesis. Minerals cannot be made by plants on their own, but rather come from the ground.

ARE MINERALS IMPORTANT?

You bet! Consider calcium. In addition to giving your skeletal system its structural strength, calcium allows your muscles to contract or move. This includes your heart and the smooth muscles of the digestive system. Without calcium, your gears are stuck in park. Research also shows a correlation between calcium deficiencies and colon cancer.

MINERAL-DEPLETED FOOD

Our food's mineral content may be decreasing. Soil is mineral-poor because of the large number of crops cycled through the ground each year without replenishing needed minerals.

Currently the only elements regularly replaced in the soil are nitrogen, phosphorus, and potassium, which are usually included within the fertilizers. Cost prevents many farmers from replacing minerals and still being able to remain

competitive in the marketplace. Therefore, we could be eating genetically engineered tomatoes that are huge, red and perfect, yet have the same nutritional value as Styrofoam — not to mention about as much taste.

WHY IS THIS IMPORTANT TO YOU?

Have you noticed people are appearing to get gray hair at earlier ages? Many times this can be partially due to a deficiency in mineral copper.

How about colds? While we really are still unsure of the actual cause of the common cold, the best treatment is sublingual zinc lozenges combined with a dose of vitamin C and Echinacea. Echinacea is an herb which can be obtained in any pharmacy or health food section. The liquid forms are most effective but can have a nasty taste. It's best to use a flavored type such as cherry or orange, unless you have a palate that can take anything. The zinc should be allowed to dissolve under the tongue and not just swallowed as a tablet. It, too, can taste much like sucking on a galvanized nail, so choose a flavored tablet.

Magnesium is another important mineral. Deficiencies can result in hypertension, osteoporosis, and fatigue. Magnesium is part of the chlorophyll molecule in plants, and can be found in nuts, milk, and whole grains.

Phosphorus is important for bone and tooth development and is one of the few minerals found in just about every type of food. It's required to be replaced by farmers. Incidence of deficiencies are rare. Iron, as most women know, is the

major component in the synthesis of hemoglobin (blood). Deficiencies can cause cold, tingling hands and feet, fatigue, irritability and palpitations. Major natural sources are grains, meats, and soy.

Have you ever wondered why bruises turn green? The answer is copper. Copper is part of what is called Superoxide, which is the enzyme synthesis of hemoglobin. The green color in the bruise is due to oxidation of the copper in the damaged tissue. Go outside and find an old copper pipe. Its color is green for the same reason. Deficiencies of copper have also been linked to heart problems.

If you know someone who appears chronically ill, or has bad teeth and brittle nails, they could have a lack of sufficient selenium. Selenium works to help maintain the health of muscles, functions as an antioxidant, and aids in cancer prevention. Natural sources are yeast, garlic, eggs, whole grains, and liver.

Finally, chromium has been getting a lot of press lately, mostly as an aid for weight loss (this is generally marketed in the form of chromium picolinate). Chromium helps to preserve muscle mass while at the same time helping to metabolize fats. Chromium also maintains the glucose tolerance factor, which is essential in preventing diabetes. There are no known toxicity levels or symptoms of too much chromium that I am aware of, so if you know someone with diabetes, it may be in their best interest to try supplementing.

MINERAL SUPPLEMENTS

There are currently three forms of

supplements on the market. The pure form is ground up and shoved in a capsule or made into a tablet. These are cheap, but the body does not readily absorb this type well. The second type is the salt form, which is more readily absorbed but a little more expensive and usually combined with a vitamin. The third type is colloidal, which is generally in liquid form, although some companies advertise a colloidal tablet. These are the most readily absorbed by the body because of the charges they carry in molecular form. However, these can be expensive — over $1.00 a day.

So what do we as consumers do? Probably the most cost effective strategy is to purchase supplements which contain strictly minerals. Initially this may appear more expensive than buying a combination vitamin/mineral, but you need to bear in mind vitamins have a shelf life, while minerals do not. You can therefore buy larger quantities of minerals for less and not worry about them losing their strength or decomposing. You should also weigh the cost benefits of the various forms. It may very well be that the cheapest is not the most effective for you. You need to decide this for yourself. ■

Fighting the Common Cold

John H. Knowles, M.D., past president of the Rockefeller Foundation, former professor of medicine at Harvard, and former director of the Massachusetts General Hospital in Boston, wrote, *"Eighty percent of the doctors work consists of treating colds, minor injuries, gastrointestinal upsets, backaches, arthritis and anxiety. One out of four people is emotionally tense and worried about insomnia, fatigue, too much or too little appetite, and his ability to cope with modern life. Since these conditions account for 80 percent of the work for a typical family-care physician in the late 20th century, it stands to reason these conditions account for 80 percent of the average American's time and money spent on seeking a physician's care."*

Typical American consumers can drastically reduce both the levels of suffering in their households and bills from their physicians for treatment of relatively minor yet costly and inconvenient illnesses, particularly the common cold. Reducing your vulnerability to the common cold will save you both time and money.

PUBLIC ENEMY #1
The number one reason Americans will visit a doctor's office this winter is due to the misery of the common cold.

The best that can be said for the common cold is that it is a serious waste of time, capable of making its victim miserable and unproductive for days on end. The good news is that you no longer have to become a victim of a cold virus. Vitamin C is sufficient to prevent or hold in check even the most stubborn of viruses, but you can't be timid or sloppy with vitamin C.

Peak cold seasons are September/October, January/February, and late spring. If you maintain a steady dose of vitamin C supplementation during the year, it will make fighting off a viral invasion much easier. The optimum daily intake of vitamin C is anywhere from 500 to 5,000 mg daily. If you have cancer, frequent colds, allergies, circulatory disorders, asthma, exposure to pollutants, or gum disease, you will need to take the higher daily doses of vitamin C. The average person may do well on 500 mg to 1,000 mg as a daily preventative dose. If you are a smoker you need to remember that every cigarette depletes blood levels of vitamin C by 65 to 100 mg. The pack-a-day smoker needs at least 2,000 mg daily of vitamin C just to keep from having signs of deficiency.

KNOW YOUR ENEMY
To master a cold you must know your monster. Viruses enter healthy cells and live off their nutrients. Once a virus is inside a cell, it can replicate into large numbers and explode the cell, moving on to destroy other healthy cells. It is thought vitamin C works to inhibit the action of viruses by oxidizing them. At the onset of a viral invasion your body releases a protective substance known as interferon. Interferon interferes with the work of the virus, but does not reach its highest level until day four of five of a viral attack. This explains why the early use and work of vitamin C is so effective and so necessary at the very

beginning of a viral invasion.

THE BIG GUN!

Taking a buffered vitamin C or an esterified form of vitamin C (as opposed to an ascorbic acid type of vitamin C) increases the absorption of vitamin C four-fold. Esterified C also decreases the undesirable side effects of large doses of vitamin C such as diarrhea, mineral loss, and stomach irritation. This form of vitamin C also comes in a powder that you can easily mix with juice, making it easier to take than tablets, every one to two hours. It's also important to maintain a high intake of water and fresh vegetables when fighting a virus.

Children should take the buffered form of vitamin C. Their doses should be half, or less, of an adult dose. Never treat a child's cold with aspirin, as this could lead to Reyes syndrome. But do give your children the popular zinc, vitamin C, vitamin A, and echinacea or slippery elm lozenges that are available. They are usually found in the health food stores and are a great way to support the child's vitamin needs while fighting a cold.

Smokers and the family members of smokers have more colds because cigarette smoke dries out the nose and throat tissues, which make them more susceptible to viral attack. Cigarette smoke is a pollutant the body detoxifies with vitamin C. Smoking or breathing cigarette smoke lowers the body's stores of vitamin C by 65 to 100 mg per cigarette. Smokers and their family members have more allergies, sinus infections, ear, nose, and throat infections, and frequent colds than the nonsmoking population.

In conclusion, make sure your vitamin C is fresh and not left over from last winter. Drink 10 to 12 glasses of water daily when fighting a cold. The vitamin C formula for fighting the common cold is shown in studies to be about 95 percent effective in eliminating most or all cold symptoms when followed correctly. ■

Appendix F

Additional Resources

Some Definitions
Some Facts and Stats
How Rent-To-Own Deals Can Be Costly
Still Denying You're In Debt? Take This Quick Quiz
A Horror Classic: "The Loan Principal That Wouldn't Go Away"
Newsletters That Rate Mutual Fund Performance
Asset Management Accounts That Offer Visa Debit Cards
Other Important Phone Numbers

APPENDIX F

Facts, Stats, and Resources

Some Definitions

Financial Freedom: Being able to work if I want, do what I want, and live where I want, as long as I want.

Financial Freedom Date: The exact day when I'll be completely debt-free, operate 100% on cash, and be able to live off the interest on my investments.

Retirement: Traditionally referred to as the time when I quit working. The concept of retiring at age 65 was invented in the 1930's when the U.S. government instituted Social Security. The goal of the Debt-FREE & Prosperous Living™ strategy is to be able to spend my time doing what I love to do (I may or may not want to continue working), so a better definition of retirement is when I'm financially free (see definition of "financial freedom" above).

Value: The worth I place on the things I buy, do, or give.

Some Facts and Stats

- A 1992 Federal Reserve study showed that 43% of U.S. families spent more than they earned.

- According to the National Association of Realtors®, the average homeowner stays in their home for 7.1 years (1993 statistic). With an 8% mortgage, they will sell their home still owing over 90% on their mortgage. **If they were to continue on this trend, they would NEVER pay off a mortgage in their lifetime.**

- Only 2% of homes in America are paid for.

- On average, Americans can expect to receive just 37% of the annual retirement income they will need to live comfortably. [*America's Retirement Crisis: The Search for Solutions* — Oppenheimer Funds Dist., Inc. 1993.]

- Americans save just 4% of their disposable income, compared to 8.7% in England, and 15.9% in Japan.

- As of 1995, 92% of U.S. family disposable income is spent on paying debts, up from 65% in 1975. [Federal Reserve]

- According to a *USA Today* headline article (5/8/95), the average baby boomer who makes $50,000 today will need one million dollars to replace that income in retirement. If this person had 20 years to retirement, they would need to start saving $2,397 per month IMMEDIATELY.

- In 1993 half of all families had less than $1,000 in net financial assets.

- For the year ending June 30, 1996, personal bankruptcies totaled more than ONE MILLION for the first time ever in a 12-month period. That's almost one bankruptcy for every 100 U.S. households.

- On average, you'll spend 112% more on a credit card purchase than when using cash.

- The average household has four credit cards with balances around $4,800, up from two cards and $2,340 in balances five years ago. [RAM Research, 1996]

- Most credit card companies set their minimum payments at only 2% of the outstanding balance or $10 per month. [CardTrak of America]

- Making the minimum payment on a $4,800 balance (average balance of

U.S. cardholders) at the average annual 17% interest rate, it would take you 39 years and seven months to pay off. You would pay $10,818.63 in interest alone, and a total of $15,619 for the privilege of charging the $4,800!

- Nearly half of all Americans (46%) have less than $10,000 saved for their retirement. And 39% of Americans are anxious about their ability to achieve their desired retirement lifestyle. [*Miles To Go: A Status Report on Americans' Plans for Retirement* — Public Agenda, 1997]

- *"The virtue of saving appears to have escaped most Americans, although the* 'just charge it' *mentality is thriving. Our access to consumer goods is considered an American success story, but could we have gone too far? The ethic of consumption is driving many Americans to leverage their futures by relying on credit, and many may face bitter disappointment and anxiety over the quality of their retirement years."* [Deborah Wadsworth, Executive Director, Public Agenda]

- 76% of the general public feel they should be putting more money aside for their retirement. [*Miles To Go: A Status Report on Americans' Plans for Retirement* — Public Agenda, 1997.]

[The statistics listed below are from a survey conducted by Intuit's Quicken Financial Network, 1997]

- 32% of survey respondents have simply stopped saving all together.

- 20% routinely get overdue notices from creditors.

- 17% don't have enough money to pay their taxes.

- 10% ask family, friends, or colleagues for loans.

- 4% declared personal bankruptcy in the past year.

- 14% don't know the interest rate on their credit cards.

- 9% get cash advances from one credit card to pay off debt on another.

- 9% post-date personal checks so they won't bounce.

- 6% borrow for regular, everyday essentials such as groceries, clothing, and gasoline for their car.

How Rent-To-Own Deals Can Be Costly

Rent-to-Own stores cater to people who crave "instant gratification," and who often don't have the available resources to make a cash purchase. But rent-to-own is just another form of credit — with disastrous consequences for the purchaser. Below are four examples of how "buying" an item through a rent-to-own contract can be many times more expensive than buying cash in a department store:

- 19" RCA color TV: Buy $218, Rent-to-Own $9.99 per week for 78 weeks = $780!

- 14-cubic-ft. refrigerator: Buy $517, RTO $1,321 over 78 weeks or 18 months.

- Packard Bell Pentium PC with color monitor, CD-ROM, 16 Mb of RAM: Buy $1,700, RTO $39.99 per week for 100 weeks = $4,000.

- Bassett sofa and loveseat set: Buy $1,170, RTO $25 per week for 91 weeks = $2,275.

Sources: U.S. Public Interest Research Group, Knight-Ridder research.

Calculating the annual rate on the TV example above shows a 230 percent interest rate! A recent *Miami Herald* article confirms this, stating that *"rates...average 100 percent, and can go as high as 275 percent...citing a study released in June by USPIRG, a non-profit consumer organization."*

A rent-to-own industry spokesman claimed that listing the total purchase price *"is more meaningful than an annual percentage rate... Rent-to-own stores serve people by making goods available that otherwise would be 'out of reach.'"*

We ask, *"If it weren't for instant gratification, why would anyone pay almost four times as much for a TV — and be paying for a year and a half — when they could save the same money for less than six months and purchase the same TV?"*

Still Denying You're In Debt?
Take this Quick Quiz

Phase 1 in the Debt-FREE & Prosperous Living™ strategy is to get out of debt. Whether you've recently subscribed to the Debt-FREE & Prosperous Living™ ranks, and don't yet realize the danger in your economic situation, or you are a seasoned reader and have yet to get started on your road to financial freedom, take this 10-question quiz to see if you're in — or headed for — certain financial disaster.

1. Do you owe more than 20 percent of your annual after-tax income (excluding rent or mortgage and car loan)?

2. Do you take cash advances on your credit card to pay daily expenses? (NOTE: Many lenders compute the interest starting from the day you take the advance.)

3. Do you extend repayment schedules on your bills?

4. Do you get loans to pay off other loans?

5. Do you make minimum payments on revolving charges?

6. Do you use credit for products and services you used to pay for with cash?

7. Do you work overtime or a second job just to stay ahead of the bill collector?

8. Do you find yourself worrying a lot about bills?

9. Do you regularly pay your bills late?

10. Is the subject of money the most frequent cause of arguments with your spouse?

If you answered "yes" to even one of these questions, you need to keep working on your Financial Freedom Strategy. If you answered yes to five of these questions, reread your *Debt-FREE & Prosperous Living™ Basic Course* and recommit yourself to achieving financial independence through our comprehensive plan. If you answered "yes" to more than five of these questions, you're either a member of Congress or you need to pour through back issues of the *Debt-FREE & Prosperous Living™* newsletter, reread your *Debt-FREE & Prosperous Living™ Basic Course*, and start today to make a difference in the way you manage your finances.

A Horror Classic: "The Loan Principal That Wouldn't Go Away"

WARNING: The following information is not for the squeamish. If you're faint of heart, please turn the page.

Look at the chart below to determine how much of your principal is remaining on your home mortgage. You'll see that, in most cases, you're well past the half-life of your mortgage before your payments begin to whittle away appreciably at the principal amount. Almost all of your payments for the first half of your mortgage term go toward paying interest (profit) to your friendly lending institution.

L O A N   R E M A I N I N G   A F T E R

Interest rate	5 years	10 years	15 years	20 years	25 years	30 years
Life of mortgage — 30 years						
7%	94%	86%	74%	57%	33%	0%
7.5%	95%	87%	75%	59%	34%	0%
8%	95%	88%	77%	60%	36%	0%
9%	96%	89%	79%	63%	39%	0%
10%	97%	91%	82%	66%	41%	0%
Life of mortgage — 25 years						
7%	91%	79%	61%	36%	0%	
7.5%	92%	80%	62%	37%	0%	
8%	92%	81%	64%	38%	0%	
9%	93%	83%	66%	40%	0%	
10%	94%	85%	69%	43%	0%	
Life of mortgage — 20 years						
7%	86%	67%	39%	0%		
7.5%	87%	68%	40%	0%		
8%	87%	79%	41%	0%		
9%	89%	71%	43%	0%		
10%	90%	73%	45%	0%		

Newsletters That Rate Mutual Fund Performance

Moneyletter
1217 St. Paul Street
Baltimore, MD 21202
800/433-1528

Mutual Fund Forecaster
3471 North Federal
Fort Lauderdale, FL 33306
800/442-9000

Mutual Fund Investing
7811 Montrose Road
Potomac, MD 20854
301/424-3700

Fund Profit Alert
1259 Kemper Meadow Drive
Suite 100
Cincinnati, OH 45240
800/327-8833

The Mutual Fund Letter
680 North Lake Shore Drive
Suite 2038
Chicago, IL 60611
800/326-6941

Louis Rukeyser's Mutual Funds
1750 Old Meadow Road
McLean , VA 22102
800/892-9702

Asset Management Accounts That Offer Visa Debit Cards

Company	Account Name	Initial Deposit	Phone No.
Schwab	Schwab One	$5,000	800/435-4000
Kemper	Money Plus	$5,000	800/621-1048
Edward D. Jones	Full Service	$1,000	314/515-2000

Other Important Phone Numbers

WASHINGTON
President and Vice President:
(202) 456-1414 or
(202) 456-1111
Members of House and Senate:
(202) 224-3121

U.S. CAPITOL SWITCHBOARD
(800) 962-FLAG (3524)

SENATE AND HOUSE BILL STATUS
(202) 225-1772

**FOR CAMPAIGN FINANCE AND
GOVERNMENT REFORM SENATE
GOVERNMENT AFFAIRS
COMMITTEE:** (202) 224-4751
House Judiciary Committee:
(202) 225-3951

STRENGTH OF BANK OR S&L
Weiss Research: (800) 289-9222
Veribanc: (617) 245-8370

**STRENGTH OF INSURANCE
COMPANY**
Weiss Research: (800) 289-9222

**HELP WITH INSURANCE POLICY
PROBLEMS**
National Insurance Consumer
Helpline: (800) 942-4242

TERM LIFE INSURANCE QUOTES
Insurance Quote Services, Inc. (free):
(800) 972-1104
TermQuote (free):
(800) 444-TERM (8376)

CONSUMER PROTECTION
(general)
Federal Trade Commission (FTC):
(202) 326-2180
For your state consumer protection
department or Attorney General's
offic, dial 411

**CHECK ON INVESTMENTS,
ADVISERS, BROKERS**
Security and Exchange Commission
(SEC): (202) 272-7210
National Association of Securities
Dealers (NASD): (800) 289-9999

USED CAR MARKET PRICE INFO
Consumer Reports Used Car Price
Service: (900) 446-0500 (typical call,
$8.75)

**CREDIT COUNSELING AND
CREDITOR INTERVENTION**
National Foundation for
Consumer Credit
(800) 388-CCCS

**DEBT-FREE & PROSPEROUS
LIVING™ CUSTOMER SERVICE**
(608) 375-3103

Index